JAVA/J2EE INTERVIEW QUESTIONS

With Ready ANSWERS

JAVA/J2EE INTERVIEW QUESTIONS

With Ready ANSWERS

ARUNESH GOYAL
Topper, B.Sc. (H) Mathematics
Hitherto, Hon. Director, Institute for Studies in Mathematics
and
Related Sciences in Computers (ISMRSC), Delhi

M.C.A., University of Delhi, DELHI - 110 007

Formerly
Computer Analyst/Consultant, St. Stephen's Hospital, Delhi

KHANNA BOOK PUBLISHING CO. (P) LTD.
::: *Publisher of Engineering and Computer Books* :::

Head Office : 4C/4344, Ansari Road, Darya Ganj, New Delhi-110002
Phone: 011-23244447/48 Fax: 011-23244447
Regd. Office : 1694-95, Nai Sarak, Delhi-110006
Phone: 011-23283211 Fax: 011-23256658
E-Mail : contact@khannabooks.com
Website : www.khannabooks.com

JAVA/J2EE Invterview Questions

ARUNESH GOYAL

ISBN: 978-93-81068-84-7
First Edition: 2013

Published by :
Khanna Book Publishing Co. (P) Ltd.
4C/4344, Ansari Road, Darya Ganj, New Delhi-110002
Phone : 011-23244448 Telefax : 011-23244447
E-mail : contact@khannabooks.com
Website : www.khannabooks.com

Regd. Off : 1694-95, 1st Floor, Nai Sarak, Delhi-110006 (India)
Phone : 011-23283211 Telefax : 011-23256658

Printed in India by:
S.P.S. Printers & Binders, Delhi

To

My Parents

The Origin !!!

The Sustainer !!

The Destination !

PREFACE

As is clear from the title, this book intends to take you through the nitty-gritty of Interview Questions from the Java/J2EE point of view; and additionally, from the general viewpoint as well as the C#.Net viewpoint. I shall briefly describe the structure and composition of the book in the following paragraphs.

The first chapter forms the core of the book as it deals extensively with "Core Java & OOP" The various concepts covered amongst others are the portability and cross-platform feature of Java via bytecodes through the use of JVM besides the object-oriented paradigm consisting of encapsulation, inheritance, and polymorphism. It goes on to discuss the various technical points associated with core Java in a subtle way besides including some interesting and fascinating Java puzzlers.

The second chapter succinctly describes the significance of "Applets" from the interview point of view. Since the concept of "Applets" is of vital significance, it has been allotted a separate chapter.

The third chapter discusses "Networking" in its various nuances including the client-server model, proxy servers, throughput, firewalls, encryption and digital certificates.

"Threading" forms part of the next chapter. Herein, the concepts of thread life-cycle, multithreading, daemon threads, thread synchronization, deadlocks and monitors have been brought out briefly.

"Databases" have become, of late, one of the most important aspects of modern programming languages. This is what is precisely discussed in the fifth chapter of the book, namely "Databases & JDBC". This chapter is especially important for first-timers while the seniors might like to brush up their knowledge of the key concepts discussed herein.

With the sixth chapter of the book – "Servlets & JSP" - we move on to the relatively more advanced concepts in the realm of Java. In the same vein, we move on to the seventh chapter of the book, namely "EJB". The various features of servlets & Java Server Pages, and Enterprise Java Beans are covered in these two chapters, respectively.

The eighth chapter of the book is on "Struts" and is to be considered extremely important from the Interview viewpoint as "Struts" is the current design trend in the industry. The next chapter, viz. "Web Services & XML" is once again very important in this context and covers aspects like AOP, SOA, SOAP, WSDL, UDDI, JMS, JAXR, OR mapping, XPath, XLink, XPointer, XSLT and XQuery, to name a few.

We move on to "Internationalization" and "JNI", respectively in the next two chapters. In this modern era, "Internationalization" is of vital significance, since we want to write code independent of the specific locales, countries, and regions. Java Native Interface allows us to include native methods from other languages such as C in our Java code and thus, cancels out the need for rewriting code, and promotes code reuse, which is a very critical aspect of any object-oriented language such as Java.

The "Architecture (including Design Patterns)" and "UML" form part of the twelfth and thirteenth chapters, respectively. While the J2EE architecture, JNDI architecture, design patterns like Singleton, Façade, Factory, Abstract Factory and MVC are discussed in the former, the Object Model, UML elements, and UML diagrams, especially the Use Case Diagrams have been thoroughly described in the latter.

"Project Management" and "The Software Development Process" have been described in detail in the next two chapters, viz. the fourteenth and the fifteenth, respectively. Besides the general concepts, "Project Management" discusses organizational behavior in its various facets such as 'Taylorism', Theory X & Theory Y, Maslow's Hierarchy of needs, Herzberg's two-factor theory, motivation, leadership, egoless programming and stress. "The Software Development Process" scientifically elaborates the SDLC, SRS, the OO Life Cycle Modeling, the various case scenarios wherein you have to enact the roles of the various people involved in the SDLC such as the system analyst, the system designer, and so on. Besides, it has many a multiple choice problems pertaining to "The Software Development Process", which you would enjoy trying your hand at!

The final sixteenth chapter of the book includes exactly one hundred "Bonus Interview Questions on C#.Net". It takes into account the various similarities and differences between C# and Java. Although a complete discussion of these was not possible in this book owing to time and space constraints, you can refer to my works – "The Essentials of C# 4.0" and "The Essentials of Java" – in this context.

The appendix contains the essence of the JAVAAPI package which includes fifty-nine libraries in all. The acronyms and the glossary sections are for your ready reference. They have been so designed as to enable you to understand much of the computer jargon associated not only with the Java environment, but in general as well, in a big way!

– Arunesh Goyal

ACKNOWLEDGEMENTS ....

I would like to laud the role played by each and every one who came into interaction with me during the course of writing this book, nay the whole cosmos, as otherwise this work may perhaps would never have been possible.

In particular, I take this opportunity to thank and acknowledge Mr. Mukul Seth, proprietor, M/s Khanna Publishing Co. (P) Ltd. But, above all, I would like to put on record the role played by my Sad_Guru_Dev, Shri Siddheshwar Baba (Formerly, Sh. B.S. Goel, M.A., Ph.D.; founder of Third Eye Foundation of India) for constantly encouraging me whenever my spirits were down and out. It is, indeed, rightly said:

"Gurura Brahma, Gurura Vishnu, Gurura Devo Maheshwara,
Gurura Sakshat Para_Brahma, Tasmai Shri Guruvey Namah:"!

– Arunesh Goyal

A Word From The AUTHOR ....

"It is not said vainly that the best way to learn is do practically whatever you know theoretically. This idea would become clearer by taking up an analogy. A new cook on special duty was told to prepare three cups of tea by following the procedure as outlined below.

Take 2 cups of water and add 1 cup of milk, 3 spoonfuls of sugar and one & a half spoonfuls of tea leaves. Finally, put this entire mixture on the stove and thus, make tea.

Now, the cook did everything right but didn't light the stove! It is needless to add that the guests had to leave without having tea as planned even after waiting for more than 3 hours!"

In the light of the above analogy, it's only imperative that my dear readers put into actual practice and implementation whatever precepts and ideas they pick up from this manual lest their effort, time and energy is put to total, sheer and abysmal waste!!

Thanks a lot!!!

– Arunesh Goyal

You can also refer the following books by the same author and publisher :

- SEE THRU C++
- The Essentials of JAVA
- The Essentials of C# 4.0

CONTENTS

(At a Glance)

CONTENTS

(In Detail)

Q.56 What is the Object class in Java?

Q.57 Define an interface in Java.

Q.58 What is the similarity and difference between interfaces and abstract classes?

Q.59 How will you choose between an interface and an abstract class?

Q.60 What is an exception handler?

Q.61 Can you elaborate on the consequences of an uncaught exception?

Q.62 What is the major benefit of exception handling?

Q.63 Can you have a try block followed by a finally block with no catch clauses?

Q.64 Explain the concept of an inner class.

Q.65 Explain the concept of anonymous classes.

Q.66 What types of variables are allowed in an interface?

Q.67 Are there any restrictions imposed on interfaces vis-à-vis classes?

Q.68 What is a stream in Java?

Q.69 Compare and contrast byte streams with character streams.

Q.70 Elucidate the benefits of the streams.

Q.71 Name the predefined I/O streams in Java.

Q.72 Name the two byte streams and the two character streams related to File I/O in Java, respectively.

Q.73 How is binary data read and written?

Q.74 Name the two classes at the top of the byte stream classes.

Q.75 Name the two classes at the top of the character stream classes.

Q.76 Does Java have a generalized console input formatter akin to the standard C function scanf() or the C++ input operators?

Q.77 Elucidate the New I/O system.

Q.78 What types of comments are supported by Java? Does it support documentation comments?

Q.79 Define a package.

Q.80 Can you create a hierarchy of packages?

Q.81 What does the Math class contain?

Q.82 What do you mean by generics?

Q.83 How is java.util useful?

Q.84 Elucidate the utility of collections.

Q.85 On what principle does a Stack operate?

Q.86 What is the principle behind the Queue?

Q.87 What is a Hashtable?

Q.88 What is the ArrayList class?

Q.89 Should collections be limited to "large jobs" such as corporate databases, inventory systems, or mailing lists?

Q.115 Can you explain the difference between the StringBuffer and StringBuilder classes of Java?

Q.116 What do you understand by hash code? How can you determine the hash code of an object?

Q.117 Can a class in Java be declared private?

Q.118 What do you understand by factory methods? Elucidate.

Q.119 In what different ways can you create an object in Java?

Q.120 What is the main point of difference between method overloading and method overriding?

Q.121 Can you name the super class for all classes inclusive of your classes as well?

Q.122 Can you write an interface without any methods?

Q.123 Can you name the method used in cloning?

Q.124 What is an abstract method/class?

Q.125 Can you forcibly implement only the features of your class; if yes, how?

Q.126 Can one interface be implemented from another?

Q.127 Do you think you need to write both the following statements:

(i) import java.awt.event.*;

(ii) import java.awt.*;

Or, the second one alone is sufficient? Give appropriate reason(s) for your answer.

Q.128 What do you understand by CLASSPATH? Elucidate.

Q.129 What do you understand by a JAR file?

Q.130 What is the scope of the default access specifier?

Q.131 Bring out the difference between an exception and an error.

Q.132 Bring out the difference between throw and throws.

Q.133 Can you name the Wrapper class with only one constructor?

Q.134 Can a primitive data type be stored into a collection?

Q.135 Bring out the major difference between ArrayList and Vector.

Q.136 What do you understand by serialization? Are there any variables which cannot be serialized?

Q.137 What do you understand by enumerations?

Q.138 What do you understand by annotations?

Q.139 What do you understand by a generic type?

Q.140 Bring out the major difference between window and frame.

Q.141 Elucidate the MVC architecture in JFC/swing.

Q.142 Enumerate the various window panes available in swing.

Q.143 What do you understand by a layout manager?

Q.144 Consider the following Method whose sole purpose is to find out if the argument passed to it is odd:

```
public static boolean odd(int k)
{
        return k % 2 == 1;
        }
```

Does the Method work?

Q.145 Can you provide declarations for two variables z and k such that:

```
z+= k;
```

is legal while

```
z = z + k;
```

is illegal?

Q.146 Can you provide declarations for two variables z and k such that:

```
z+= k;
```

is illegal while

```
z = z + k;
```

is legal?

Q.147 Consider the following Program:

```
public class Hurrah
{
        public static void main(String args [])
        {
                System.out.println("H" + "A");
                System.out.println('H' + 'A');
        }
}
```

What does the Program print?

Q.148 Consider the following Program:

```
public class Browser
{
        public static void main(String args [])
        {
                System.out.print("explore":);
                http://www.yahoo.mail;
                System.out.println(":maximize");
        }
}
```

What does the Program print?

Q.149 Consider the following Program:

```
public class Increase
{
    public static void main(String args [])
    {
        int z = 0;
        for (int y = 0; y < 100; y++)
        z = z++;
        System.out.println(z);
    }
}
```

What does the Program print?

Q.150 Can you provide declaration for a variable z such that the loop:

```
while (z != z + 0)
{ }
```

becomes an infinite loop (note that you are not allowed to declare z to be of type double or float)?

Q.151 Consider the following Program:

```
public class Indecision
{
    public static void main(String args [])
    {
        System.out.println(indecisive());
    }
        static boolean indecisive()
    {
        try
        {
            return false;
        }
        finally
        {
            return true;
        }
    }
}
```

What does the Program print?

Q.152 Consider the following Program:

```
public class World
{
        public static void main(String args [])
        {
                try
                {
                        System.out.println("Bye");
                        System.exit(0);
                }
                finally
                {
                        System.out.println("Arunesh");
                }
        }
}
```

What does the Program print?

Q.153 Consider the following Program:

```
public class World
{
        public static void main(String args [])
        {
                ((null) null).Bye();
        }
        public static void Bye()
        {
                System.out.println("Arunesh");
        }
}
```

What does the Program print?

Q.154 Consider the following Program:

```
public class World
{
        public static void main(String args [])
        {
                System.out.println(Bye.Arunesh.Hello);
        }
}
class Bye
{
        static class Arunesh
        {
                static String Hello = "Arunesh";
        }
                static Z Arunesh = new Arunesh();
}
class Z
{
        String Hello = "Bye";
}
```

What does the Program print?

Q.155 Consider the following Program:

```
class World
{
        public static final String ITEM = "10,000";
}
        public class Hello extends World
{
public static final String ITEM = "1";
        public static void main(String args[])
        {
                System.out.println(Hello.ITEM);
        }
}
```

What does the Program print?

Q.156 Consider the following code:

```
for (int y = 0, int z = 0; y < 10; y++) { }
```

Will the code compile?

Q.157 Consider the following Program:

```
class Hello
{
        public static void main(String args[])
        {
                boolean b = 1;
                System.out.println(b);
        }
}
```

Will this program compile?

Q.158 Consider the following Program:

```
class Hello
{
        public static void main(String args[])
        {
                System.out.println(args[3]);
        }
}
```

What does the Program print when run with the following command line?

```
java    Hello    VERY    GOOD    MORNING
```

(i) Hello
(ii) VERY
(iii) GOOD
(iv) MORNING
(v) exception raised:java.lang.ArrayIndexOutOfBoundsException:3

Q.159 Which of the following statements is true?

(i) Methods cannot be overridden to be more private.

(ii) static methods cannot be overloaded.

(iii) Private methods cannot be overloaded.

(iv) An overloaded method cannot throw exceptions which are not checked in the super/base class.

Q.160 Consider the following Program:

```
class base { }
class sub1 extends base { }
class sub2 extends base { }
public class cexcp
{
        public static void main(String args[])
        {
                base b = new base();
                sub1 s1 = (sub1) b;
        }
}
```

What will happen if this program is compiled and executed?

(i) Compile and run without any error

(ii) Compile-time exception is raised

(iii) Run-time exception is raised

Q.161 Consider the following Program:

```
class base
{
        public void a_mthd(int z) { }
}
public class scope extends base
{
        public static void main(String args[])
        {
        }
        // Method HERE
}
```

Which of the following methods can be legally inserted in place of the comment//Method HERE?

(i) void a_mthd(int z) throws Exception { }

(ii) void a_mthd(long z) throws Exception { }

(iii) void a_mthd(long z) { }

(iv) public void a_mthd(int z) throws Exception { }

Q.162 Consider the following Program:

```
public class Hello
{
    public static void main(String args[])
    {
        /* Modifier at ZZ */ class InnerHello { }
    }
}
```

What modifiers would be legal at ZZ in this program?

(i) public
(ii) private
(iii) static
(iv) friend

Q.163 You need to create a class that will store unique object elements. You do not need to sort these elements but they must be unique.

What interface might be most suitable to satisfy this need?

(i) List
(ii) Set
(iii) Map
(iv) Vector

Q.164 Describe a java source file.

Q.165 What is Bytecode?

Q.166 Why does the main method need a static identifier?

Q.167 Will the program compile if the main method doesn't have the static identifier?

Q.168 Which is the default parent class for a Java class?

Q.169 How are java objects passed to a method?

Q.170 What are native methods?

Q.171 What is the order of declaring class, package and import statements within a java file?

Q.172 Can a variable be an unsigned integer?

Q.173 Can a private method be static?

Q.174 Enumerate and elucidate the various bit wise operators.

Q.175 Explain the use of 'instanceof' operator.

Q.176 What are the access modifiers available for a class, method, and variable?

Q.177 Elucidate widening and narrowing conversions.

Q.178 How do you create Java API documentation?

Q.179 Explain the concept of jar, war and ear files.

Q.273 Does the performance of a JDBC program depend on the driver? Elucidate

Q.274 What do you understand by an RDBMS?

Q.275 What do you mean by SQL?

Q.276 What are the different types of DBMS?

Q.277 Enumerate the main features of a relational database.

Q.278 What do you understand by an Entity-Relationship (E-R) diagram?

Q.279 What do you mean by referential integrity?

Q.280 What do you understand by a primary key?

Q.281 What do you mean by a foreign key?

Q.282 What is an alternate key in a table?

Q.283 Elucidate the concept of normalization.

Q.284 Elucidate the First Normal Form (**1**NF).

Q.285 Elucidate the Second Normal Form (**2**NF).

Q.286 Elucidate the Third Normal Form (**3**NF).

Q.287 Elucidate the concept of denormalization.

Q.288 Elucidate the SQL Data Manipulation Language (DML).

Q.289 Elucidate the SQL Data Definition Language (DDL).

Q.290 Explain the concepts of transaction and ACID properties.

Q.291 Bring out the difference between DELETE TABLE and TRUNCATE TABLE commands.

Q.292 What are constraints? Enumerate the different types of constraints.

Q.293 What are cursors? Enumerate the different types of cursors.

Q.294 What is a join? Enumerate the different types of joins.

Q.295 What do you mean by a self-join? Illustrate with the help of an example.

Q.296 How does JDBC help in accessing databases?

Q.297 What are the steps involved in using JDBC in general?

Q.298 Enumerate and elucidate the various types of JDBC drivers.

Q.299 Can the ResultSet be used even after closing the connection?

Q.300 Can a connection object be serialized and used from another machine?

Q.301 How do you get hold of the column names fetched in a ResultSet?

Q.302 Elaborate setAutoCommit(true).

Q.303 Can a ResultSet be updated?

Q.304 How can you call a stored procedure from JDBC?

Q.305 What do you understand by connection pooling?

Q.306 Will the following code compile?

Q.395 Elucidate UDDI.

Q.396 Elucidate JAXR.

Q.397 Elucidate SOA. Are SOA and EJB mutually exclusive?

Q.398 Are SOA and Web Services the same? Elaborate.

Q.399 Elucidate SOAP.

Q.400 Elucidate WSDL.

Q.401 Explain service-oriented architecture with Web services.

Q.402 Can you explain the concept of Web services in the form of an equation?

Q.403 Elucidate JMS.

Q.404 What is an Object-Relational (OR) mapping? Elaborate.

Q.405 Elucidate publish/subscribe messaging domain.

Q.406 What criteria would you employ while choosing between servlets and stateless session beans as Web service endpoints?

Q.407 Elucidate Aspect-Oriented Programming (AOP).

Q.408 Does the EJB world uses AOP techniques?

Q.409 Is AOP different than OOP?

Q.410 Elucidate XML.

Q.411 Is XML merely an extension of HTML? Elaborate.

Q.412 What are the inherent advantages in using XML?

Q.413 When would you use XML with EJB?

Q.414 In the XPath data model, what is an XML tree?

Q.415 Is an XML document just a tree structure, just a textual representation, or both?

Q.416 Elucidate XPath.

Q.417 Elucidate XPointer and XLink.

Q.418 Elucidate XSLT.

Q.419 Elucidate XQuery.

Q.420 Evaluate XQuery vis-à-vis XSLT.

Q.421 Can you elucidate the relation between Web services and XML?

Q.422 Give one feature each of SOAP, WSDL and UDDI.

13. UML 154

Q.448 What do you understand by an Object Model?

Q.449 What do you understand by UML?

Q.450 Enumerate the various UML diagrams.

Q.451 What does an UML class element comprise of?

Q.452 Enumerate the various relationships between classes in UML.

Q.453 (a) Who is an actor? Explain with the help of suitable examples wherever necessary.

(b) What are Use Cases? Explain with reference to the case of a vending machine.

(c) What are Use Case Diagrams? Explain with reference to the Use Case in (b).

(d) What guidelines would you suggest for use case models? Elaborate.

Q.454 (a) What do you understand by Use Case Relationships? Explain with the help of suitable examples wherever necessary.

(b) What guidelines would you suggest for use case relationships? Elaborate.

Q.455 Can we have a combination of Use Case Relationships? If yes, elaborate with the help of a suitable example.

14. PROJECT MANAGEMENT 162

Q.456 What do you understand by a project?

Q.457 Enumerate the main characteristics of a project.

Q.458 Consider the following:

(i) Producing an edition of a newspaper;

(ii) Putting a robot vehicle on Mars to search for signs of life;

(iii) Getting married;

(iv) Amending a financial computer system to deal with a common European currency;

(v) A research project into what makes a good human-computer interface;

(vi) An investigation into the reasons why a user has a problem with a computer system;

(vii) A second-year programming assignment for a computing student;

(viii) Writing an operating system for a new computer;

(ix) Installing a new version of a word processing package in an organization;

Some of the above would appear to merit the description 'project' more than the others. Put them into an order that most closely matches your ideas of what constitutes a project. For each entry in the ordered list, describe the difference between it and the one above which makes it less worthy of the term 'project'.

Q.459 Enumerate the activities covered by software project management.

Q.460 What are the problems generally faced by software projects? Enumerate at least ten.

Q.461 What does the mnemonic SMART stand for as regards the objectives of a project.

Q.462 Bearing in mind the above discussion of objectives, comment on the appropriateness of each of the following 'objectives' for software developers.

(i) To implement the new application on time and within budget;

(ii) To implement the new software application with the fewest possible software errors that might lead to operational failures;

(iii) To design a system that is user-friendly;

(iv) To produce full documentation for the new system.

Q.463 How would you go about initiating a new software project? Elaborate.

Q.464 What do you understand by cost-benefit analysis? Can all benefits and costs be quantified and valued? Elaborate.

Q.465 IIT, Delhi is considering the replacement of the existing payroll service, operated by a third party, with a tailored, off-the-shelf computer-based system. List some of the costs it might consider under the headings of:

(i) Development costs

(ii) Setup costs

(iii) Operational costs

List some of the benefits under the headings:

(i) Quantified and valued benefits

(ii) Quantified but not valued benefits

(iii) Identified but not easily quantified benefits

For each cost or benefit, explain how, in principle, it might be measured in monetary terms.

Q.466 What do you understand by Parkinson's Law and Brooks' Law regarding effort estimation?

Q.467 How are effort, system size and productivity rate related to each other?

Q.468 What do you understand by COCOMO as regards software effort estimation?

Q.469 What do you understand by risk? How would you assess it?

Q.470 Match the following causes (a – d) to their possible effects (i – iv). The relationships are not necessarily one-to-one. Explain the reason(s) for each match.

Causes :

(a) Staff inexperience

(b) Lack of top management commitment

(c) New technology

(d) Users uncertain of their requirements

Effects :

(i) Testing takes longer than planned
(ii) Planned effort and time for activities exceeded
(iii) Project scope increases
(iv) Time delays in getting changes to plans agreed

Q.471 Give the full forms of PERT and CPM?

Q.472 Enumerate the three principles of 'Taylorism' as regards organizational behavior.

Q.473 Enunciate Theory X and Theory Y regarding human behavior and management as proposed by McGregor.

Q.474 According to Maslow's Hierarchy of Needs Theory of Motivation, where does the need for 'self-actualization' stand?

Q.475 What do you understand by Herzberg's two-factor theory about job satisfaction?

Q.476 What is your personal motivational factor?

Q.477 Distinguish between structured and unstructured decisions.

Q.478 On what does the style of leadership depend upon?

Q.479 What is your personal preferred style of leadership?

Q.480 What do you understand by egoless programming?

Q.481 What causes stress in general? Is stress always a negative factor towards the quality of work? Elucidate.

Q.482 Outline the steps involved in software development process.

Q.483 Elaborate the software development life-cycle.

Q.484 Outline the steps involved in feasibility study.

Q.485 What does the systems design entail?

Q.486 What are the characteristics of a good SRS (Software Requirement Specifications)?

Q.487 How is a request for a new system reviewed and selected?

Q.488 How would you handle an infeasible project?

Q.489 Suppose you are the systems analyst. How would you arrive at feasible solutions from the candidate solutions?

Q.490 Suppose you have to design an on-line human-computer interface. How would you go about doing it?

Q.491 Suppose you have to design the documentation for a new system. How would you go about doing it?

Q.492 Suppose you are responsible for the quality assurance of the new software developed? What factors would you bear in mind to ensure the quality of the

Q.493 Suppose you are one of the system designers. What factors would you bear in mind to ensure the moral and ethical quality of the product?

Q.494 Suppose you are responsible for maintenance of the new system developed. What issues would weigh on your mind while carrying out this responsibility?

Q.495 Suppose the company has deputed you to purchase new hardware and software. Discuss the specific and general criteria while selecting any equipment (hardware or software) from a vendor.

Q.496 Supposing that you are the systems analyst, what role would you have to play in the development of new software?

Q.497 What do you understand by Object Oriented Life Cycle Modeling? Explain and Elucidate.

Q.498 Compare and contrast the Object-Oriented and Module-Oriented approaches for Systems Design.

Q.499 From amongst the following multiple choice questions, select the best alternative:

(1) System analyst is:
- (a) an agent of change
- (b) a communicator
- (c) a problem solver
- (d) all of the above

(2) On-line data entry is most suitable in:
- (a) entering monthly journal entries
- (b) payroll master updation
- (c) processing for payments of cheques in a bank
- (d) none of the above

(3) The System Development phase associated with creation of test data is:
- (a) system analysis
- (b) system acceptance
- (c) physical design
- (d) logical design

(4) Prototype is a:
- (a) mini-model of the existing system
- (b) mini-model of the proposed system
- (c) working model of the existing system
- (d) none of the above

(5) Which of the following is a part of the Software Development Life Cycle?
- (a) requirements analysis
- (b) bench marking
- (c) program specifications
- (d) all of the above

(6) Entities, attributes, and relationships are associated with:
- (a) logical concepts of data
- (b) physical concepts of data
- (c) persons of an organization
- (d) none of the above

(7) File conversion is a part of:
- (a) system cut-over
- (b) day-to-day activity of data processing
- (c) system design
- (d) none of the above

(8) Software quality pertains to:
- (a) reliability
- (b) efficiency
- (c) maintainability
- (d) all of the above

(9) Objects may be viewed as:
- (a) clients in a system
- (b) servers in a system
- (c) both (a) & (b)
- (d) neither (a) nor (b)

(10) In a Unified Modeling Language (UML) diagram, an object:
- (a) can't be represented
- (b) is irrelevant
- (c) is represented as an attribute
- (d) is represented as a result of an operation

(11) The components that make up any system are known as:
- (a) system boundary
- (b) system description
- (c) system environment
- (d) all of the above

(12) A distributed data processing system:
- (a) attempts to capture advantages of centralized processing
- (b) attempts to capture advantages of decentralized processing
- (c) allows greater flexibility
- (d) provides slow access of data
- (e) both (a) & (b)
- (f) none of the above

(13) "Back up" refers to:
- (a) delay in production of outputs
- (b) accumulation of programs in memory
- (c) job scheduling failures
- (d) all of the above
- (e) none of the above

(14) Cost of error correction is least in the stage of:
- (a) requirements analysis
- (b) system design
- (c) evaluating the tangible factors

(d) evaluating the intangible factors
(e) both (c) & (d)
(f) all of the above
(g) none of the above

(15) An object is selected for modeling, if:
(a) its attributes are invariant during operation of the system
(b) it has numerous attributes
(c) its attributes change during operation of the system
(d) it has no attributes relevant to the system
(e) none of the above

(16) Tangible benefits, by their very nature, require:
(a) subjective evaluation
(b) feasible evaluation
(c) quantifiable evaluation
(d) none of the above

(17) A menu-driven software:
(a) helps the user to reduce errors during data entry
(b) is developed for planning meals at a restaurant
(c) contains options for the user to enter his choice
(d) all of the above
(e) none of the above

(18) While designing a report layout, which of the following should be avoided?
(a) report should be read from top to bottom
(b) report should be read from left to right
(c) the most important items must come first
(d) use of abbreviations
(e) none of the above

(19) A business accounting system includes:
(a) order entry
(b) shipping / billing
(c) sales analysis
(d) all of the above

(20) In a modern supermarket using computerized systems, which of the following would be found in use?
(a) Point-of-Sale (POS) terminal
(b) scanner
(c) bar code reader
(d) all of the above
(e) none of the above

(21) Open systems interact with the:

(a) system environment

(b) system boundary

(c) closed systems

(d) feedback

(22) Information is:

(a) data

(b) computer output

(c) manipulated input

(d) processed data

(23) The first step in Software Development Life Cycle (SDLC) is:

(a) system design

(b) database design

(c) feasibility study

(d) preliminary investigation and analysis

(e) none of the above

(24) On-line data entry is preferable to batch data entry because:

(a) it is faster

(b) it ensures better accuracy of input

(c) it reduces human effort in checking control totals, checklists etc.

(d) all of the above

(e) none of the above

(25) If the requirements analysis phase of a software development project is not conducted properly, then the:

(a) resulting system would be delivered before the deadline

(b) output reports won't be easy to decipher and make out

(c) system might fail to address the real needs of the users

(d) all of the above

(26) The detailed study / investigation of the existing system is often referred to as:

(a) system planning

(b) feasibility study

(c) system analysis

(d) none of the above

(27) System specifications are mainly concerned with:

(a) how the functions are performed

(b) what functions are to be performed

(c) both (a) & (b)

(d) neither (a) nor (b)

(28) In data processing, classifying, calculating and summarizing data pertain to:

(a) capturing of input data

(b) managing output results

(c) manipulation of data

(d) all of the above

(e) none of the above

(29) In case a data dictionary is not included in the system analysis and design of a software project, then the following task(s) can't be carried out well:

(a) over-all cost-benefit analysis

(b) bench marking of equipment to be acquired

(c) cross referencing and consistency checks of various data

(d) all of the above

(e) none of the above

(30) In a Railway Reservation System, which of the following is the most critical?

(a) Ease of programming

(b) Response time

(c) GUI

(d) none of the above

(31) Tactical information is needed to:

(a) carry out day-to-day routine operations

(b) meet government requirements

(c) perform long range planning

(d) perform short range planning

(e) none of the above

(32) Operational information is required by:

(a) middle managers

(b) line managers

(c) top managers

(d) all workers

(33) Inheritance in object modeling can be used to:

(a) generalize classes

(b) specialize classes

(c) both (a) & (b)

(d) neither (a) nor (b)

(e) create new classes

(34) Object-oriented modelling:

(i) allows easy integration of subsystems

(ii) promotes reuse of code

(iii) allows modification of some objects by other objects

(iv) allows data structures in objects to be modified by other objects

State whether:

(a) (i) & (ii) are true

(b) (i), (ii) & (iv) are true

(c) (ii), (iii) & (iv) are true

(d) (i), (ii), (iii) & (iv) are true

(35) Loss of data integrity implies that data is:

(a) outdated

(b) unsuitable for running in an integrated environment

(c) repeated

(d) inconsistent

(e) all of the above

(f) none of the above

(36) The main advantage of normalized relations in relational DBMS is that they:

(a) are highly secure

(b) occupy minimal storage

(c) do not suffer from anomalies during delete and update operations

(d) all of the above

(37) Digital signatures are used in:

(a) data communications

(b) floppy disk marking

(c) programming

(d) none of the above

(38) Which one of the following statements is incorrect?
(a) a report format file can show any object within a box
(b) a report format can show vertical lines in the report
(c) current date can be shown both in page header and footer
(d) none of the above

(39) A system design is said to be functionally modular if:
(a) system is able to handle all functions of the application
(b) system is developed through structured programming using languages like PASCAL or COBOL
(c) system makes extensive use of function keys for maximum user assistance
(d) each module performs a specific function and can be developed independently by programmers

(40) In considering the total cost associated with desired information, cost of data collection, data input and computer processing are:
(a) recurring costs
(b) one-time costs
(c) temporary costs
(d) permanent costs
(e) none of the above

(41) The present trend in data processing systems is towards:
(a) real-time processing
(b) remote processing
(c) distributed processing
(d) none of the above

(42) Whether a proposed system can provide right information for the organization's personnel or not, would fall under the study of:
(a) economic feasibility
(b) technical feasibility
(c) operational feasibility
(d) all of the above
(e) none of the above

(43) A class, in object-oriented programming, is a:
(a) template for objects of a particular type
(b) group of objects
(c) classification of objects
(d) none of the above

(44) Encapsulation in object modeling is useful because:

(a) it hides implementation details of the methods

(b) it allows improving methods of an object, independent of other parts of the system

(c) it allows for an easy design

(d) it encapsulates attributes and operations of objects

(45) In a motor car manufacturing company, following information is tactical:

(a) assessing competitor's car

(b) decision on introducing a new model

(c) computing sales tax collected

(d) scheduling production

(46) A Management Information System (MIS) is required because:

(a) the size of the organization has become too large

(b) computers are available economically

(c) it is difficult for clerks to process data

(d) timely decisions have to be taken based on available data

(47) The term used to refer to checking of outputs of a computer with the corresponding input documents is called:

(a) auditing around the computer

(b) auditing through the computer

(c) regression testing

(d) process control

(48) Bench mark is used during:

(a) computer contract

(b) software selection

(c) hardware selection

(d) both (b) & (c)

(e) neither (b) nor (c)

(49) Smart card pertains to:

(a) system project management

(b) return on investment

(c) GUI

(d) structured design

(e) none of the above

(50) A use case diagram is a classic case of:

(a) flow chart

(b) what-if analysis

(c) interaction between system and its environment

(d) gathering qualitative information

(e) none of the above

Q.500 Illustrate the software development life cycle with the help of a suitable diagram.

16. BONUS INTERVIEW QUESTIONS ON C#.NET 201

Q.501 Compare in brief C++, Java, and C#.

Q.502 Discuss the evolution of the various versions of C#.

Q.503 Give two compelling reasons for the creation of C#.

Q.504 Mention two main points as to how C# relates to the .NET Framework.

Q.505 Distinguish between managed and unmanaged code.

Q.506 What are the value types allowed by C#?

Q.507 What is the decimal data type intended for?

Q.508 Is there any special significance of the char data type in C#?

Q.509 What do you understand by a widening and a narrowing conversion?

Q.510 What is the difference between the use of the prefix increment ++x and the use of the postfix increment x++ in C# and Java?

Q.511 What is the difference between short-circuit logical operators | | OR and && AND in C# and Java?

Q.512 Can you name an operator in C# that takes three operands?

Q.513 Can you create a 'for' loop without any conditional expressions? What does it amount to?

Q.514 What does the foreach loop do?

Q.515 What do the break and continue statements do? Bring out the main point of difference between them.

Q.516 Explain the use of the keyword new.

Q.517 Can new be used with value types?

Q.518 Point out the difference between C++ and C# as regards release of previously allocated memory.

Q.519 What is the purpose of the destructor in C#?

Q.520 What do you understand by 'this'?

Q.521 Can you elaborate on the concept of jagged arrays?

Q.522 Can you point out the main difference between C/C++ strings and C# strings?

Q.523 Can the contents of strings in C# be changed?

Q.524 What are C#'s access modifiers?

Q.525 What is the use of the ref and out keywords?

Q.526 Is it possible to have a variable number of arguments in C#?

Q.527 What is the use of the object initializers?

Q.528 Can you elaborate on the use of the optional arguments?

Q.529 Can optional arguments result in ambiguity?

Q.530 What do you understand by named arguments?

Q.531 Specify the forms of the Main () method available in C#.

Q.532 Elucidate the role of the keyword static.

Q.533 Point out any two restrictions on static methods?

Q.534 When an operator is overloaded, does its original meaning get lost?

Q.535 What are indexers used for?

Q.536 What are properties used for?

Q.537 Are indexers and properties related to each other?

Q.538 Can you overload an indexer?

Q.539 Does an indexer require an underlying array?

Q.540 What is the main difference between a private variable and a property?

Q.541 What do you mean by an auto-implemented property?

Q.542 Can properties be overloaded?

Q.543 Can a property be passed as a ref or out parameter to a method?

Q.544 Can you use a different access modifier with the get and set accessors than the one used for their indexer / property?

Q.545 Both the base class and the derived class can have their own constructors. So, what constructor is responsible for building an object of the derived class – the one in the base class, or the one in the derived class, or both?

Q.546 How does a derived class call a constructor defined in its base class?

Q.547 In what order are constructors called in a class hierarchy?

Q.548 What do you mean by method overriding?

Q.549 What do you understand by dynamic method dispatch?

Q.550 Can properties / indexers be modified by the keyword virtual and overridden using override?

Q.551 Can you give one good reason for using overridden methods?

Q.552 Can an abstract method have a body?

Q.553 Can you use virtual and abstract together?

Q.554 Can you create an object of an abstract class using new?

Q.555 What are the two uses of the keyword sealed?

Q.556 What do you mean by boxing and unboxing?

Q.557 Is the object class a universal data type? If it is, what are its pitfalls?

Q.558 Define an interface in C#.

Q.559 What is the main point of difference between structures and classes?

Q.560 What is the similarity and difference between interfaces and abstract classes?

Q.561 How will you choose between an interface and an abstract class?

Q.562 When would you prefer to use a structure instead of a class?

Q.563 Can an enumeration be used to control a switch statement or as a control variable in a 'for' loop?

Q.564 What are an exception and an exception handler?

Q.565 Can you elaborate on the consequences of an uncaught exception?

Q.566 What is the major benefit of exception handling?

Q.567 What are the pitfalls of using the 'catch all' handler as a means of dealing with exceptions?

Q.568 Can you have a try block followed by a finally block with no catch clauses?

Q.569 Elucidate the use of the checked and unchecked keywords.

Q.570 What is a stream in C#?

Q.571 Name the standard console I / O streams.

Q.572 How is binary data read and written?

Q.573 Define a delegate and an event.

Q.574 What do you understand by multicasting?

Q.575 In what way are delegates useful?

Q.576 Name the two types of lambda expressions.

Q.577 How does an event work?

Q.578 Define a namespace.

Q.579 Can namespaces be nested, one inside another?

Q.580 List the C# preprocessor directives.

Q.581 What do you mean by generics?

Q.582 Can properties/indexers/operators be generic?

Q.583 Explain in brief the utility of LINQ.

Q.584 What do you understand by nullable types?

Q.585 Differentiate between dynamic type and the object class.

Q.586 How can you create a string in C# that is mutable?

Q.587 What do you understand by multithreading?

Q.588 What is meant by TPL?

Q.589 What is meant by PLINQ?

Q.590 While using the TPL, what are the two basic ways in which you can add parallelism?

Q.591 Elucidate the utility of collections.

Q.592 What is the ArrayList class?

Q.593 What is a Hashtable?

Q.594 Define a SortedList.

Q.595 On what principle does a Stack operate?

Q.596 What is the principle behind the Queue?

Q.597 What is a BitArray?

Q.598 Elaborate on the role of the enumerator.

Q.599 What is the utility of the collection initializers?

Q.600 What types of comments are supported by C#? Does it support XML documentation comments?

1

CORE JAVA & OOP

Q. 1 Discuss the significance of the Java language.

ANS. Java is the preeminent language of the Internet. Apart from this, many of its features are influencing upcoming languages such as C#. Java not only opened the door to immense possibilities on the Internet, but is inherently suitable for administrative data processing (via database processing), for development using client/server architectures as well as for something it was tailor-made: industrial and loaded data processing.

Without any doubt, we can say that Java shall remain a popular programming language for many a future years to come.

Q. 2 Elaborate briefly upon the evolution of Java.

ANS. A research team at Sun Microsystems was working on the development of home automation applications that could be integrated into cellular telephones and real-time portable systems all of which were developed using C++. This type of development imposed certain restrictions due to the differing hardware architectures, interconnection problems between different machines etc. C++ was not particularly suitable for this kind of development as it is greedy on memory, lacks portability across processes, and pointer management risks the deletion of data vital to the operation of the application.

Given such problems, one of the team members, namely James Gosling endeavoured to write a new programming language. Given its application domain, this language needed to be object-oriented, high performance oriented, fast and such as to ensure portability between different types of hardware. At first, it was called C++--, then Oak, and finally Java - a slang term for "coffee" - due to the amount of coffee consumed by the developers.

Q. 3 Compare in brief C/C++, C#, and Java.

ANS. Java derives its syntax from C. Many of the object-oriented features of Java were strongly influenced by C++. But, it would be improper to consider Java as the "Internet version of C++". C# and Java are similar in the sense that they both share the same C++ syntax, support distributed programming, and both make use of the same object model. But, in spite of this, there are stark differences between the two.

We have already stated that Java is closely related to both C and C++, deriving its syntax from C and the object-oriented features from C++. Now, we shall see in what ways it differs from them in terms of programming.

Differences between Java & C:

- Java does not have the C keywords: *sizeof, typedef, auto, extern, register, signed, unsigned.*
- Java adds new operators such as *instanceof* and >>> (unsigned right shift).
- Java adds labelled break and continue statements.
- Java does not support the data types *struct* and *union.*
- Java does not have an explicit *pointer* type.
- Java does not have a *preprocessor* and thus, does not support any preprocessor directive such as *#define, #include, #ifdef* etc.

Differences between Java & C++:

- Java does not support *operator overloading.*
- Java does not allow *default arguments.*
- Java does not support *multiple inheritance.*
- Although Java supports constructors, it does not have *destructors*. Instead, it has a *finalize()* function.
- Java does not allow the *goto.*
- Java does not have the *delete* operator.
- Java does not support *global variables/functions* as all the code in a Java program is encapsulated within one or more classes.
- The << and >> in Java are not overloaded for I/O operations.
- In Java, objects are passed by *reference* only. In C++, they could be passed by reference as well as by value.
- Java adds *multithreading, packages, interfaces,* a third comment type: the *documentation comment* that begins with /** and ends with */, and a built-in string type called *String.*
- Java does not have C++ type libraries but has its own set of *API* (Application Program Interface) classes.
- While both Java and C++ support a boolean data type, their implementation is different.
- In C++, a nonzero value is true while zero value is false. But, in Java, true and false are treated as *predefined literals.*
- In a C++ class, the access operators apply to a group of statements while in Java, they apply only to the *declarations* they immediately precede.
- Both Java and C++ support exception handling. But, in C++, there is no particular requirement that a thrown exception be *necessarily caught* as is the case in Java.

Q. 4 Elaborate on the main features of Java.

ANS. Some of the main features of Java include the following:-

(i) Simple and secure

(ii) Portable and architecture-neutral

(iii) *Object-oriented*
(iv) *Robust and multithreaded*
(v) *Interpreted and high performance*
(vi) *Distributed and dynamic*

Q. 5 Name and enumerate the three Object-Oriented Programming (OOP) principles.

ANS. The three object-oriented programming (OOP) principles are:-
(i) *Encapsulation*
(ii) *Inheritance*
(iii) *Polymorphism*

These three principles work together in unison.

Q. 6 Distinguish between "call-by-value" and "call-by-reference".

ANS. There are, in general, two ways that a computer language can pass an argument to a subroutine. The first way is referred to as "call-by-value" while the second is known as "call-by-reference". In "call-by-value", the method copies the value of an argument into the formal parameter of the subroutine, and whence, changes made to the parameter of the subroutine have no effect on the argument. In contrast to this, a reference to an argument, and, not the value of the argument is passed to the parameter in the "call-by-reference" approach. Inside the subroutine, this reference is then used to access the actual argument specified in the call so that changes made to the parameter will affect the argument used to call the subroutine.

In Java, when a simple type is passed to a method, it is done through "call-by-value" whereas objects are passed through "call-by-reference".

Q. 7 What is recursion? Does Java support recursion?

ANS. Recursion is the process of defining something in terms of itself. Java does support recursion as it allows a method to call itself. Such a method is said to be recursive. A classic case of recursion is computing the factorial of a number.

Q. 8 How can you determine the size of an array?

ANS. The size of an array, that is to say, the number of elements it can hold, is found in its length instance variable.

Q. 9 How are command-line arguments passed in Java?

ANS. In Java, all command-line arguments are passed as strings only. If you wish to pass numeric values, they must be converted to their internal forms manually.

Q. 10 What is the difference between the prefix increment ++x and the postfix increment x++?

ANS. The statement:-

```
y = y + x++;
```

adds the current values of x and y and assigns this result back to y. The value of x is only incremented after the value of y has been thus obtained.

On the other hand, the statement:-

```
y = y + ++x;
```

obtains the value of x, increments x, then adds that value to the current value of y, and this result is assigned to y.

You can see for yourself (by assigning some initial values to x and y) that simply changing ++x to x++ changes the results quite substantially when both of the above statements are run over a loop.

Q. 11 What is the use of short-circuit logical operators || OR and && AND?

ANS. Contrary to the normal counterparts | and &, the short circuit operators | | and && evaluate the second operand only when necessary. That is to say, the result of the OR operation will always be true if the first operand is true irrespective of the second operand. Similarly, the result of the AND operation will always be false if the first operand is false irrespective of the second operand. In both these cases, | | and && do not evaluate the second operand unlike their normal counterparts | and &, which evaluate both the operands in all situations.

Q. 12 Can you name an operator in Java that takes three operands?

ANS. The ternary operator with the most general form:-

exp1 ? exp2 : exp3;

(if exp1 is true, exp2 becomes the value of the whole expression else exp3 becomes the value of the whole expression)

Q. 13 Can you create a 'for' loop without any conditional expressions? What does it amount to?

ANS. Leaving the conditional expressions in a 'for' loop makes it an infinite loop that will run forever:-

```
for ( ; ; )        // intentional infinite loop
{
            ..............................
            ..............................
}
```

Q. 14 Can Objects be passed as parameters just like simple types?

ANS. Yes! The answer to this query is in the affirmative.

Q. 15 What do the break and continue statements do? Bring out the main point of difference between them.

ANS. The break statement causes an early termination of the loop whereas the continue statement causes an early iteration of the loop.

Q. 16 Explain the use of the keyword new.

ANS. The keyword new is used to create objects, e.g.

House building = new House ();

Here, building by itself does not contain the object (House). Rather, it contains a reference to it.

On the other hand, consider:

int i = 100;

Here, i contains the value 100 since i is a variable of type *int*, which, in turn, is a value type.

Again, consider:

House building1 = new House ();

House building2 = new House ();

building2 = building1;

House building3 = new House ();

building2 = building3;

After the execution of this sequence, building2 refers to the same object (House) as building3. The object (House) referred to by building1 is unchanged.

Q. 17 What are the two uses of the keyword super?

ANS. *(i)* A subclass can call a constructor defined in its superclass by using the keyword super.

(ii) The second use of super relates to situations in which member names of a subclass hide members by the same name in the superclass. In such a case, you can refer to the superclass member by using super.member.

Q. 18 Point out the difference between C++ and Java as regards release of previously allocated memory.

ANS. In C++, the delete operator is used to free memory that was previously allocated. But, Java uses a different, more trouble-free approach, viz. garbage collection.

Q. 19 What is the purpose of the finalize() method in Java?

ANS. We can define a method in Java that shall be called just prior to the object's final destruction by the garbage collector. This method is known as the *finalize()* method, which can be used in some highly specialized situations to ensure that the object is destroyed / terminated cleanly.

Q. 20 What do you understand by 'this'?

ANS. When a method is called, it is, by itself, passed a reference to the invoking object, i.e. the object on which the method is called. This reference is referred to as 'this'.

Q. 21 Can you elaborate on the concept of jagged arrays?

ANS. In general, when we create a two-dimensional array, we are creating what is a rectangular array with the length of each row being the same for the entire array, e.g. a 2 x 3 array implies an array of two rows with three elements in each row. But, Java allows you to create a special two-dimensional array called a jagged array, which is an array of arrays, where the length of each array can differ. In this way, we can have a table where the lengths of the rows differ, e.g.

```
int jag [ ] [ ] = new int [4] [ ];
jag [0] = new int [10];        // length of first array is ten
jag [1] = new int [2];         // length of second array is two
jag [2] = new int [5];         // length of third array is five
jag [3] = new int [8];         // length of fourth array is eight
```

Q. 22 Can you point out the main difference between C/C++ strings and Java strings?

ANS. In C/C++, strings are simply arrays of characters terminated by the '\0' null character whereas in Java, string is a built-in data type. In fact, in Java, strings are objects and thus, reference types.

Q. 23 Can the contents of strings in Java be changed?

ANS. No, strings in Java are immutable. This might seem to be a drawback but since unused string objects are automatically garbage-collected, you can simply create a new string with the desired changes. (Refer Q. 92 also)

Q. 24 What are Java's access modifiers?

ANS. In Java, member access control is achieved through three access modifiers, namely, public, private, and protected. The protected modifier applies only in case of inheritance. When a member of a class is modified by the public specifier, then that member can be accessed by any code in your program. If a member of a class is specified to be private, it can then only be accessed by other members of its class so that methods in other classes will not be able to access a private member of another class.

Q. 25 Which feature of C/C++ is similar to overridden methods in Java?

ANS. Overridden methods in Java are similar to virtual functions in C/C++.

Q. 26 Is it possible to have a variable number of arguments in Java?

ANS. Yes, this is a recently added new feature to Java. It was added by JDK 5. The addition of this feature has enabled formatted output in Java akin to the *printf()* family of functions in C.

We might also mention here that it is possible to have a normal parameter along with the variable-length parameter but in such cases, the variable length parameter must be the last one in the method declaration. Moreover, you cannot have a method with more than one variable-length parameter.

Q. 27 Can you declare a class as both abstract and final?

ANS. An abstract class is incomplete by itself and relies upon its subclasses to provide complete implementation. Whence, it is illegal to declare a class as both abstract and final.

Q. 28 When do you declare an element as protected?

ANS. In Java, if you want to allow an element to be visible outside your current package, but only to classes that subclass your class directly, then you declare that element as protected.

Q. 29 Where does the package statement occur in a Java source file?

ANS. The package statement must be the first statement in a Java source file.

Q. 30 Where does the import statement occur in a Java source file?

ANS. The import statement in a Java source file must occur immediately after the package statement, if any, and before any class definitions.

Q. 31 Specify the forms of the Main () method available in Java.

ANS. The following four versions of Main () are currently available in Java:-

(i) public static void main ()

(ii) public static int main ()

(iii) public static void main (String args[ ])

(iv) public static int main (String args[ ])

Q. 32 Elucidate the role of the keyword static.

ANS. In general, a class member has to be accessed through an object of its instance. But, it is possible in Java to create a member that can be used by itself, without any reference to a specific instance. To create such a member, you have to precede its declaration with the keyword static.

Q. 33 Point out any four restrictions on static methods?

ANS. First, a static method cannot have a 'this' reference. Second, a static method cannot refer to super in any way. Third, a static method can directly call only other static methods. Finally, a static method can have access only to static data.

Q. 34 Which feature of Java is akin to multiple inheritance in C++?

ANS. Interfaces in Java provide most of the functionality associated with multiple inheritance in C++.

Q. 35 Can Java interfaces be inherited?

ANS. The answer to this query is indeed in the affirmative.

Q. 36 Give a one line definition of an exception. What do you mean by checked and unchecked exceptions?

ANS. An exception is a run-time error.

Most of the exceptions are directly available from the JVM (such as *ArithmeticException*, *ArrayIndexOutOfBoundsException* etc.) and need not be specified in the throws list of any method. All these exceptions are known as unchecked exceptions. Then, there are other exceptions such as *IllegalAccessException* defined by *java.lang*, which must be specified in the throws statement in case a method generates them but does not handle them by itself. Such exceptions are called checked exceptions.

Q. 37 Which class is at the top of the exception hierarchy?

ANS. Throwable.

Q. 38 Which are the two important subclasses of Throwable?

ANS. Exception and Error.

Q. 39 Can you name the all important subclass of Exception?

ANS. RuntimeException.

Q. 40 What is RuntimeException?

ANS. *RuntimeException* is a subclass of *Exception* and includes such run-time programming error conditions such as divide-by-zero and invalid array index.

Q. 41 What does the throws clause do?

ANS. A *throws* clause lists all the types of exceptions that a method might *throw* but does not handle them by itself.

Q. 42 How is java.lang related to exceptions?

ANS. Inside its standard package *java.lang*, Java defines several exception classes. The most general of these exceptions are subclasses of the standard type *RuntimeException*. Since *java.lang* is implicitly imported into all Java programs, most of the exceptions derived from *RuntimeException* are automatically available and need not be included in the throws list of any method. In terms of Java, these are known as unchecked exceptions since the Java compiler does not check to see if a method handles or throws these exceptions.

Q. 43 Can you create your own custom exceptions in Java?

ANS. Although Java's built-in exceptions are capable of handling the most common errors, there will still be occasions when you would like to create your own exception types specific to your applications. This is quite simply done by defining a subclass of *Exception*, which, in turn, is in fact a subclass of *Throwable.*

Q. 44 What do you understand by chained exceptions?

ANS. Java 2, version 1.4 added the feature of chained exceptions to the exception subsystem of Java. This feature allows you to associate one exception with another where the second exception describes the cause of the first exception. For instance, take the case when an ArithmeticException occurred because of an attempt to divide-by-zero. But, the actual cause of the problem was that an I/O error occurred, which caused the divisor to be set to zero. In such a scenario, the method must certainly throw an Arithmetic Exception but you also might want to let the calling code know that the underlying cause was an I/O error: chained exceptions allow you to do this and any similar situation where layers of exceptions exist, thus forming a chain.

Q. 45 Both the subclass and the superclass can have their own constructors. So, what constructor is responsible for building an object of the subclass – the one in the superclass, or the one in the subclass, or both?

ANS. The constructor for the superclass constructs the superclass part of the object and the constructor for the subclass builds the subclass portion of the object.

Q. 46 How does a subclass call a constructor defined in its superclass?

ANS. A subclass can call a constructor defined in its superclass by using the super keyword in the following manner:-

super (param_list);

where, param_list specifies any parameters required by the constructor in the superclass. Note that super must always be the first statement executed inside a subclass' constructor.

Q. 47 In what order are constructors called in a class hierarchy?

ANS. In a class hierarchy, constructors are called in their order of derivation, that is, from superclass to subclass.

Q. 48 What do you mean by method overriding?

ANS. When a method in a subclass has the same name, return type, and signature as that in the superclass, it is said to override the method in the superclass and this phenomenon is referred to as method overriding in Java.

Q. 49 What do you understand by dynamic method dispatch?

ANS. Dynamic method dispatch is the means by which a call to an overridden method is resolved at run-time rather than at compile time. It is important since Java implements run-time polymorphism this way.

Q. 50 Can you give one good reason for using overridden methods?

ANS. Overridden methods are another way that Java implements the 'one interface, multiple methods' aspect of polymorphism.

Q. 51 Can an abstract method have a body? Can an abstract class have concrete methods (other than abstract ones)?

ANS. While the answer to the first query is in the negative the answer to the second query is in the affirmative.

Q. 52 Can you create an object of an abstract class using new?

ANS. An abstract class does not specify a complete implementation and whence, there can be no objects of an abstract class. Therefore, attempting to create an object of an abstract class using new will lead to a consequent compile time error.

Q. 53 What are the three uses of the keyword final?

ANS. (i) You can use final to prevent a class from being inherited by preceding the class declaration with the keyword final.

(ii) You can use final to prevent further overriding of a method by preceding its declaration with the keyword final.

(iii) The keyword final can be used to create what are known as final named constants.

Q. 54 What do you mean or understand by type wrappers?

ANS. In Java, simple types such as int or char are not part of the object hierarchy. They are passed by value to methods and cannot be directly passed by reference. Moreover, there is no way for two methods to refer to the same instance of an int. There will be occasions when you need to create an object representation for one of these simple types, e.g., there are the enumeration classes, which deal only with objects, and thus, to store a simple type in one of these classes, you must wrap the simple type in a class. To take care of this need, Java provides for classes that correspond to each of these simple types. These classes essentially encapsulate or wrap the simple types within a class and whence, they are commonly referred to as type wrappers.

Q. 55 What do you mean by autoboxing and auto-unboxing?

ANS. Beginning with JDK 5, Java added two important features, namely, autoboxing and auto-unboxing. Auto-boxing is the process by which a primitive type is automatically encapsulated ("boxed") into its equivalent type wrapper whenever an object of that type is required. There is thus, no need to construct an object explicitly as such.

Auto-unboxing is the process by means of which the valued of a "boxed" object is automatically extracted ("unboxed") from a type wrapper when its value is required. There is thus, no need to explicitly invoke a method such as *intValue()* or *doubleValue()* etc.

Q. 56 What is the Object class in Java?

ANS. There is one special class, Object, defined by Java, which is a superclass of all other classes. This means that a reference variable of type Object can refer to object of any other class. Moreover, since arrays are implemented as classes in Java, a variable of type Object can also refer to any array.

Q. 57 Define an interface in Java.

ANS. An interface defines a set of methods that will be implemented by a class. An interface, by itself, does not implement any method. In this way, we see that an interface is a purely logical construct that describes functionality without defining any implementation whatsoever.

Q. 58 What is the similarity and difference between interfaces and abstract classes?

ANS. Interfaces are syntactically similar to abstract classes. But, in an interface, no method can have a body. Thus, an interface does not provide any implementation at all. It tells what is to be done but is completely silent about how it is to be done. Once an interface is specified, any number of classes can implement it. Moreover, one class may implement any number of interfaces.

Q. 59 How will you choose between an interface and an abstract class?

ANS. When you can fully describe the concept in terms of 'what it does' without any need to specify 'how it does it', you should use an interface. However, if you need to include at least some implementation details, you should use an abstract class to represent your concept.

Q. 60 What is an exception handler?

ANS. As we have already stated in the answer to Q. 36, an exception is an error which occurs at run-time. Exception handling streamlines error handling by allowing the program to specify a block of code, called an exception handler, which is executed automatically in case of an error. Exception handler eliminates the need to manually check the success / failure of each specific operation or method call. In case an error occurs, it is processed / handled by the exception handler gracefully.

Q. 61 Can you elaborate on the consequences of an uncaught exception?

ANS. In general, if your program does not catch an exception, it will be caught by the run-time system, which, in turn, will report an error and terminate the program abnormally / ungracefully.

Q. 62 What is the major benefit of exception handling?

ANS. One of the major benefits of exception handling is that it enables your program to respond to an error and then continue running, that is, handle the error gracefully, and then continue further.

Q. 63 Can you have a try block followed by a finally block with no catch clauses?

ANS. Syntactically, when a finally block follows a try block, no catch clauses are technically required. In such a case, the finally block gets executed after exit from the try block, but no exceptions are handled in such a case / event.

Q. 64 Explain the concept of an inner class.

ANS. Classes present inside another class are termed inner classes. A point to note is that inner classes increase the complexity of code and must be used only if absolutely necessary. In this context, it would be worthwhile to mention that inner classes are used to implement adapters in an AWT program.

```
class X
    {
        int x;
        public void do()
        {   }
        // Inner class
        Class Y
        {
            public void done()
            {
                /* can access the instance variables of the outer class */
                x = 100;
            }
        }
    }
```

Q. 65 Explain the concept of anonymous classes.

ANS. An anonymous class is an inner class without a name. An anonymous class, in general, makes the code difficult to read and understand. Its use must be limited to very small classes (with a method or two) and whose use is well understood such as in the case of the AWT event-handling adapter classes.

Q. 66 What types of variables are allowed in an interface?

ANS. All the variables in an interface must be public, static and final, that is to say, constants.

Q. 67 Are there any restrictions imposed on interfaces vis-à-vis classes?

ANS. An interface is akin to a class with a few restrictions including the following:-

(1) As mentioned in the previous problem, all variables in an interface must be public, static and final, i.e. constants.

(2) All methods in an interface are implicitly declared public and abstract.

Another point to note is that a class can inherit multiple interfaces.

Q. 68 What is a stream in Java?

ANS. Java programs perform Input / Output through streams. A stream is an abstraction that produces / consumes information. A stream is liked to a physical device by the I/O system. It is useful to note that all streams behave in the same manner irrespective of the physical device they might be linked to.

Q. 69 Compare and contrast byte streams with character streams.

ANS. The following four are the major points of difference between Byte Streams and Character Streams:-

(1) *java.io.InputStream and java.io.OutputStream are the base byte streams while java.io.Reader and java.io.Writer are the base character streams.*

(2) *Byte streams are 8 bit streams while character streams are 16 bit Unicode streams.*

(3) *In byte streams, method names end with the suffix InputStream or OutputStream while in case of character streams, method names end with the suffix Reader or Writer.*

(4) *Since character streams are Unicode, they are internationalized and more efficient than byte streams.*

Q. 70 Elucidate the benefits of the streams.

ANS. The streaming interface to I/O in Java provides a clean abstraction for a complex and often cumbersome task. The composition of the filtered stream classes allows you to dynamically build the custom streaming interface to suit your data transfer requirements. Java programs written to adhere to the abstract, high-level InputStream, OutputStream, Reader, and Writer classes will function properly even in the future when new and improved concrete stream classes are invented. This model works very well even when we switch from a file system-based set of streams to the network and socket streams. Moreover, serialization of objects is expected to play an increasingly important role in the future Java programming. In fact, Java's serialization I/O classes provide a portable solution to this sometimes tricky task/proposition.

Q. 71 Name the predefined I/O streams in Java.

ANS. *System.in*, *System.out*, and *System.err* are the three predefined I/O streams in Java. By default, *System.in* refers to the keyboard while *System.out* and *System.err* refer to the console.

Q. 72 Name the two byte streams and the two character streams related to File I/O in Java, respectively.

ANS. *FileInputStream & FileOutputStream* are the two byte streams and *FIleReader & FileWriter* are the two character streams, respectively, related to File I/O in Java.

Q. 73 How is binary data read and written?

ANS. Binary data is read and written using the *DataInputStream* and *DataOutputStream* streams, respectively.

Q. 74 Name the two classes at the top of the byte stream classes.

ANS. *InputStream* and *OutputStream*.

Q. 75 Name the two classes at the top of the character stream classes.

ANS. *Reader* and *Writer.*

Q. 76 Does Java have a generalized console input formatter akin to the standard C function scanf() or the C++ input operators?

ANS. Yes, added by JDK 5 recently, Java has the Scanner class which reads formatted input and converts it into its binary form. The Scanner class is the complement of the Formatter class of Java which has made formatted output in Java very easy akin to the *printf()* style of functions in C/C++.

Q. 77 Elucidate the New I/O system.

ANS. Java 2, version 1.4 added a new way to handle I/O operations. Called the new I/O APIs, it supports a channel-based approach to I/O operations. The new I/O (NIO) system is built on two foundational items, viz. buffers and channels. A buffer holds data. A channel represents an open connection to an I/O device, such as a file or a socket. In general, to use the NIO system, you obtain a channel to an I/O device and a buffer to hold data. You then operate on the buffer, inputting / outputting data as needed. We must, at this stage, sound a caveat as to whether NIO is the future of I/O handling? The channel/buffer based NIO approach is currently designed to supplement, and not supplant the traditional and standard stream-based I/O mechanisms.

Q. 78 What types of comments are supported by Java? Does it support documentation comments?

ANS. Java supports three types of comments – the first two are // and /* */. The third type is called a documentation comment. A documentation comment begins with /** and ends with */. Using such documentation comments, you can embed information about your program into the program itself; and, later on, you can use the *javadoc* utility program to extract this information and put it into an HTML file.

Q. 79 Define a package.

ANS. A package is a container for classes that is used to keep the class name space compartmentalized.

Q. 80 Can you create a hierarchy of packages?

ANS. You can indeed create a hierarchy of packages. To do so, simply separate each package name from the one above it by using a period. The most general form of a multileveled package statement is as follows:-

package pkg1[.pkg2[.pkg3.[pkg4]]];

Note that a package hierarchy must be reflected in the file system of your Java development system.

Q. 81 What does the Math class contain?

ANS. The Math class contains all the floating-point functions that are used for geometry and trigonometry such as *sin()*, as well as several general-purpose methods such as *sqrt()*.

Q. 82 What do you mean by generics?

ANS. Generics imply parameterized types. They provide a streamlined and type-safe approach to deal with different data types as also promote reusability of code. Generics were introduced by JDK 5 and are somewhat similar to templates in C++.

Q. 83 How is java.util useful?

ANS. The *java.util* package contains one of Java's most powerful subsystems, viz. collections. In addition to collections, *java.util* contains a wide assortment of classes and interfaces, which support a broad range of functionality such as generating pseudorandom numbers, manipulating date and time, observing events, manipulating sets of bits, and tokenizing strings. These classes and interfaces are used throughout the core Java packages and are, of course, available for use in the programs you write.

Q. 84 Elucidate the utility of collections.

ANS. Collections simplify many programs by providing off-the-shelf solutions to several common but at times difficult to develop data structures. For instance, there are built-in collections that support dynamic arrays, linked lists, stacks, queues, and hash tables.

Q. 85 On what principle does a Stack operate?

ANS. Stack is a First-in, Last-out list. To visualize a stack, imagine a stack of plates on a table. The first plate put down is the last one to be retrieved.

Q. 86 What is the principle behind the Queue?

ANS. Queue is a First-in, First-out list, i.e. the first item put in a queue is the first item retrieved from it. Queues are common in real life, e.g. lines at a bank or railway reservation center are queues.

Q. 87 What is a Hashtable?

ANS. Hashtable creates a collection which uses a hash table for 'storage (the hash table, in turn, stores information using a mechanism known as hashing).

Q. 88 What is the ArrayList class?

ANS. The ArrayList class supports dynamic arrays, which can grow or shrink as per the user requirements.

Q. 89 Should collections be limited to "large jobs" such as corporate databases, inventory systems, or mailing lists?

ANS. Collections need not be reserved for only the "large jobs" such as corporate databases, inventory systems, or mailing lists. They are equally effective when applied to smaller jobs, e.g., a TreeMap would be ideal to hold the directory structure of a set of files and a TreeSet would be an excellent choice for storing project-management information.

Q. 90 How can you obtain an Array from an ArrayList?

ANS. When working with *ArrayList*, you might want to obtain an actual array, which contains the contents of the list. You can easily accomplish this by calling the *toArray()* method.

Q. 91 Are the == and the equals() method the same? If not, point out the difference between the two.

ANS. It is important to understand that the *equals()* method and the = = operator perform two different operations. While the *equals()* method compares the characters inside a String object, the = = operator compares two object references to see whether they refer to the same instance.

Q. 92 How can you create a string in Java that is mutable?

ANS. A mutable string in Java can be created by means of the *StringBuffer* class. In the *StringBuffer* class, characters can be inserted in the middle or appended to the end of a string.

Q. 93 Can an enumeration be used to control a switch statement?

ANS. Yes, enumerations can easily be used to control a switch statement. Of course, all of the case statements must use constants from the same *enum* as that used by the switch expression.

Q. 94 Can you assign floating point values to integers in Java as in C/C++?

ANS. No! Not at all!! This is due to the fact that Java is a very strongly typed language unlike C/C++.

Q. 95 How will you declare a three-dimensional array of shorts and a string variable called surname in Java? How will you determine the size of an array?

ANS. A three-dimensional array of shorts can be declared in Java in the following manner:-

```
short s_arr[][][];
```

A string variable called surname can be declared as:-

```
String surname[];
```

In Java, the size of an array can be determined by means of the property called length.

Q. 96 Can variables in the inner scope have the same name as the ones in the outer scope in Java as in C/C++?

ANS. No! Not at all!! In C/C++, there is no such restriction. However, the designers of Java opined that such "name hiding" could very well lead to programming errors and whence, disallowed it.

Q. 97 Does Java have a foreach loop like C#?

ANS. JDK5 introduced the *for-each* style loop as a simple enhanced version of the *'for'* loop unlike C# which uses the foreach keyword. The major advantage of this is that no keyword is required and no pre-existing legacy code is broken.

The most general form of for-each style loop is:

```
for (var_type var_name : coll)
{
statement(s);
}
```

where, var_type and var_name specify the type and name of the iteration variable and the collection being cycled through is referred to by coll.

Q. 98 What are the two uses of the keyword 'super'?

ANS. The Java keyword, *super*, can be used in two distinct ways. Its first use is to call/ invoke a super class constructor. Its second use lies in accessing a member of the superclass that has been hidden by a member of the subclass having the same name.

A subclass can call a constructor defined in its immediate superclass by using super as given below:

super(argument_list);

where, *argument_list* specifies any arguments needed by the constructor in the superclass. Note that *super()* must be the first statement executed in the constructor of the subclass always. Also, note that since constructors can be overloaded, *super()* can be invoked using any form defined by the superclass. The constructor that matches the parameters/arguments shall be the one to get executed.

Now, we introduce you to the second use of *super* that acts in a manner similar to *this* except for the fact that it always refers to the superclass of the subclass in which it is used. The most general form of this usage is:

super.member

where, *member* can either be an instance variable or a method. This form of *super* applies mostly to cases in which member names of a subclass hide members by the same name in the superclass.

Q. 99 Does Java support formatted output akin to the printf() style function in C/C++? If yes, when did Java begin to have this facility and why it could not provide it earlier?

ANS. With the release of JDK 5 (*Java Development Kit 5*), Java added a new capability, viz. the ability to easily create formatted output akin to the *printf()* style of functions in C/C++. This feature was implemented using the *Formatter* class of Java.

You might wonder why Java was not able to earlier provide such a facility. The simple reason was that the *printf()* style formatting requires the use of variable-length arguments (*varargs*), which Java did not support before JDK 5.

Once *varargs* became available with the release of JDK 5, it was easy pickings to add a general-purpose formatter. At the roots of Java's formatted output is the *Formatter* class, which provides format conversions that let you display numbers, strings, date and time in almost every format as per your requirements very much similar in fashion to the *printf()* function of C/C++.

The *Formatter* class works by converting the binary form of data used by a program into formatted text. It stores this text in a buffer from where it can be obtained any time you need. The buffer may be supplied explicitly or you can let the *Formatter* supply it on its own. *Formatter* may be constructed in a variety of ways including the following:-

Formatter()

Formatter(Appendable buf)

Formatter(String file) throws FileNotFoundException

Formatter(File outF) throws FileNotFoundException

Formatter(OutputStream outStrm)

where, *buf* specifies a buffer for the formatted output, *file* specifies the name of the file which shall receive the formatted output, *outF* specifies a reference to an output file which shall receive the output, and *outStrm* specifies a reference to an output stream which shall receive the output.

After creating the *Formatter*, you can use the following *format()* method to create a formatted string:-

Formatter format(String fmtString, Object ... args)

where, *fmtString* contains either characters which are copied as such to the output buffer or *format specifiers* such as *%d* for integers, *%f* for floating-point data and *%s* for strings.

An integer placed between the % sign and format conversion code acts as the minimum field-width specifier. The default padding is done with spaces. If you want to pad with 0's, place a 0 before the field-width specifier, e.g., *%05d* will pad a number of less than five digits with 0's so that its length is five.

By default, all output is right-justified. You can force output to be left-justified by placing a minus sign directly after the % sign, e.g., *%-10.2f* left-justifies a floating point number with two decimal places in a *10*-character field.

When displaying large numbers, it is often useful to add a comma separator/flag, e.g., *4337788990.23* is more easily read as *4,337, 788,990.23*. *Formatter* lets you achieve this very easily. *Formatter* also includes a very useful feature that lets you specify the argument to which a *format specifier* applies. In other words, it allows you to use an *argument index*.

Q. 100 Can you elaborate on the 'why' of Java?

ANS. Java serves both as a programming language as well as a platform. As a programming language, Java is simple, object-oriented, distributed, interpreted, robust, secure, architecture-neutral, portable, high performance based, multithreaded and dynamic. By definition, a platform is a hardware/software environment in which a program can be run. The majority of present day platforms are a combination of hardware (the machine) and software (the operating system).

The Java platform is quite different in the sense that it consists only of a software component that can be run on varying hardware. It consists of the Java Virtual Machine (JVM) and the Java Application Programming Interface (JAVAAPI).

Java is simple with syntax similar to that of C and C++ but without their semantic complexity that make them confusing and insecure. Thus, there is no need for pointer management etc. Java is object-oriented unlike C but likewise C++.

Java is distributed in the sense that network access protocols like TCP/IP, UDP, HTTP, and FTP are supplied with it that allows for the development of client/server model in order to access data on a distant/remote machine. Once again, a Java program does not operate in the normal way.

Rather, it is interpreted by the JVM. Java achieves robustness by strict program checking during compilation as well as execution. The Java code is verified both during compilation and run-time by the interpreter making it free from errors and ensuring security.

Java is inherently architecture-neutral as the Java compiler produces Java bytecodes independent of any specific environment. The primary data in Java is primarily of the same size (generally IEEE754) ensuring portability across varying platforms. Although the Java program is interpreted resulting in it being slow to a degree but, still, Java uses JIT (Just In Time), a code interpretation optimizing technique resulting in almost the same performance as C++.

Java introduces multithreading, a concept that allows for many things/applications being run simultaneously and increases response time. Finally, in Java, one doesn't have to edit links (mandatory in C++) resulting in executables having a lower memory size. Thus, Java is dynamic as well!

The Java Virtual Machine (JVM) is the base of the Java platform and is essential for running the Java programs. It is compatible with any type of computer machine. The JVM undertakes the loading of Java bytecodes, classes, memory management, security management and, if necessary, interfacing with native code such as C. The JAVAAPI package contains a collection of prefabricated software components that supply a number of functions like the management of graphical interface etc.

The Java Application Interface is organized as a collection of packages just as libraries in C/C++. Each package has Java classes that are predefined language objects directly reusable. The Java platform consisting of the JVM and the JAVAAPI is the link between the hardware and the Java program.

To compile Java source code, we need to use the compiler dedicated to our machine. After compilation, the file remains independent of the hardware platform and the operating system. The interpreter runs Java programs.

To run Java applets, the interpreter is incorporated into Java compatible Web browsers such as HotJava (refer Chapter 2), Netscape Navigator etc. To run independent stand alone Java applications, we need to run the virtual machine (JVM) supplied with the Java development Kit (JDK) or the Java runtime Environment (JRE).

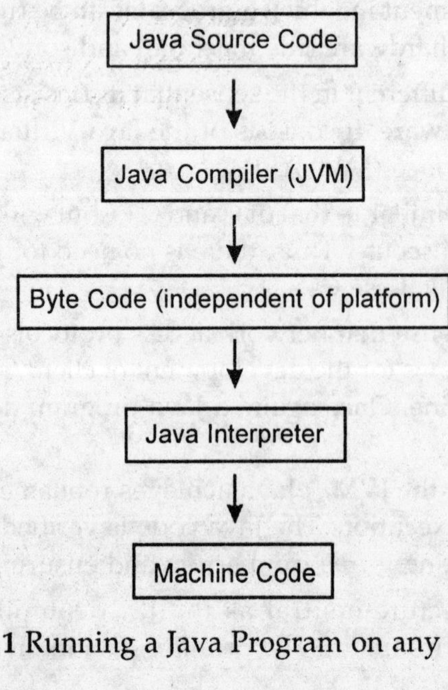

Figure 1 Running a Java Program on any Platform

As discussed above, a Java program is independent of the operating system/platform on which it is run. This is achieved by means of the Java Virtual Machine (JVM) that converts the original source code into bytecodes (which is platform independent). Finally, the Java interpreter on the concerned operating system converts these bytecodes into machine code which can be run on that particular machine. Figure 1 illustrates all this.

Q. 101 Can you explain the difference between a .class file and an .exe file?

ANS. There is basically one main point of difference between the two. While a .class file contains bytecodes for the JVM and is thus system independent, an .exe file contains machine language for the microprocessor and is thus system dependent.

Q. 102 What do you understand by an API document? Elucidate.

ANS. An API document is essentially an *.html* file having complete details of all the features of a software/product/technology. It is very much handy for the users in using the relevant software/product/technology.

Q. 103 Can you explain the difference between the #include statement of C/C++ and the import statement of Java?

ANS. The import statement of Java is a much better option than the #include statement of C/C++ since the import statement makes the JVM go to the standard Java library, run the code over there, and finally, substitute the result into the Java program thus avoiding any wastage of memory/processor's time while the #include directive of C/C++ makes the compiler go to the standard C/C++ library and copy the code from the header files into the C/C++ program leading to a considerable increase in the program size, which, in turn, results in wastage of memory and the processor time.

Q. 104 Suppose, String args [] is not written in the main() method; will the program still run? Elucidate.

ANS. Suppose, we write the main() method without String args [] as follows:-

public static void main()

The compiler will not report any error in such a case but the Java Virtual Machine environment, which always looks for the main() method with String args [] as parameter, will not be able to recognize the main() method in such a case and, whence, the program shall not run/ execute.

Q. 105 Is it possible in Java to call the main() method of a class from another class? Elucidate.

ANS. Yes! It is very much possible!! This is achieved by the use of the relevant *classname.main()*. Note that at the time of calling *main()*, you will have to pass a string type array to it.

Q. 106 Is it possible in Java to compile and run a program without the main() method? Elucidate.

ANS. Yes! It is very much possible!! This is achieved by the use of a static block in the relevant Java program.

Q. 107 Can you explain the difference between the float and double data types of Java?

ANS. The float data type can store up to seven digits after the decimal point accurately; on the other hand, the double data type can store up to fifteen digits after the decimal point accurately.

Q. 108 Can you explain the difference between the return statement and the System.exit(0) statement of Java?

ANS. The *return* statement can be used anywhere in a method to come out of it while *System.exit(0)* can be used anywhere in a method to come out of the Java program itself.

Q. 109 Can you explain the difference between the System.exit(1) statement and the System.exit(0) statement of Java?

ANS. The *System.exit(1)* statement is used to exit the Java program abnormally because of some error encountered during its execution while *System.exit(0)* is used to exit the Java program normally without any error.

Q. 110 Can you explain the difference between the System.err and System.out?

ANS. Although both *System.out* and *System.err* send messages to the monitor, by default, the difference lies in the fact that *System.out* displays normal output while *System.err* displays error messages.

Q. 111 What are the types of memory available in Java; incidentally, on which memory are arrays created in Java?

ANS. There is no static memory in Java; there is only dynamic memory. As such, everything (objects, variables) as well as arrays are created on dynamic memory only.

Q. 112 Can you consider class as a data type?

ANS. Yes! Indeed, a class is a user-defined data type.

Q. 113 What, according to you, is String – a class or a data type?

ANS. String is a class in *java.lang* package. But as mentioned in the previous question, a class can be taken to be a data type as well. Whence, String can be considered as a data type too.

Q. 114 Can you explain the difference between the String class and the StringBuffer class of Java?

ANS. There are two points of difference between *String* and *StringBuffer* classes of Java:-

(i) *String* class objects are immutable so that their contents are not modifiable; *StringBuffer* class objects are mutable so that their contents are modifiable.

(ii) The methods that directly manipulate the contents of objects are available only in the *StringBuffer* class.

Q. 115 Can you explain the difference between the StringBuffer and StringBuilder classes of Java?

ANS. *StringBuilder* is identical to *StringBuffer* with one important exception, viz. it's not synchronized, which, in turn, implies that it's not thread-safe. The main advantage and benefit of *StringBuilder* is faster performance. But, there is a caveat. In cases where you are using multithreading, you must make use of *StringBuffer* instead of *StringBuilder* since only *StringBuffer* is synchronized.

Q. 116 What do you understand by hash code? How can you determine the hash code of an object?

ANS. Hash code is a unique identification number assigned to objects by the JVM. It is created based on the basis of the location of the object in memory and is unique for all objects with the sole exception of String objects. The hash code of an object can be determined using the *hashCode()* method of the Object class in java.lang package.

Q. 117 Can a class in Java be declared private?

ANS. By declaring a class as private, it becomes unavailable to the Java compiler resulting in a compile-time error. However, inner classes can be declared to be private.

Q. 118 What do you understand by factory methods? Elucidate.

ANS. A method that creates and returns an object to the class to which it belongs is known as a factory method. A single factory method can replace several different constructors in the class by accepting different options from the user while in the process of creating the object.

Q. 119 In what different ways can you create an object in Java?

ANS. You can create an object in Java in any of the following ways:-

(i) By the use of the new operator;

(ii) By cloning an already available object;

(iii) By the use of the *newInstance()* method; and,

(iv) By the use of factory methods.

Q. 120 What is the main point of difference between method overloading and method overriding?

ANS. Writing two or more methods with the same name but different signatures is referred to as method overloading while writing two or more methods with the same name and the same signatures is referred to as method overriding.

Q. 121 Can you name the super class for all classes inclusive of your classes as well?

ANS. The Object class.

Q. 122 Can you write an interface without any methods?

ANS. YES!

Q. 123 Can you name the method used in cloning?

ANS. The *clone()* method of the Object class.

Q. 124 What is an abstract method/class?

ANS. An abstract method is simply a method without any body. It is generally used when the same method has to carry out different tasks based upon the object calling it. An abstract class is simply a class with one or more abstract methods.

Q. 125 Can you forcibly implement only the features of your class; if yes, how?

ANS. This can be easily achieved by using an abstract class or by the use of an interface.

Q. 126 Can one interface be implemented from another?

ANS. NO! Not at all!!

Q. 127 Do you think you need to write both the following statements:

(i) import java.awt.event.;*

(ii) import java.awt.;*

Or, the second one alone is sufficient? Give appropriate reason(s) for your answer.

ANS. *event* is a sub-package of *java.awt* package. However, when a package is imported, its sub-packages are not imported into the program by themselves. Whence, for every package or sub-package, you need to write a separate *import* statement. Therefore, if you want to import the classes and interfaces of both the *java.awt.event* and *java.awt* packages, you should include both the *import* statements in your program.

Q. 128 What do you understand by CLASSPATH? Elucidate.

ANS. *CLASSPATH* is an environment variable which tells the Java compiler as to where to look for the class files to import.

Q. 129 What do you understand by a JAR file?

ANS. *A JAR or Java Archive file,* as it is called, is a file containing compressed versions of different .class files, audio files, image files, and directories.

Q. 130 What is the scope of the default access specifier?

ANS. Default members are available within the same package but not outside it.

Q. 131 Bring out the difference between an exception and an error.

ANS. An exception is an error that can be handled gracefully but an error means a condition that cannot be handled and the program can do nothing to handle the situation.

Q. 132 Bring out the difference between throw and throws.

ANS. throw is used to throw an exception explicitly and handle it using a try-catch block while throws is used to throw the exception out of a method without handling it there and then.

Q. 133 Can you name the Wrapper class with only one constructor?

ANS. Character wrapper class.

Q. 134 Can a primitive data type be stored into a collection?

ANS. NO! Not at all!! Collections can store only objects.

Q. 135 Bring out the major difference between ArrayList and Vector.

ANS. *ArrayList* object is not synchronized by default while *Vector* object is synchronized by default.

Q. 136 What do you understand by serialization? Are there any variables which cannot be serialized?

ANS. Serialization is essentially the process of storing object contents into a file; static and transient variables cannot be serialized.

Q. 137 What do you understand by enumerations?

ANS. Enumerations were added to Java with the release of JDK 5. An enumeration is a way of assigning names to integer constants.

To give you a practical example of the need for enumerations, imagine a scenario where you wanted to represent the seasons of the year in a program. You could very well use the integers *0*, *1*, *2*, and *3* to represent *spring*, *summer*, *autumn*, and *winter* respectively. This solution would work but it is not very innovative, e.g., if you used the integer value *0* in the program code, it would not be very obvious that a particular *0* represented *spring*.

Furthermore, it would also not be a very robust solution to the problem, e.g., if you declare an integer variable called *season*, there is nothing to prevent you from assigning the variable *season* any legal integer value other than *0*, *1*, *2*, or *3*. Enumerations offer a much better solution. You can create an enumeration (sometimes called an *enum* type), whose values would be limited to a set of symbolic names, e.g. in this particular case, it could be:

enum season{spring, summer, autumn, winter}

The most general form of an enumeration is:

enum enum_name {enum_list } // notice the keyword *'enum'*!

where, *enum_name* is the name of the said enumeration and *enum_list* is a comma separated list of identifiers.

Java enumerations are class types. Although an *enum* is not instantiated using new, it has more or less the same capabilities as other classes. This feature adds to the power of Java enumerations in a big way, e.g., you can give them constructors, add instance variables/methods, and even implement interfaces.

It is important to realize that each *enum* constant is an object of its enumeration type so that when you define a constructor for an *enum*, the constructor is invoked when each enum constant is created.

Q. 138 What do you understand by annotations?

ANS. JDK 5 introduced a new feature into the Java language, viz. annotations (metadata) by means of which you could embed supplemental information into a source file.

In fact, this information is itself called an annotation, which leaves the semantics/actions of a program unchanged but can be used by various tools both during deployment and development, e.g., an annotation can be processed by a source-code generator.

An annotation is created by means of a mechanism based on the *interface*. To declare an annotation, say, *MyAnnotation*, we proceed as follows:

```
// A simple annotation type
@interface MyAnnotation
{
String s();
int value();
}
```

Take note of the @ preceding the keyword interface. This indicates to the compiler that an annotation is being created. Now, take note of the two members, *s()* and *value()*. All annotations solely consist of method declarations. But, you don't provide bodies for these methods; Java implements these methods instead. Also, the methods act much like fields as we shall see shortly.

Once an annotation is declared, it can be used to annotate any declaration, which means that any type of declaration can have an annotation associated with it, e.g., classes, methods, fields, parameters, and *enum* constants may be annotated. In fact, even an annotation may be annotated. In all cases, the annotation comes before the rest of the declaration. When applying an annotation, its members are given values, e.g., here is an example of *MyAnnotation* being applied to a method:

```
// Annotate a method
@MyAnnotation(s = "string", value = 999)
public static void myMethod()
{
//..................
}
```

Thus, *MyAnnotation* is linked with the method *myMethod()*. Take note of the annotation syntax. The name of the annotation, preceded by a @, is followed by a parenthesized list of member initializations. Also, take note of the fact that no parentheses follow *s* or *value* in this assignment of initial values so that annotation members act like fields in this regard.

Q. 139 What do you understand by a generic type?

ANS. A generic type is a class/interface which can act on any data type. In other words, it is type-safe.

Q. 140 Bring out the major difference between window and frame.

ANS. A *window* is a frame without any borders/title while a *frame* does have borders/title.

Q. 141 Elucidate the MVC architecture in JFC/swing.

ANS. MVC or *Model-View-Controller*, as it is called, is essentially a model used in swing components, wherein, *Model* is the data of the component, *View* is its appearance while *Controller* is a mediator between the model and the view.

In other words, MVC is the separation of the model of an object from its view as well as how it is controlled.

Q. 142 Enumerate the various window panes available in swing.

ANS. The various window panes available in swing are enumerated below:-

(i) *Content pane;*
(ii) *Glass pane;*
(iii) *Layered pane;* and,
(iv) *Root pane.*

Q. 143 What do you understand by a layout manager?

ANS. A *layout manager* essentially is a class helpful in arranging components (in a specific/ particular way) in a frame/container.

Q. 144 Consider the following Method whose sole purpose is to find out if the argument passed to it is odd:

```
public static boolean odd(int k)
{
    return k % 2 == 1;
}
```

Does the Method work?

ANS. An odd number is any integer that leaves 1 as remainder when divided by 2. The expression *k* % 2 computes this remainder; so, it looks like that this Method ought to work. But, it returns the wrong answer one quarter of the time. This is so since half of the integer values are negative and when half of these negative integer values are divided by 2, the remainder is -1, not 1.

Q. 145 Can you provide declarations for two variables z and k such that:

```
z+= k;
    is legal while
z = z + k;
    is illegal?
```

ANS. Consider:

```
short z = 0;
int k = 1234;
The compound assignment:
z += k;          // contains a hidden cast
                 // but compiles without error
while the corresponding simple assignment:
z = z + k;       // requires explicit cast
                 // and won't compile
                 // due to possible loss of precision
```

Q. 146 Can you provide declarations for two variables z and k such that:

```
z+= k; is illegal
while
z = z + k;  is legal?
```

ANS. Consider:

```
Object z = "BE";
String k = "YOURSELF ALWAYS!";
The compound assignment:
z += k;        // is illegal
               // since LHS has an object reference type
               // other than String
while the corresponding simple assignment:
z = z + k;     // is legal since RHS is of type String
               // and String is an assignment
               // compatible with Object
```

Q. 147 Consider the following Program:

```
public class Hurrah
{
    public static void main(String args [])
    {
        System.out.println("H" + "A");
        System.out.println('H' + 'A');
    }
}
```

What does the Program print?

ANS. *HA*
137

Q. 148 *Consider the following Program:*

```
public class Browser
{
    public static void main(String args [])
    {
        System.out.print("explore":);
        http://www.yahoo.mail;
        System.out.println(":maximize");
    }
}
```

What does the Program print?

ANS. *explore::maximize*

Q. 149 Consider the following Program:

```
public class Increase
{
    public static void main(String args [])
    {
        int z = 0;
        for (int y = 0; y < 100; y++)
        z = z++;
        System.out.println(z);
    }
}
```

What does the Program print?

ANS. *0*

Q. 150 Can you provide declaration for a variable z such that the loop:

```
while (z != z + 0)
{ }
```

becomes an infinite loop (note that you are not allowed to declare z to be of type double or float)?

ANS. *z can be initialized to any value of type String:*

```
String z = "BECOME YOURSELF ALWAYS!";
```

The integer value 0 is converted to the string value "0" and appended to z. The resulting string is not equal to the original as computed by the equals() method ; so, it can't be surely identical, as computed by the == operator. Whence, the boolean expression:

(z != z + 0)

evaluates to true always and the loop never terminates.

Q. 151 Consider the following Program:

```
public class Indecision
{
    public static void main(String args [])
    {
        System.out.println(indecisive());
    }
        static boolean indecisive()
    {
        try
    {
        return false;
    }
    finally
    {
    return true;
    }
  }
}
```

What does the Program print?

ANS. *true*

Q. 152 Consider the following Program:

```
public class World
{
    public static void main(String args [])
    {
        try
        {
            System.out.println("Bye");
            System.exit(0);
        }
        finally
        {
            System.out.println("Arunesh");
        }
    }
}
```

What does the Program print?

ANS. *Bye*

Q. 153 Consider the following Program:

```
public class World
{
    public static void main(String args [])
    {
        ((null) null).Bye();
    }
        public static void Bye()
    {
        System.out.println("Arunesh");
    }
}
```

What does the Program print?

ANS. *Arunesh*

Q. 154 Consider the following Program:

```
public class World
{
    public static void main(String args [])
    {
        System.out.println(Bye.Arunesh.Hello);
    }
}
class Bye
{
    static class Arunesh
    {
        static String Hello = "Arunesh";
    }
    static Z Arunesh = new Arunesh();
}
class Z
{
    String Hello = "Bye";
}
```

What does the Program print?

ANS. *Bye*

Q. 155 Consider the following Program:

```
class World
{
    public static final String ITEM = "10,000";
}
    public class Hello extends World
{
    public static final String ITEM = "1";
    public static void main(String args[])
    {
        System.out.println(Hello.ITEM);
    }
}
```

What does the Program print?

ANS. 1

Q. 156 Consider the following code:

```
for (int y = 0, int z = 0; y < 10; y++) { }
```

Will the code compile?

ANS. No! You can declare the data type of at most one variable in the initialization section of the 'for' loop. The correct statement is:-

for (int y = 0, z = 0; y < 10; y ++) { }

Q. 157 Consider the following Program:

```
class Hello
{
    public static void main(String args[])
    {
        boolean b = 1;
        System.out.println(b);
    }
}
```

Will this program compile?

ANS. No! Boolean variables can only take the values – true, false!!

Q. 158 Consider the following Program:

```
class Hello
{
    public static void main(String args[])
    {
        System.out.println(args[3]);
    }
}
```

What does the Program print when run with the following command line?

java Hello VERY GOOD MORNING

(i) *Hello*

(ii) *VERY*

(iii) *GOOD*

(iv) *MORNING*

(v) *exception raised:java.lang.ArrayIndexOutOfBoundsException:3*

ANS. Unlike C/C++, java doesn't start the parameter count with the program name. It does however start with zero. So, in this case, zero starts with VERY, GOOD would be 1, MORNING would be 2 and there is no parameter 3; hence, an exception would be raised, and thus, the correct answer is:-

(v) *exception raised:java.lang.ArrayIndexOutOfBoundsException:3*

Q. 159 Which of the following statements is true?

(i) Methods cannot be overridden to be more private.

(ii) static methods cannot be overloaded.

(iii) Private methods cannot be overloaded.

(iv) An overloaded method cannot throw exceptions which are not checked in the super/ base class.

ANS. *(i)* Methods cannot be overridden to be more private.

Q. 160 Consider the following Program:

```
class base { }
class sub1 extends base { }
class sub2 extends base { }
public class cexcp
{
    public static void main(String args[])
    {
        base b = new base();
        sub1 s1 = (sub1) b;
    }
}
```

What will happen if this program is compiled and executed?

(i) Compile and run without any error

(ii) Compile-time exception is raised

(iii) Run-time exception is raised

ANS. *(iii)* Run-time exception is raised.

Q. 161 Consider the following Program:

```
class base
{
        public void a_mthd(int z) { }
}
public class scope extends base
{
        public static void main(String args[])
        {
        }
        // Method HERE
}
```

Which of the following methods can be legally inserted in place of the comment // Method HERE?

(i) *void a_mthd(int z) throws Exception { }*

(ii) *void a_mthd(long z) throws Exception { }*

(iii) *void a_mthd(long z) { }*

(iv) *public void a_mthd(int z) throws Exception { }*

ANS. *(ii)* void a_mthd(long z) throws Exception { }

(iii) void a_mthd(long z) { }

Q. 162 Consider the following Program:

```
public class Hello
{
        public static void main(String args[])
    {
            /* Modifier at ZZ */ class InnerHello { }
    }
}
```

What modifiers would be legal at ZZ in this program?

(i) *public*

(ii) *private*

(iii) *static*

(iv) *friend*

ANS. (i) public; (ii) private & (iii) static.

Q. 163 You need to create a class that will store unique object elements. You do not need to sort these elements but they must be unique.

What interface might be most suitable to satisfy this need?

(i) *List*

(ii) *Set*

(iii) *Map*

(iv) *Vector*

ANS. *(ii)* Set

Q. 164 Describe a java source file.

ANS. A java source file must have "*.java*" extension. Also, it should have at least one top level public class definition and any number of non-public class definitions. The file name (without the extension) must match the public class name.

Q. 165 What is Bytecode?

ANS. Every java program is converted into one or more class files. The content of each class file is a set of instructions referred to as Bytecode to be executed by the JVM. Java introduces Bytecode to produce platform independent program/code.

Q. 166 Why does the main method need a static identifier?

ANS. The main method needs a static identifier since static methods and members do not require an instance of their class to invoke them and main is the first method that is called/invoked.

Q. 167 Will the program compile if the main method doesn't have the static identifier?

ANS. The program will still compile; but it can't be executed or run.

Q. 168 Which is the default parent class for a Java class?

ANS. *java.lang.Object.* By default, all java classes extend *java.lang.Object* unless they have their own parent class. Moreover, the package named *java.lang* is imported (by default) into all java files.

Q. 169 How are java objects passed to a method?

ANS. Java passes both the primitive types and objects by value. During object passing, the object's reference is copied.

Q. 170 What are native methods?

ANS. Native methods are methods implemented in some other programming language such as C/C++. The Java Native Interface (JNI) is the API to invoke these native methods from a class in java.

Q. 171 What is the order of declaring class, package and import statements within a java file?

ANS. The order should be the following:-

(1) package
(2) import statements
(3) class definition

Q. 172 Can a variable be an unsigned integer?

ANS. No! Not at all!!

In java, all data types are signed numeric numbers.

Q. 173 Can a private method be static?

ANS. YES!

A private method can indeed be static.

Q. 174 Enumerate and elucidate the various bit wise operators.

ANS. The various bit wise operators are:-

(1)	*~a*	*complement*
(2)	*a & b*	*bit wise AND*
(3)	*a | b*	*bit wise OR*
(4)	*a ^ b*	*bit wise exclusive OR (XOR)*
(5)	*a << n*	*left shift n places*
(6)	*a >> n*	*right shift n places*
(7)	*a >>> n*	*unsigned right shift n places*

Q. 175 Explain the use of 'instanceof' operator.

ANS. The *'instanceof'* operator verifies whether its first operand is an instance of its second operand.

Op1 instance of Op2 (Op1 must be the name of an object and Op2 must be the name of a class/interface/array type)

An object is considered to be an instance of a class if that object descends from that class directly/indirectly.

Example

Code:

```
class X
{ }
class Y extends class X
{ }
X x = new Y();
if (x instance of X)
{
    System.out.println("Instance of X");
}
if (x instance of Y)
{
    System.out.println("Instance of Y");
}
```

Output:

```
Instance of X
Instance of Y
```

Q. 176 What are the access modifiers available for a class, method, and variable?

ANS. *public, private, protected,* and *default* access.

Q. 177 Elucidate widening and narrowing conversions.

ANS. A widening conversion occurs when we try to cast an object of lesser size to an object of larger size, e.g. *short to long*. A narrowing conversion, on the other hand, occurs when we try to cast an object of larger size to an object of lesser size, e.g. *long to short*.

Q. 178 How do you create Java API documentation?

ANS. Java API documentation can be created using the **javadoc** utility which parses the declarations and documentation comments in a set of Java source files and produces a corresponding set of HTML pages describing (by default) the public and protected classes, nested classes (but not anonymous inner classes), interfaces, constructors, methods, and fields.

Q. 179 Explain the concept of jar, war and ear files.

ANS. *jar* is Java Archive File used to package classes, property files etc. as a single file. To create a *jar* file we can use the *jar* command just like the *zip* command in windows, e.g. to create a *jar* file with all class files under the current directory, we can use:-

*jar –cvf jarfilename.jar *.class*

war is a Web Archive File used to package a web application, i.e. classes, JSP's, property files etc. as a single file.

ear is an Enterprise Archive File. This format is used to package EJB, JSP, Servlets, property files etc. It is generally used to package an entire enterprise application. It can consist of multiple *war* files.

Each *war* and *ear* will have its own deployment descriptor which is a XML based file.

Q. 180 How many JVM's can run on a single machine?

ANS. A JVM is like any other process. Whence, there is no limit on the number of JVM's which can run on a single machine.,

Q. 181 Explain the Just-In-Time (JIT) compiler.

ANS. The Java interpreter on any platform will interpret the compiled *bytecode* into instructions understandable by the particular hardware. However, the JVM handles one *bytecode* instruction at a time. The java JIT (Just-In-Time) compiler compiles the *bytecode* into the particular machine code as if the program had been compiled initially on that platform. Once the code has been (re)-compiled by the JIT compiler, it will, in general, run more quickly on that system.

Q. 182 Can you retrieve Java code from Bytecode?

ANS. YES!

Class files can be decompiled using utilities such as JAD, which takes the class file as an input and generates a java file. This feature comes especially handy when you are confused as to which version of the java file was used to generate the class file in a multi-user environment.

Q. 183 Explain the concept of garbage collector.

ANS. When an object is no longer required and its reference count is zero, it needs to be cleaned up and freed. The garbage collector does exactly this.

In fact, the garbage collector is a thread running as a part of the JVM process. This thread scans the program for objects that will never again be accessed and releases their resources back to the system. The basic garbage collector uses the mark and sweep algorithm (which marks all the unused variables whose reference count is zero and sweeps them).

Q. 184 Can you force the garbage collector to run?

ANS. NO!

There is no way that guarantees that the garbage collector will indeed run. It runs as and when appropriate.

Q. 185 Bring out the difference between:

(i) *String s1 = new String("xyz");*

(ii) *String s2 = "xyz";*

ANS. *"xyz"* is known as a string literal.

In the first case, a new memory space is allocated in the heap on account of the *'new'* and also allocated in the string pool on account of the literal *"xyz"*

In the second case, when the statement is being compiled, a pointer to the string literal *"xyz"* is stored in *s2*.

Q. 186 When intern() method on a String object is invoked, what happens?

ANS. Interned strings avoid duplicate strings. There is only one copy of each String that has been interned, no matter how many references point to it. The process of converting duplicated strings to shared ones is called interning and is accomplished by means of the *intern()* method.

Q. 187 Bring out the purpose of the StringTokenizer class.

ANS. The *StringTokenizer* class allows an application to break a string into tokens. The *StringTokenizer* methods do not distinguish between identifiers, numbers, and quoted strings, nor do they recognize and skip comments. The set of delimiters (the characters which separate tokens, one from the other) can be specified either at creation time or on a pre-token basis.

Example

Code:

```
StringTokenizer strtok = new StringTokenizer("Testing IT OUT!");
while (strtok.hasMoreTokens()
{
    System.out.println(strtok.nextToken());
}
```

Output:

```
Testing
IT
OUT!
```

Q. 188 Which collection sorts data?

ANS. *TreeMap.*

Q. 189 Bring out the difference between Hashtable and HashMap.

ANS. The main point of difference between *Hashtable* and *HashMap* is that while in a *Hashtable*, methods are synchronized and thus thread safe, in a *HashMap*, methods are not synchronized, not thread safe, making it faster.

Q. 190 Bring out the difference between Enumeration and Iterator interface.

ANS. The main point of difference between *Iterators* and *Enumerations* is that *Iterators* allow the caller to remove elements from the underlying collection during the iteration but *Enumerations* do not allow any such provision.

Q. 191 What do you understand by the Throwable class?

ANS. The *Throwable* class is the superclass of all errors/exceptions in the Java language so that only objects that are instances of the *Throwable* class or one of its subclasses are thrown by the JVM. Thus, only the *Throwable* class or one of its subclasses can be the argument type in a catch clause.

Q. 192 How can you write your own customized exceptions?

ANS. Customized exceptions can be written by extending the *java.lang.Exception* class. In this context, it would be worthwhile to mention that the *toString()* method should be overridden to print an appropriate error message.

Q. 193 Suppose an exception goes uncaught; what happens in such a case?

ANS. An uncaught exception results in the *uncaughtException()* method of the thread's *ThreadGroup* being called, which ultimately causes the termination of the program in which it is thrown.

Q. 194 What gets printed when the printStackTrace() method is invoked?

ANS. *public void printStackTrace()*

Prints this throwable and its backtrace to the standard error stream. This method prints a stack trace for this Throwable object on the error output stream that is the value of the field System.err. The first line of this output contains the result of the toString() method for this object while the remaining lines represent data previously recorded by the fillInStackTrace() method. The exact format of all this information is implementation dependent but the following may be regarded as a typical case:-

```
java.lang.NullPointerException
    at Cls.much(Cls.java: 9)
    at Cls.lunch(Cls.java: 6)
    at Cls.main(Cls.java: 3)
```

The above output was produced by executing the following program:-

```
class Cls
{
    public static void main(string args[])
    {
        lunch(null);
    }
        static void lunch(int [] x)
    {
        much(x);
    }
        static void much(int [] y)
    {
        System.out.println(y[0]);
    }
}
```

Q. 195 How do you use this() and super() methods with constructors? Bring out the difference between their use.

ANS. *this()* method within a constructor is used to invoke another constructor in the same class while the *super()* method within a constructor is used to invoke its immediate superclass constructor.

Q. 196 Does java support operator overloading?

ANS. No! Not at all!!

However, java internally supports operator overloading in the form of performing String concatenation using the '+' operator.

Q. 197 Compare and contrast Interfaces with Abstract classes.

ANS. In this context, consider the following main points:-

(1) Neither interfaces nor abstract classes can be instantiated.

(2) Direct multiple inheritance is not allowed in Java unlike C++. But, java provides for interfaces to take care of this problem. A class can implement any number of interfaces, but can extend only one class.

(3) An interface has all public members and no implementation whatsoever. An abstract class is a class which may have the usual features of class members such as private, protected etc. but has some abstract methods.

(4) Interfaces should be used as much as possible and an abstract class must be used only when you want to provide some but not complete implementation.

Q. 198 Can you instantiate an abstract class? Elaborate.

ANS. As mentioned in the previous problem, we cannot instantiate an abstract class. In order to declare an abstract class, we use the modifier or keyword abstract before the class keyword in our class definition, e.g.

```
abstract public class Form
{
    ........................
    ........................
}
class Circle extends Form
{  }
```

If you try to create an instance of the abstract class *Form*, the compiler reports an error!

Q. 199 Can you declare an abstract class as final? If not, why not?

ANS. An abstract class cannot be declared as final.

The purpose of having an abstract class is that its subclasses can extend its functionality and this very purpose of declaring an abstract class will be defeated in case an abstract class is allowed to be declared as final.

Q. 200 Bring out the use of the 'transient' keyword.

ANS. On Object Serialization, if any of the object's members need not be serialized, they must be declared as *transient*.

■

2

APPLETS

Q. 201 Define an applet in Java.

ANS. There are two classes of programs in Java, namely, the applications and the applets. Applications are the normal programs while applets are small applications that are accessed on an Internet server, transported over the Internet, automatically installed, and run as part of a Web document.

Q. 202 What are the two packages that all applets must import?

ANS. *(i) java.applet*; and,

(ii) java.awt.

Q. 203 What do you understand by double buffering?

ANS. Images are not only useful for storing pictures, but you can also use them as offscreen drawing surfaces. This allows you to render any image, including text and graphics, to an offscreen buffer which you can display later on. The main advantage of doing this is that the image is seen only when it is complete. Drawing a complicated image could take several milliseconds or more, which can be seen by the user as flashing/flickering. This flickering/flashing is distracting and causes the user to perceive your rendering as slower than it actually is. Use of an offscreen image to reduce flicker is known as double buffering, since the screen is considered as a buffer for pixels, and the offscreen image is the second buffer, where you can prepare pixels for display.

Q. 204 What are the methods called in order when an applet begins and ends, respectively?

ANS. When an applet begins, the AWT calls the following methods in order:-

(i) init()

(ii) start()

(iii) paint()

When an applet terminates/ends, the following order of methods comes into play:-

(i) stop()

(ii) destroy()

Q. 205 What is HotJava?

ANS. HotJava is a Web browser fully programmed in Java developed by the two Sun programmers, Patrick Naughton and Jonathan Peayne. HotJava enabled the running of Java applets in web pages. Subsequently, Java applets became implementable in other Web browsers such as Netscape Navigator.

Q. 206 Why is Java important to the Internet?

ANS. Java's ability to create and run applets and its portability because of its ability to create bytecodes to be run by the Java Virtual Machine (JVM) render it extremely suitable for the internet.

Q. 207 Does Java support pointers? If not, why not?

ANS. Java does not support or allow pointers. The reason for that is simple. Java cannot allow pointers as by doing so, Java applets would be able to breach the firewall between the Java Runtime Environment and the host computer (this is because pointers can be assigned any address in memory - even those outside the Java runtime systems).

C/C++ programmers make extensive use of pointers and they might be inclined to think that their loss puts Java at a significant disadvantage. But, this is false. Java is designed in such a manner that as long as one stays within the boundaries of its execution environment, he will never feel the need to use a pointer. Moreover, he would not get any additional benefit by doing that either.

We must also add here that C/C++ code making use of pointers can be converted conveniently to Java code that makes no use of such pointers.

Q. 208 Can you enumerate the tag used to embed an applet into a WEB/HTML page?

ANS. The relevant tag used is *<APPLET>*.

Q. 209 Where are the applets executed?

ANS. Applets are executed by the applet engine similar in working to a virtual machine existing in the web browser at the client side.

Q. 210 Enumerate the main points of difference between an application and an applet.

ANS. There are basically two main points of difference between an application and an applet enumerated as under:-

(i) Applets are useful for creating dynamic and interactive web applications. An applet runs under the control of a browser whereas an application runs as a stand-alone program on the desktop.

(ii) An applet is subjected to tougher security restrictions in terms of file and network access whereas an application can easily access the file system and network.

■

3

NETWORKING

Q. 211 What is the client/server model in the context of networking?

ANS. The term client/server is often heard in the context of networking. A server is anything that has some resource which can be shared. Thus, there are compute servers which provide computing power; print servers which manage a collection of printers; disk servers which provide networked disk space; and web servers which store web pages. And, a client is simply any other entity that wants to gain access to a particular server.

A network can have several clients and servers and this architecture is aptly called the *client/server* architecture. Figure 2 shows a simple *client/server* model. In this simple model, it can be easily seen that the client sends a request to the server and the server responds upon receiving the request.

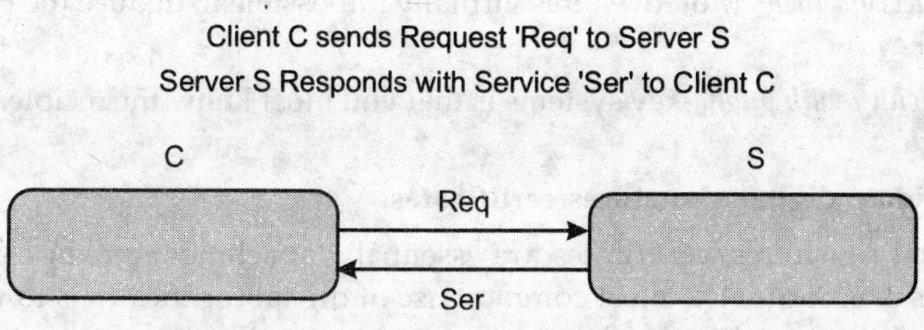

Figure 2 A Network with a single Client and a single Server

Q. 212 Elaborate on the advantages of a network.

ANS. There is essentially one chief advantage that we derive by using a network, viz. it helps in the optimal utilization of the available system resources by making resource sharing possible amongst the connected systems on the network.

Q. 213 What do you mean by 'throughput'?

ANS. In computer parlance, throughput is the amount of work a computer network can perform during a given period of time.

Q. 214 What do you understand by a firewall?

ANS. A firewall is simply a mechanism which isolates a network from the rest of the Internet, allowing only specific traffic to pass through it.

Q. 215 Why is data encryption required?

ANS. Data traversing unsecured networks is open to many kinds of attacks. Data can be read, altered, or forged by anybody who has access to the route your data takes, e.g. a protocol analyzer (sniffer) can read packets and gain classified information, or, an intimidating party can tamper with packets and cause damage by hindering, reducing, or preventing network communications within your organization.

Encryption provides a means to safeguard network data that travels from one router to another across unsecured networks. Encryption is particularly important if certain confidential/critical data is being sent.

Q. 216 What do you understand by public key encryption?

ANS. Any cryptographic system essentially employs two keys for encryption/decryption, viz. the public key known to everyone and a private (secret) key known only to the recipient of the message. When device X wants to send a secure message to device Y, it uses device Y's public key to encrypt the message. Device Y then uses its private key to decrypt the message sent by device X.

An important element to the public key system is that the public and private keys are related in such a manner that only the public key can be used to encrypt the messages and only the corresponding private key can be used to decrypt them. Moreover, it is virtually impossible to deduce the private key if you know the public key.

The only difficulty with public-key systems is that you must know the recipient's public key to encrypt a message.

Q. 217 Elucidate digital signatures/certificates.

ANS. Digital signatures/certificates are essentially attachments to an electronic message used for purposes of security. The most common use of digital certificates is to verify that a user sending a message is the one he/she claims to be, and to provide the receiver with the means to encode a reply.

An individual wishing to send an encrypted message applies for a digital certificate from a Certificate Authority (CA). The CA issues an encrypted digital certificate containing the applicant's public key and a variety of other identification information. The CA makes its own public key readily available through print publicity or perhaps on the Internet.

The recipient of an encrypted message uses the CA's public key to decode the digital certificate attached to the message, verifies it as issued by the CA and then obtains the sender's public key and identification information held within the certificate. With this information, the recipient can send an encrypted reply.

The most widely used standard for digital certificates is ***X.509***.

Q. 218 What is the use of the URLs?

ANS. The Uniform Resource Locators (URLs) provide a reasonably intelligible form to uniquely identify/address information on the Internet.

Q. 219 What is the most widely used protocol on the Internet?

ANS. *HyperTextTransferProtocol* (HTTP) is the most widely used protocol on the Internet. Using this protocol, the text from one machine to another is sent / received.

Q. 220 Why is Java suitable for the Internet?

ANS. Java suits the Internet just about in possible way. But, there are specifically two main reasons. First Java, being system independent, is portable and can be run on any kind of system on the Internet. In other words, Java's versatility is the mainstay of the Internet. And, secondly, Java with its strong type checking and lack of pointers is especially suitable for the Internet by eliminating most of the security concerns of the Internet.

Q. 221 What do you understand by a socket?

ANS. A socket is essentially a connection point between a client and a server on the same network.

Q. 222 Does the port number identify a socket uniquely?

ANS. Yes! It does!!

Q. 223 What do you understand by IP address?

ANS. An IP address is a unique identification number allotted to every computer on a network/Internet. It contains some unique bytes identifying the network and the actual inside the network.

Q. 224 What do you understand by DNS?

ANS. DNS or Domain Naming Service, as it is called, is a service provided by the Internet that helps in mapping the IP addresses with their corresponding website names.

Q. 225 What is the full form of JSSE?

ANS. *Java Secure Socket Extension.*

Q. 226 What are proxy servers?

ANS. A proxy server speaks the client side of a protocol to another server. This is often required when clients have certain restrictions on which servers they can connect to. Thus, a client would connect to a proxy server, which did not have such restrictions, and the proxy server would, in turn, communicate for the client.

■

4

THREADING

Q. 227 What do you understand by multithreading?

ANS. Java has built-in support for multithreaded programming. A multithreaded program contains two or more parts that can run concurrently. Each such part is called a thread, and each thread defines a separate path of execution. A text editor formatting its text and printing at the same time is a good example of multithreading. In this way, we see that multithreading is a specialized version of multitasking.

Q. 228 Can multithreading lead to problems at times?

ANS. Multithreading can lead to problems at times especially when you create too many threads. In such a case, you actually degrade the performance of your program rather than enhance it as multithreading is supposed to do. This is because some overhead is always associated with context switching. If you create too many threads, more CPU time will be spent changing contexts rather than executing your program! You must always remember and be aware of this vital fact.

Q. 229 What is the use of the isAlive() method?

ANS. How can one thread know when another thread has ended? You can call *isAlive()* on the thread. This method is defined by Thread, and its most general form is as follows:-

final boolean isAlive()

The *isAlive()* method returns true if the thread upon which it is called is still running and false otherwise.

Q. 230 What is the use of the join() method?

ANS. There is a second way to know when a thread has ended apart from the *isAlive()* method described above in **Q.** 229. While *isAlive()* is occasionally useful, the method, which you will more often use to wait for a thread to finish is called *join()*, whose most general form is as follows:-

final void join() throws InterruptedException

This method waits until the thread on which it is called terminates/finishes. Its name comes from the concept of the calling thread waiting until the specified thread joins it. Apart from the form of *join()* elaborated above, there are additional forms, which allow you to specify the maximum amount of time that you want to wait for the specified thread to terminate/finish.

Q. 231 What do you mean by a deadlock?

ANS. There is a special type of error relating specifically to multitasking that you need to avoid. It is known as a deadlock, which occurs when two threads have a circular dependency on a pair of synchronized objects.

Q. 232 Can the thread priority be changed? What is the default priority assigned to a thread?

ANS. The thread priority can indeed be changed ranging from a minimum one to a maximum one; the default priority assigned to a thread is 5.

Q. 233 Elucidate the daemon thread.

ANS. A continuously executing thread such as the one providing background processing (e.g. the garbage collector thread) is referred to as a daemon thread; daemon threads act as service providers for other objects/threads.

Q. 234 Explain the thread lifecycle.

ANS. A thread : is created using the new Thread() statement

is executed using the start() method

now, enters the 'runnable state'

when blocked on I/O or when wait()/sleep() methods are used, enters 'not runnable state'

comes back into 'runnable state' continuing to run/execute the statements

finally, 'dies' after coming out of the run() method

ALL THE AFOREMENTIONED TRANSITION STATES OF A THREAD ARE REFERRED TO AS ITS LIFECYCLE (Figure 3).

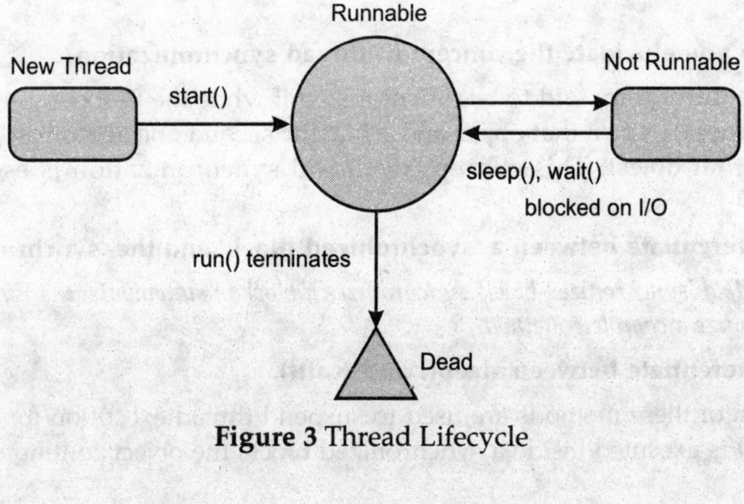

Figure 3 Thread Lifecycle

Q. 235 What do you understand by a monitor?

ANS. A monitor is a lock on an object which allows only one thread to access or modify the contents of that object.

Q. 236 How can you make code thread-safe?

ANS. The keyword *'synchronized'* is used to temporarily lock an object to have exclusive access to it. It marks a block of code or an entire method as *critical section*. Only one thread can execute at any point in time. Other threads will *wait* for their turn to use the *critical section*.

When an instance method is synchronized, the synchronized code can be run by many threads on different objects simultaneously, since the locking is on the object. For a synchronized class method, the locking is on the class object, which thus limits to only one thread executing that particular code.

Q. 237 What is the purpose behind Thread.wait()?

ANS. *Thread.wait()* and *Thread.notify()* methods are used for inter-thread communication. *Thread.wait()* makes the thread go to sleep until some other thread wakes it up using the *Thread.notify()* method.

Q. 238 Bring out the difference between Thread.notify() and Thread.notifyall().

ANS. *Thread.notify()* : This method can only be called from within a synchronized method/block. It wakes up a single thread that is waiting on the object's lock. In case there is more than one thread waiting, the choice is arbitrary, i.e. there is no particular way to determine which of the waiting threads should be awakened.

Thread.notifyAll() : This method wakes up all the waiting threads. The JVM scheduler then decides as to which of the awakened threads will execute.

Q. 239 How do you invoke a thread's run() method?

ANS. After a thread is started through its *start()* method or that of the Thread class, the JVM scheduler invokes the thread's *run()* method once the turn comes for this thread to run/ execute.

Q. 240 Can you elucidate the concept of thread synchronization?

ANS. Two threads are said to be synchronized if while the first one is acting on an object, the second one doesn't act on that object and while the second one acts on an object, the first one doesn't act on that object. This concept of thread synchronization is especially handy in multithreading.

Q. 241 Differentiate between a 'synchronized block' and the 'synchronized' keyword.

ANS. *While a 'synchronized block' synchronizes a block of statements, the 'synchronized' keyword is used to synchronize a complete method.*

Q. 242 Differentiate between sleep() and wait().

ANS. Both of these methods are used to suspend thread execution for a specified period. But, when *sleep()* is executed inside a synchronized block, the object continues to be under lock;

on the other hand, when *wait()* is executed inside a synchronized block, the lock is removed. In general, *sleep()* is used to make a thread wait for some time while *wait()* is used alongside *notify() / notifyAll()* in multithreading.

Q. 243 Does the thread execute any method by default; if yes, which one?

ANS. Yes, it does! The *public void run()* method.

Q. 244 Differentiate between "implements Runnable" and "extends Thread"

ANS. Functionally, both of them are same but by using "extends Thread", we cannot extend another class since Java doesn't support multiple inheritance; on the other hand, if we use "implements Runnable", we can still extend another class. This feature is especially handy when we want to use threads as well as access the characteristics of another class.

```
class class1 extends Thread, class2                  // not okay
class class1 extends class2 implements Runnable      // okay
```

Q. 245 Can you stop a thread in Java; if yes, how?

ANS. Yes, it is indeed possible to stop a thread in Java. This can be achieved by creating a boolean type variable that is initialized to 'false' and later on, when we want to stop the thread, we should make its value 'true'; the status of this variable is checked in the *run()* method and since it is true, the thread executes the return statement and then stops executing.

Q. 246 Which is the thread that always runs in a Java program by default?

ANS. The *main* thread.

Q. 247 In how many ways can you create a thread? Elaborate.

ANS. There are essentially two ways of creating a thread:-

(1) *The first method involves extending the Thread class.* This should only be done in case the class doesn't need to be extended from another class.

```
import java.lang.*;
public class Cntr extends Thread
{
    public void run()
    { ...................... }
}
```

Here, a new class Cntr is being created that extends the Thread class ana overrides the Thread.run() method. The run() method is where all the work of the Cntr class thread is being done.

(2) *The second way involves implementing the interface Runnable.*

```
import java.lang.*;
public class Cntr implements Runnable
{
```

```
        Thread T;
        public void run()
        { .................... }
    }
```

In this case, the abstract method run() is defined in the Runnable interface and is being implemented. Note that we have an instance of the Thread class as a variable of the Cntr class.

The only difference between the two methods is that by implementing Runnable, there is greater flexibility in the creation of the class Cntr, i.e. there still is an opportunity to extend the class Cntr, if needed.

Q. 248 What is the purpose of Thread.start()?

ANS. *Thread.start()* creates the system resources necessary to run the thread and schedules it to run. After the start method has returned, the thread is actually in the Runnable state. When a thread gets the CPU time, it will be executed.

Q. 249 Explain the concept of thread prioritization.

ANS. Execution of multiple threads on a single CPU, in some order, is called scheduling. The Java runtime supports a very simple, deterministic scheduling algorithm known as fixed priority scheduling. This algorithm schedules threads based on their priority relative to other runnable threads.

When a java thread is created, it inherits its priority from the thread that created it. A thread's priority can also be modified at any time after its creation using the *setPriority()* method.

Thread priorities are integers ranging between MIN_PRIORITY (1) and MAX_PRIORITY (10). The value 5 is the default priority. The greater the integer, the higher the priority of the corresponding thread.

At any given time, when multiple threads are ready to be executed, the java runtime system chooses the runnable thread with the highest priority for execution. Only when that mthread stops, yields or becomes not runnable for some reason will a lower priority thread start executing.

If two threads of the same priority are waiting for the CPU, the scheduler chooses one of them in a round-robin fashion. The chosen thread will run until a higher priority thread becomes runnable, or, it yields (or, its run method exits), or, its time allotment has expired (on systems that support time-slicing). Then, the second thread is given a chance to run, and so on, until the interpreter exits.

Java runtime system's thread scheduling algorithm is preemptive as well. Thus, if at any time, a thread with a higher priority than all other runnable threads becomes runnable, the runtime system chooses the new higher priority thread for execution. This new higher priority thread is said to have preempted the other threads.

Q. 250 Bring out the difference between yield() and sleep() methods.

ANS. When a thread invokes its *yield()* method, it returns to its ready state. On the other hand, when a thread invokes its *sleep()* method, it returns to its waiting state.

Q. 251 Bring out the difference between preemptive scheduling and time slicing.

ANS. Under preemptive scheduling, the highest priority thread executes until it enters its waiting or dead states or a higher priority thread comes into existence. On the other hand, under time slicing, a thread executes for a predefined slice of time and then re-enters the pool of ready threads. The scheduler then determines which thread should execute next, based upon priority and other factors.

Q. 252 Explain in brief the concepts of synchronized methods and synchronized statements.

ANS. Synchronized methods are methods that are used to control access to an object. A thread only executes a synchronized method after it has acquired the lock for the method's object or class.

Synchronized statements are similar to synchronized methods. A synchronized statement can only be executed after a thread has acquired the lock for the object or class referenced in the synchronized statement.

This means that no other thread can access the object till the current thread releases the object. This is used to make the code thread safe and prevent dirty reads.

Q. 253 Under what condition(s) do you use synchronized statements?

ANS. Synchronized statements are good to use in two cases:-

(1) *It is sufficient to synchronize only part of a method, e.g.*

```
void mthd()
{
    // some statement
    Synchronized(this)
    {
        this.x = 100;
    }
        // some statement
}
```

(2) *If a class whose object to be locked is part of a third part jar file, e.g.*

```
void mthd()
{
    // some statement
    Synchronized(thirdPartyObject)
```

```
        {
            thirdPartyObject.x = 100;
        }
        // some statement
    }
```

Q. 254 Can you restart a dead thread; if yes, how?

ANS. A dead thread cannot be restarted.

Q. 255 Under what condition(s) does a thread go out of the runnable state?

ANS. A thread becomes *Not Runnable* when one of the following events occurs:-

(1) Its sleep method is invoked.

(2) The thread is blocking on Input/Output.

(3) The thread calls the wait method to wait for a specific condition to be fulfilled.

■

(5)

DATABASES & JDBC

Q. 256 What do you understand by a database?

ANS. A database is a permanent, self-descriptive store of data that is contained in one or more files. Self-description is what sets a database apart from ordinary files. A database contains the data structure or 'schema' – description of data – as well as the data.

Q. 257 What do you understand by DBMS?

ANS. A *database management system* (*DBMS*) is the software for managing access to a database. Some of the reasons for using a DBMS are:-

- *Data Protection:* A DBMS protects data from accidental loss due to hardware crashes, disk media failures, and application errors.
- *Efficiency:* A DBMS has efficient algorithms for managing large quantities of data.
- *Sharing between users & sharing between applications:* Multiple users can access the database at the same time. Multiple application programs can read/write data to the same database.
- *Data quality:* You can specify rules that data must satisfy.
- *Data distribution:* You can partition data across various sites, organizations, and hardware platforms. The DBMS keeps the fragmented data consistent.
- *Security:* A DBMS can restrict reading/writing of data to authorized users only.

Q. 258 How do you implement one-to-one, one-to-many, and many-to-many relationships while designing tables?

ANS. One-to-one relationship can be implemented as a single table and very rarely as two tables with primary and foreign key relationships. One-to-many relationship can be implemented by splitting the data into two tables with primary and foreign key relationships. Many-to-many relationship can be implemented using a junction table with the keys from both the tables forming the composite primary key of the junction table.

Q. 259 Bring out the difference between a primary key and a unique key.

ANS. Both primary key and unique key enforce uniqueness of the column on which they are defined. But, by default, primary key creates a clustered index on the column whereas unique key creates a non-clustered index by default. Also, primary key doesn't permit NULL value while unique key permits NULL value, but only one.

Q. 260 What do you understand by a stored procedure? What are its advantages?

ANS. A stored procedure is a set of pre-compiled T-SQL statements, which can be executed whenever required. These are similar to procedures in any other programming language and whence, can accept input parameters, return output parameters, and can even return status values to the calling procedure or batch to indicate success/failure along with the reason for failure, if any.

The main advantages of using stored procedures are:-

(i) Increased modularized programming;

(ii) Faster execution since they are pre-compiled;

(iii) Reduce the network traffic by sending the call to the stored procedure, instead of sending hundreds of T-SQL lines of code which are embedded in the stored procedure.

Q. 261 What do you mean by triggers? How do you invoke a trigger on demand?

ANS. Triggers are a special kind of stored procedures that get executed automatically when an INSERT/UPDATE/DELETE operation takes place on a table. Triggers cannot be invoked on demand. They get triggered automatically as mentioned already. Triggers can be used to extend the referential integrity checks also, but wherever possible, constraints should be used for this purpose instead of triggers since constraints are much faster.

Q. 262 Bring out the difference between a stored procedure and a trigger.

ANS. Trigger is a special type of stored procedure that cannot be called directly by the user. At the time of creating the trigger, it is defined to be executed when a specific type of data modification such as Insert/Update/Delete is made against a specific table/column.

Q. 263 What do you understand by JDBC?

ANS. JDBC or *Java Database Connectivity*, as it is called, is an Application Programming Interface (API), which makes it possible for Java programs to connect to any database, retrieve the data/information from the database and utilize this data for themselves.

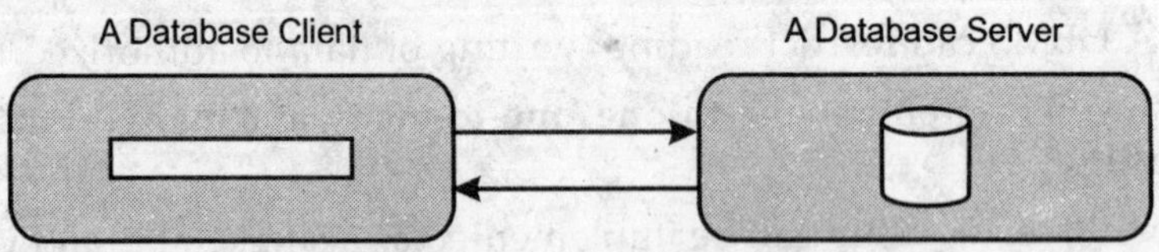

Figure 4 A Database Client and A Database Server

Q. 264 What do you understand by DSN?

ANS. DSN or *Data Source Name*, as it is called, is the unique name given to database in order to identify it in a Java program. It is linked with the actual location of the database.

Q. 265 What do you understand by ResultSet?

ANS. *ResultSet* is an object containing the rows (results) of executing an SQL statement upon a database.

Q. 266 What do you understand by stored procedures?

ANS. A stored procedure means a set of statements stored and executed at the database server and sending the results to the client.

Q. 267 What do you understand by BLOB?

ANS. BLOB or *Binary Large Object*, as it is called, represents an SQL datatype which helps in storing LARGE volumes of binary data into the database. By means of BLOBS, you can even store images in the database.

Q. 268 What do you understand by CLOB?

ANS. CLOB or *Character Large Object*, as it is called, represents an SQL datatype which helps in storing LARGE volumes of text data into the database. By means of CLOBS, you can even store text files in the database.

Q. 269 Can you explain the use of the CallableStatement?

ANS. The *CallableStatement* is used to call stored procedures and functions that run at a database server and get the results into the client.

Q. 270 What do you understand by parsing?

ANS. Parsing means checking the syntax and grammar of a Java statement as a whole as well as word by word.

Q. 271 What do you understand by a database driver?

ANS. A database driver represents a set of classes/interfaces written in accordance with the JDBC API in order to communicate with a given database.

Q. 272 How do you register a database driver? Elaborate.

ANS. A database driver can be registered in any of the following ways:-

(i) By using System class *getProperty()* method;

(ii) By creating an object to the driver class;

(iii) By sending the driver class name to the *Class.forName()* method; or,

(iv) By sending the driver class object to the *DriverManager.registerDriver()* method.

Q. 273 Does the performance of a JDBC program depend on the driver? Elucidate.

ANS. Yes! It does!! Each driver performs differently.

Q. 274 What do you understand by an RDBMS?

ANS. RDBMS or *Relational Database Management System*, as it is called, is a way to store the information in a database, creating relationships amongst different, related data in order to enable the user to query among different factors and get the maximum range of data from a single query. To put it more simply, it's a system which organizes data into related rows and columns.

Q. 275 What do you mean by SQL?

ANS. SQL or *Structured Query Language*, as it is called, enables:-

(i) ACCESS TO A DATABASE;

(ii) INSERTION/UPDATION/DELETION OF RECORDS IN A DATABASE;

(iii) RETRIEVAL OF DATA/INFORMATION FROM A DATABASE.

Q. 276 What are the different types of DBMS?

ANS. DBMS (Database Management System) is essentially of the following kinds:-

(i) Hierarchical

(ii) Network

(iii) Relational

(iv) Object

(v) Object-Relational

Of all these, Relational DBMS is the most widely used one.

Q. 277 Enumerate the main features of a relational database.

ANS. Relational database has essentially the following features:-

(i) It makes no presumptions about the inter-relationships between the data elements;

(ii) Relationships are represented in the form of one table containing key data from another table.

(iii) Relations are dynamic and determined as needed.

(iv) Everything in a relational database is stored in the form of tables which consist of rows and columns.

(v) Creation of these tables and their columns is performed using SQL. Similarly, storage and retrieval of data is also carried out using SQL.

(vi) In formal relational theory, tables are known as relations; whence, these came to be known as relational databases.

Q. 278 What do you understand by an Entity-Relationship (E-R) diagram?

ANS. One of the best ways to design a database is to draw an image of the tables with the relationships among them. This graphical representation of the database tables is known as an E-R diagram.

Q. 279 What do you mean by referential integrity?

ANS. Referential integrity prevents users/applications from entering inconsistent data into a table. Referential integrity rules are used when a relationship is created between two tables. Different RDBMSs have different referential integrity rules. As already mentioned, these rules help to maintain the integrity of data, e.g. if we are dealing with a 'customer' table and multiple orders from a customer, we can set referential integrity rule in such a manner that all orders from a customer should get deleted before the customer gets deleted; this is commonly referred to as **cascading delete.**

Q. 280 What do you understand by a primary key?

ANS. Primary key is used to uniquely identify a row of data in a table. This can be a single column of the table or a combination of more than one column; in the latter case, it's known as a composite primary key.

Q. 281 What do you mean by a foreign key?

ANS. A key column in a table which identifies records in a different table is referred to as a foreign key.

Q. 282 What is an alternate key in a table?

ANS. In a database table, apart from primary key column(s), some other column may need to be a key as well; these are referred to as alternate key. This column value may or may not be unique.

Q. 283 Elucidate the concept of normalization.

ANS. Normalization is the process of efficiently organizing data in a database by creating tables and establishing relationships between those tables according to certain normalization rules which have been designed to make the database more flexible by eliminating two factors, viz. redundancy and inconsistent dependency.

There are a few rules for database normalization. Each such rule is referred to as a "normal form". If the first rule is observed, the database is said to be in "first normal form", and so on.

Q. 284 Elucidate the First Normal Form (1NF).

ANS. 1NF states that:-

(*i*) Eliminate duplicate columns from same table;

(*ii*) Create a separate table for each set of related data and identify each such set of related data with a primary key.

Q. 285 Elucidate the Second Normal Form (2NF).

ANS. 2NF states that:-

(*i*) Create separate tables for sets of values that apply to multiple records;

(*ii*) Create relationships between these new tables and their predecessors through the use of foreign keys.

Q. 286 Elucidate the Third Normal Form (3NF).

ANS. 3NF states that:-

Eliminate fields that do not depend on the primary key.

Q. 287 Elucidate the concept of denormalization.

ANS. Developers can violate normal forms for good cause, such as to increase the performance for a database that is read and seldom updated. Such a relaxation is known as *denormalization*. The important issue here is to violate normal forms deliberately and only when necessary.

Q. 288 Elucidate the SQL Data Manipulation Language (DML).

ANS. As previously mentioned, SQL is syntax for executing queries and updating, inserting, and deleting records.

These query and update commands together form the DML part of SQL:-

(*i*) *SELECT* : extracts data from a database table

(*ii*) *UPDATE* : updates data in a database table

(iii) *DELETE* : deletes data from a database table

(iv) *INSERT INTO* : inserts new data into a database table

Q. 289 Elucidate the SQL Data Definition Language (DDL).

ANS. The DDL part of SQL provides syntax for creating and deleting database tables. One can also define indexes (keys), specify links between tables and impose constraints between database tables. The most important DDL statements in SQL are the following:-

(i) *CREATE TABLE* : creates a new database table

(ii) *ALTER TABLE* : alters (changes) a database table

(iii) *DROP TABLE* : deletes a database table

(iv) *CREATE INDEX* : creates an index (search key)

(v) *DROP INDEX* : deletes an index

Q. 290 Explain the concepts of transaction and ACID properties.

ANS. A transaction is a unit of work in which a series of operations occur between the BEGIN TRANSACTION and END TRANSACTION statements of an application. The term ACID stands for Atomic, Consistent, Isolated, and Durable. These properties ensure predictable behavior, reinforcing the role of transactions as all-or-none propositions designed to reduce the management load when there are many variables.

Q. 291 Bring out the difference between DELETE TABLE and TRUNCATE TABLE commands.

ANS. DELETE TABLE is a logged operation, whence, the deletion of each row gets logged in the transaction log, which makes it slow. On the other hand, TRUNCATE TABLE also deletes all the rows in a table, but it does not log the deletion of each row; instead, it logs the de-allocation of the data pages of the table, making it much faster.

Q. 292 What are constraints? Enumerate the different types of constraints.

ANS. Constraints enable the database system to enforce the integrity of the data automatically, without the need to create triggers, rules or defaults. The various types of constraints are:-

(i) NOT NULL (NOT NULL constraint on a column prevents its values from being NULL)

(ii) CHECK

(iii) UNIQUE

(iv) PRIMARY KEY

(v) FOREIGN KEY

Q. 293 What are cursors? Enumerate the different types of cursors.

ANS. A cursor is like a virtual table, with rows and columns specified by the query. A cursor also has the notion of a ***current row,*** which in essence is a pointer to the row in use in the virtual table. The different types of cursors are:-

(i) Static

(ii) Dynamic

(iii) Forward-only

(iv) Keyset-driven

Q. 294 What is a join? Enumerate the different types of joins.

ANS. Joins are used in queries to explain how different tables are related. Joins also let you select data from a table based upon data from another table. The various types of joins are:-

(i) *Inner join*

(ii) *Outer join*

(iii) *Self-join*

(iv) *Cross join*

Q. 295 What do you mean by a self-join? Illustrate with the help of an example.

ANS. In a self-join, two instances of the same table are joined in the query. We illustrate this concept with the help of an example. Suppose, there is an employee table containing rows for normal employees as well as managers. To find out the managers of all the employees, you need a self-join.

```
CREATE TABLE employee
(
    Emp_ID int,
    Mgr_ID int,
    Emp_NM char(20)
)
INSERT employee SELECT 1, 2, "Meena"
INSERT employee SELECT 2, 3, "Arunesh"
INSERT employee SELECT 3, NULL, "Harry"
SELECT temp1.Emp_NM [employee], temp2.Emp_NM [Manager]
FROM employee temp1, employee temp2
WHERE temp1.Mgr_ID = temp2.Emp_ID
```

Q. 296 How does JDBC help in accessing databases?

ANS. JDBC provides a standard library for accessing relational databases. By using the JDBC (*Java DataBase Connectivity*) API, you can access a wide variety of SQL databases with exactly the same Java syntax. It is, however, important to point out that although the JDBC API standardizes the approach for connecting to databases, the syntax for sending queries and committing transactions, and the data structure representing the result, JDBC does not attempt to standardize the SQL syntax. So, you can use any SQL extensions your database vendor supports. But, since most queries follow standard SQL syntax, using JDBC lets you change database hosts, ports, and even database vendors with minimal changes to your code.

Q. 297 What are the steps involved in using JDBC in general?

ANS. *(1)* *Load the JDBC driver:* To load a driver, you specify the classname of the database driver in the *Class.forName* method. By doing so, you automatically create a driver instance and register it with the JDBC driver manager.

(2) *Define the connection URL:* In JDBC, a connection URL specifies the server host, port, and database name with which to establish a connection.

(3) *Establish the connection:* With the connection URL, username, and password, a network connection to the database can be established. Once the connection is established, database queries can be performed until the connection is closed.

(4) *Create a Statement object:* Creating a *Statement* object enables you to send queries and commands to the database.

(5) *Execute a query or update:* Given a *Statement* object, you can send SQL statements to the database by using the *execute, executeQuery, executeUpdate, or executeBatch* methods.

(6) *Process the results:* When a database query is executed, a *ResultSet* is returned. The *ResultSet* represents a set of rows and columns that you can process by calls to next and various *getXxx* methods.

(7) *Close the connection:* When you are finished performing queries and processing results, you should close the connection, releasing resources to the database.

Q. 298 Enumerate and elucidate the various types of JDBC drivers.

ANS.

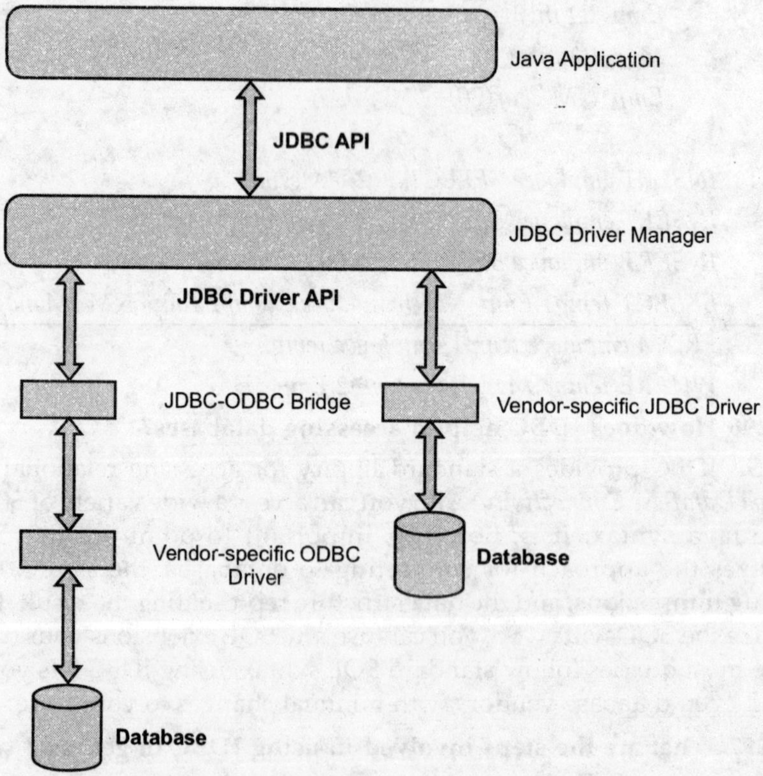

Figure 5 Two common JDBC Driver Implementations. JDK 1.4 includes a JDBC-ODBC Bridge; however, a pure JDBC Driver (provided by the vendor) yields better performance

JDBC technology drivers fit into one of the following categories according to the Sun Java developer Forum:-

Type 1 : A JDBC-ODBC bridge provides JDBC API access via one or more ODBC drivers. Some ODBC native code and in many cases, native database client code must be loaded on each client machine using this type of installation and downloading of a Java technology application is not important.

Type 2 : A native-API partly Java technology-enabled driver converts JDBC calls into calls on the client API for Oracle, Sybase, DB2, Informix, or other DBMS. Some binary code must be loaded on each client machine.

Type 3 : A net-protocol fully Java technology-enable driver translates JDBC API calls into a DBMS-independent net protocol which is then further translated to a DBMS protocol by a server. This net server middleware is able to connect all of its technology-based clients to many different databases. The specific protocol used is vendor-dependent. In general, this is the most flexible JDBC API alternative. All vendors of this solution will most likely provide products for Intranet use. In order for such products to also support Internet access, they must handle the additional requirements for security, access through firewalls etc. that the Web imposes.

Type 4 : A native-protocol fully Java driver converts JDBC technology calls into a network protocol used by DBMSs directly. This allows a direct call from the client machine to the DBMS server and is a practical solution for Intranet access. Since many of these protocols are proprietary, the database vendors themselves will be the primary source for this type/style of driver. This is the most preferred driver since it improves portability.

Q. 299 Can the Result Set be used even after closing the connection?

ANS. No! Not at all! This is due to the fact that the *ResultSet* becomes invalid once the connection is closed.

Q. 300 Can a connection object be serialized and used from another machine?

ANS. No! Not at all!! A connection object can't be serialized and used from another machine. This is due to the fact that the connection is created for the current machine IP address.

Q. 301 How do you get hold of the column names fetched in a ResultSet?

ANS. To retrieve information about the fetched *ResultSet*, you may use *con.getMetaData()*.

It returns a MetaData Object using which the various properties of the resultset can be fetched.

Q. 302 Elaborate setAutoCommit(true).

ANS. A transaction is one or more SQL statements forming a logical unit of work. Within one transaction, all the SQL statements must succeed/fail as one logical entity.

Changes are made to the database only if all statements in the transaction succeed and a COMMIT is issued. If one or more statements fail, we must issue a ROLLBACK to undo the changes. This ensures the integrity and security of the data in the database.

By setting AutoCommit to false, we prevent the connection from committing the changes unless the commit method is called in the program. We can COMMIT/ROLLBACK in the code depending upon whether all the statements within the transaction succeed/fail.

Q. 303 Can a ResultSet be updated?

ANS. Yes! Of course!! We can indeed update the database values from a *ResultSet*.

Q. 304 How can you call a stored procedure from JDBC?

ANS. We can invoke a stored procedure using *CallableStatement* as illustrated below:-

```
CallableStatement clblstmt = con.prepareCall("{call getTestData(?, ?)}");
clblstmt.registerOutParameter(1, java.sql.Types.TINYINT);
clblstmt.registerOutParameter(2, java.sql.Types.DECIMAL, 3);
clblstmt.executeQuery();
byte b = clblstmt.getByte(1);
java.math.BigDecimal bd = clblstmt.getBigDecimal(2, 3);
```

In general, calling a stored procedure in a database involves the following six basic steps:-

(1) Define the call to the database procedure: The procedure definition includes escape syntax where the appropriate ? defines input and output parameters.

(2) Prepare a *CallableStatement* for the procedure: You obtain a *CallableStatement* from a Connection by calling *prepare Call*.

(3) Register the output parameter types: Before executing the procedure, you must declare the type of each output parameter.

(4) Provide values for the input parameters: Before executing the procedure, you must supply the input parameter values.

(5) Execute the stored procedure: To execute the database stored procedure, call *execute* on the *CallableStatement*.

(6) Access the returned output parameters: Call the corresponding *getXxx* method, according to the output type.

Q. 305 What do you understand by connection pooling?

ANS. Connection pooling is a technique which allows multiple clients to share a cached set of connection objects that provide access to a database resource. It is actually implemented in different ways by different application server vendors.

Q. 306 Will the following code compile?

Give appropriate reason(s) for your answer.

```
import java.sql.*;
import java.util.*;
class TestingItOut
{
    Date dt = new Date(2012, 10, 01);
    System.out.println(dt.toString());
}
```

ANS. No! Not at all!! This is due to the fact that both *sql* and *util* packages have the *Date* class; compiler is in a fix and doesn't know which one to use!!!

6

SERVLETS & JSP

Q. 307 What are servlets? And, what purpose do they serve?

ANS.

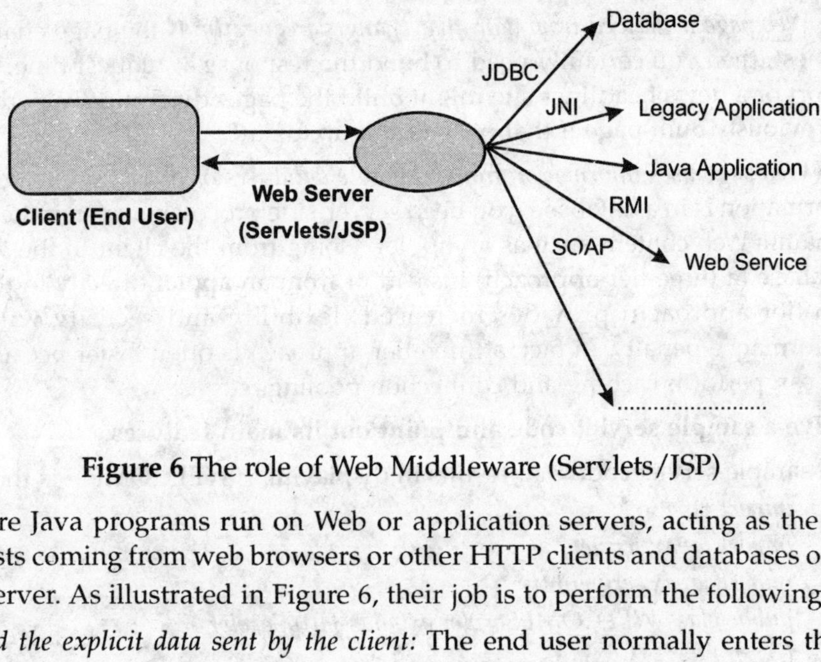

Figure 6 The role of Web Middleware (Servlets/JSP)

Servlets are Java programs run on Web or application servers, acting as the middle layer between requests coming from web browsers or other HTTP clients and databases or applications on the HTTP server. As illustrated in Figure 6, their job is to perform the following tasks:-

(1) *Read the explicit data sent by the client:* The end user normally enters this data in an HTML form on a Web page. However, the data could also come from an applet or a custom HTTP client program.

(2) *Read the implicit HTTP request data sent by the browser:* The HTTP information includes cookies, information about media types, and compression schemes the browser understands, and so on.

(3) *Generate the results:* This process may require talking to a database, executing an RMI or EJB call, invoking a Web service or computing the response directly.

(4) *Send the explicit data (i.e. the document):* This document can be sent in a variety of formats such as text (HTML or XML), binary (GIF images), or even a compressed format like *gzip* that is layered on top of some other underlying format.

(5) *Send the implicit HTTP response data:* Sending the implicit HTTP response data (besides the explicit document itself) involves telling the browser or other client what type of document is being returned (e.g. HTML), setting cookies and caching parameters, and other such tasks.

Q. 308 What is the underlying need to build web pages dynamically?

ANS. Servlets and JSP technology has become the technology of choice for developing online stores, interactive Web applications and other dynamic Web sites. There are a number of reasons why Web pages need to be built on-the-fly:-

(1) *The Web page is based on data sent by the client:* For instance, the results page from search engines and order-confirmation pages at online stores are specific to particular user requests. You never know what to display until you read the data that the user submits.

(2) *The Web page is derived from data that changes frequently:* If the page changes for every request, then you certainly need to build the response at request time, e.g. a weather report or a news headlines site might build the pages dynamically, perhaps returning a previously built page if that page is still up to date.

(3) *The Web page uses information from corporate databases or other server-side sources:* If the information is in a database, you need server-side processing even if the client is using dynamic Web content such as an applet. Going from the client to the Web tier to the database (a three-tier approach) instead of from an applet directly to the database (a two-tier approach) provides increased flexibility and security with little or no performance penalty. In fact, a three-tier approach is often faster because the middle tier can perform caching and connection pooling.

Q. 309 Give a sample servlet code and point out its main features.

ANS. A sample servlet code that results in displaying – WELCOME – is the following:-

```
import java.io.*;
import javax.servlet.*;
import javax.servlet.http.*;
public class WELCOMEServlet extends HttpServlet
{
public void doGet(HttpServletRequest request, HttpServletResponse response) throws
                                                   ServletException, IOException
{
    response.setContentType("text/html");
    PrintWriter out = response.getWriter();
    String docType = "<!DOCTYPE HTML PUBLIC \"
                          - // W3C // DTD HTML 4.0 " +
                          "Transitional // EN\ ">\n";
```

```
        out.prinlln(docType +
        "<HTML>\n" +
    "<HEAD><TITLE>WELCOME</TITLE></HEAD>\n" +
        "<BODY BGCOLOR= \ "FDF5E6\ " | n" +
        "<H1>WELCOME< /H1>\n" +
        "</BODY></HTML>");
        }
    }
```

There are essentially four points to note in the above servlet code:-

(1) *It is regular Java code:* There are new API's but no new syntax.

(2) *It has unfamiliar import statements:* The servlet and JSP API's are not part of the Java 2 Platform, Standard Edition (J2SE); they are a separate specification and are also a part of the Java 2 Platform, Enterprise Edition (J2EE).

(3) *It extends a standard class (HttpServlet):* Servlets provide a rich infrastructure for dealing with HTTP.

(4) *It overrides the doGet method:* Servlets have different methods to respond to different types of HTTP commands.

Q. 310 What are the advantages of servlets over traditional CGI?

ANS. Java servlets are more efficient, easier to use, more powerful, more portable, safer and cheaper than traditional CGI and many alternative CGI-like technologies.

Q. 311 Why is HTTP referred to as a stateless protocol?

ANS. HTTP is called a stateless protocol since every request is independent of the previous request. The server doesn't keep track of whether the same user is making repeated requests.

Q. 312 What is the order in which the life cycle methods are called in a Servlet/HttpServlet and which are the ones that can be overridden?

ANS. The order of the life cycle methods in a *Servlet/HttpServlet* is enumerated as under:-

(1) *init():* Called only once during the initialization of the Servlet.

(2) *destroy():* Called only once when a Servlet instance is about to be destroyed.

(3) *service():* Do not override this method.

(4) *doGet(), doPost(), doPut(), doDelete(), doOptions(), doTrace():* These methods are called according to the type of HTTP request received. Override them to generate your own response.

(5) *log():* Writes messages to the Servlet's log files.

(6) *getLastModified():* Override this method to return your Servlet's last modified date.

(7) *getServletInfo():* Override this method to provide a String of geneal information about your Servlet such as author, version, copyright etc.

(8) *getServletName():* Override this method to return name of the Servlet.

(9) *getInitParameter(), getInitParameterNames():* First one returns value of given initialization parameter, second one returns an Enumeration object containg the names of all initialization parameters provided.

Q. 313 Bring out the difference between GET and POST requests.

ANS. The HTML specifications technically define the difference between *"GET"* and *"POST"* so that the former means that form data is encoded (by a browser) into a URL while the latter means that the form data is to appear within a message body. Thus, we can say that *"GET'* is basically for just getting/retrieving data while *"POST"* may involve anything such as storing/updating data, ordering a product or sending an E-mail etc.

Q. 314 Bring out the difference between ServletContext and HttpSession.

ANS. The interface *ServletContext* defines a set of methods that a servlet uses to communicate with its servlet container, e.g. to get the MIME type of a file, dispatch requests or write to a log file. There is one context per "web application" per JVM that can be used as a location to share global information.

The interface HttpSession provides a way to identify a user across more than one page request or visit to a website and to store information about that user. The servlet container uses this interface to create a session between an HTTP client and an HTTP server. This interface allows servlets to:-

(1) *View and manipulate information about a session such as the session identifier, creation time and last accessed time etc.*

(2) *Bind objects to sessions, allowing user information to persist across multiple user connections.*

Q. 315 Bring out the difference between forward() and sendRedirect() methods.

ANS. *forward()* : It finds the Servlet on the local server, and calls its service (request, response) method, passing the same request and response that was used by the current page. The parameters stored in the request object are available to the called request, when we forward a request and the url in the address bar will not change.

sendRedirect() : It sends a response to the client with a meta-refresh that makes the client send a new request to the page specified. We can also make requests to pages other than those on the local server as well. The parameters stored in the request object are lost when we redirect and the url in the address bar will change.

Q. 316 Are variables declared at the class level in a servlet thread-safe? Explain in brief.

ANS. There is only one copy of the instance variables per instance of the servlet and all of the threads share this copy. In case of the multithreaded model, multiple threads may access an instance variable simultaneously, which makes it unsafe. In the case of a single-threaded model, only one thread executes the methods of a servlet instance at a time. Whence, an instance variable is thread-safe in this case.

By wrapping non-thread-safe code in a synchronized block, you can force the requesting thread to acquire the instance lock in order to gain access to the code block, thus making it safe, e.g.

```
synchronized(this)
{
    ctr++;
}
```

Q. 317 How many instances of a servlet are created?

ANS. Only one instance of a servlet gets created. And, this instance is accessed by all the requests hitting the server.

Q. 318 How can you make a servlet Single threaded and how many instances are created in this case?

ANS. A servlet can be made thread safe by implementing *SingleThreadedModel* interface. The number of instances created depends upon what Servlet container decides to do. It may just create one instance; it might create more.

Q. 319 What is the argument of the init() method? What is ServletConfig and what does it contain? Elaborate.

ANS. An object of type *ServletConfig* is passed. *ServletConfig* is an interface. A servlet configuration object is used by a servlet container to pass information to a servlet during initialization. Two of the methods available are:-

(1) getServletName()

(2) getServletContext()

Q. 320 What are the exceptions thrown by service method?

ANS. The exceptions thrown are:-

ServletException and *IOException.*

ServletException is thrown to report any problems encountered in the servlet engine trying to service the HTTP request while an *IOException* can be thrown when using the *PrintWriter* object to stream web resources back to the client browser.

Q. 321 What will happen if the service method in HttpServlet is overridden?

ANS. If we override the service method in an *HttpServlet*, we have to take care of calling the default service method. In some cases, it does make sound sense to override the service method, e.g. when you have a lot of Servlets that need to perform the same checks (like, is the session authenticated?) before processing the request. Rather than having to copy the logic into each Servlet you write, you can develop a common base class which extends *HttpServlet*. The logic inside the method is effectively as follows:-

```
service(...)
{
    common processing logic ....
    super.service(...);
}
```

Another option is to write the logic in a helper method and call it at the beginning of both the doGet and doPost methods.

Q. 322 How can you keep track of the sessions created in a servlet container? Elaborate.

ANS. The session can be kept track of using the following two objects:-

(1) *HttpSessionListener*: Implementations of this interface are notified of changes to the list of active sessions in a web application. To receive notification events, the implementation class must be configured in the deployment descriptor for the web application.

(2) *HttpSessionEvent:* This is the class representing event notifications for changes to sessions within a web application.

Q. 323 How does an object know when it is put in session?

ANS. An object can know when it is put in session by means of the following two events:-

(1) *HttpSessionBindingListener: This causes an object to be notified when it is bound to or unbound from a session. The object is notified by an HttpSessionBindingEvent object:*

(a) *The method valueBound(HttpSessionBindingEvent event) – notifies the object that is being bound to a session and identifies the session.*

(b) *The method valueUnbound(HttpSessionBindingEvent event) – notifies the object that is being unbound from a session and identifies the session.*

2) *HttpSessionBindingEvent: It has methods like getName which returns the name with which the object is bound to or unbound from the session.getSession which returns the session to or from which the object is bound / unbound.*

Q. 324 *How do you set the session time out for a session? Can you make it infinite; if yes, how?*

ANS. The method *setMaxInactiveInterval* in *HttpSession* can be used to set the timeout.

public void setMaxInactiveInterval(int interval)

where, interval specifies the time in seconds between client requests before the servlet container will invalidate this session. A negative time indicates that the session should never timeout (infinite timeout).

Q. 325 What are the methods available in HttpSessionListener?

ANS. *sessionCreated* and *sessionDestroyed* are the two methods available in *HttpSessionListener*. An *HttpSessionEvent* object is passed to these methods by the container when a new session is created or when an existing session is destroyed.

Q. 326 How do you carry out session management?

ANS. Since HTTP is a stateless protocol, we use a variety of methods to maintain information of the history of actions performed during a session. There are four ways in which we can do session management, enumerated as under:-

(1) *Cookies:* A cookie is a piece of information stored on the client machine by the browser. Cookies are widely used by various server-side programming techniques for the purpose of implementing session tracking. The cookie is a text file which is stored on the client machine. These cookies are sent to the server whenever a user makes a request to the same server from which the cookies were created. The Java API provides us various classes and methods designed to allow us to use cookies in servlets. Some of

the places where a cookie can be used are storing user preferences, shopping cart applications etc.

(2) *URL Rewriting:* In this method, the data is appended to the URL over successive requests. In addition to the current data, the values of the previous data with which the user invoked the servlet are retrieved from the incoming URL and appended to the new URL. In other words, the parameter values for each successive URL that is generated match those of the previous URL. In addition, new parameter values are added which represent the current data.

(3) *Hidden Fields:* IN HTML, we have a type of field called HIDDEN. This type of field is not visible on the browser but gets passed to the application server. Every time the client makes a request to the server, a HTML form is created and sent back to the client. Hidden fields are added to the form each time it is created. The hidden fields contain the data from the previous request that would be required by the future requests. Using this approach, the historical data is saved by embedding it in the new HTML database or in the server's file system.

(4) *HttpSession*:The *HttpSession* object is created and maintained by the application server. We can get hold of the session object using *request.getSession(true)* where the request is of type *HttpServletRequest*. Once we have a handle on this object, we can store data in this object, and this data is shared between the various requests coming from the same user in one session, i.e. from one browser window. Sessions are used to maintain state and user identity across multiple page requests. The session persists for a specified time period. We can add and retrieve objects from a session using the following two methods:

(a) *void setAttribute(java.lang.String name, java.lang.Object value);*

(b) *java.lang.Object getAttribute(java.lang.String name);*

Q. 327 Give a sample JSP code and point out its main features.

ANS. A sample JSP code that uses a request parameter to display the title of a book is the following:-

```
<!DOCTYPE HTML PUBLIC " - // W3C // DTD HTML 4.0 Transitional // EN">
<HTML>
<HEAD>
<TITLE>WELCOME</TITLE>
<LINK REL=STYLESHEET
HREF="JSP-Styles.css"
TYPE="text / css">
</HEAD>
<BODY>
<H2>Order Confirmation</ H2>
```

Thank you for the order **<I><%=request.getParameter("title") %>< /I>**!

</BODY></HTML>

There are essentially two points to note in the above JSP code:-

(1) It is mostly standard HTML.

(2) The dynamic code consists entirely of the half line depicted in bold in the code.

Q. 328 Compare and contrast the role of JSP vis-à-vis servlets.

ANS. A somewhat oversimplified view of servlets is that they are Java programs with HTML embedded inside of them. A somewhat oversimplified view of JSP documents is that they are HTML pages with Java code embedded inside of them. Thus, servlets look mostly like a regular Java class whereas a JSP document lloks mostly like a normal HTML page. Despite the huge differences, the interesting thing is that behind the scenes, both are the same. In fact, a JSP document is just another way of writing a servlet. JSP pages get translated into servlets, the servlets get compiled and it is the servlets that run at request time.

So, the question is, if JSP technology and sevlet technology are essentially equivalent in power, does it matter, which you use? Of course, yes! The issue is not power, but convenience, ease of use and maintainability. JSP is focused on simplifying the creation and maintenance of HTML whereas servlets are best at invoking business logic and performing complicated operations. A quick rule of the thumb is that servlets are best for tasks oriented towards processing while JSP is best for tasks oriented towards presentation. For some requests, servlets are the right choice; for other requests, JSP is a better option; for still others, neither JSP nor servlets alone is best and a combination of the two is best (as in MVC – Model View Controller architecture).

But, the point is that you need both JSP and servlets in your project. Almost no project will consist entirely of servlets or entirely of JSP; you want both!

Q. 329 What are the benefits and need for JSP? Elucidate.

ANS. As we have already pointed out, although JSP and servlets are equivalent behind the scenes, servlets are not so good when it comes to presentation; they excel in tasks related to programming or data processing. Servlets suffer from the following deficiencies when it comes to generating the output:-

(1) *It is hard to write and maintain the HTML;*

(2) You cannot use standard HTML tools;

(3) The HTML is inaccessible to non-Java developers.

JSP technology offers the following benefits in this context:-

(1) It is easier to write and maintain the HTML;

(2) You can use standard Web-site development tools;

(3) You can divide up your development team so that the Java programmers can work on the dynamic code while the Web developers can concentrate and focus on the presentation layer/aspect.

Q. 330 What are the common misconceptions about JSP?

ANS. Some of the common misunderstandings involving JSP are the following:-

(1) *Forgetting that JSP is server*-side technology;

(2) *Confusing translation time with request time;*

(3) Thinking JSP alone is sufficient;

(4) Thinking servlets alone are sufficient.

Q. 331 Explain in brief as to how a JSP is processed.

ANS. A JSP is converted into a Servlet by the application server and then the request is serviced. Once compiled, the Servlet object created from the JSP remains in memory just like any other Servlet. When a change is made to the JSP then the servlet object gets re-created. This could very well vary depending upon the server.

Q. 332 What is an 'include'? Enumerate the types of 'includes'.

ANS. We can use the *<jsp: include>* element to include either a static or dynamic resource in a JSP page. If the resource is static, its content is included in the calling JSP page as it is. If the resource is dynamic, it acts on a request and sends back a result that is included in the JSP page. When the include action is finished, the JSP container continues processing of the remainder of the JSP page. If the included resource is dynamic, we can use a *<jsp: param>* clause to pass the name and value of the parameter to the resource, e.g. we can pass the userId and a value to a login form that is coded in a JSP page.

Q. 333 Can you use Tag Libraries in a JSP; if yes, how?

ANS. A tag library is a set of actions that encapsulate functionality. These tags are then used within JSP pages. This helps us to reuse common functionality like connecting to a database.

```
<%@ taglib prefix="sql" url=http://java.sun.com/jstl/sql %>
```

For JSP pages that do not have a default database, <sql:setDataSource> can prepare a database for use.

The code snippet below shows how to create a data source.

```
<sql:setDataSource
    var="example"
    driver="oracle.jdbc.driver.OracleDriver"
url="jdbc:oracle:thin:@<OracleServerName>:1521:OracleInstanceName>"
    user="scott"
    password="tiger"
/>
```

Q. 334 Can you explain as to how exception handling is done in JSP?

Ans. You can specify error page in the 'page' directive. Then, if any exception is thrown, the control will be transferred to that error page where you can display a useful message to the user about what happened and also inform your sysadmin about this exception depending, of course, on how important it is.

```
<%@ page errorPage="ExceptionHandler.jsp"          %>
<%@ page isErrorPage="true"   import="java.io.*"   %>
```

Q. 335 Enumerate the implicit objects in JSP.

ANS. There are nine implicit objects that are available in a JSP enumerated as under:-

(1) ***Application*** *is the broadcast context state available. It is equivalent to ServletContext. It allows the JSP page's servlet and any Web components contained in the same application to share information.*

(2) ***Config*** *allows initialization data to be passed to a JSP page's servlet. This is equivalent to ServletConfig object passed to init method in the Servlet.*

(3) ***Exception*** *houses exception data to be accessed only by designated JSP "error pages".*

(4) ***Out*** *provides access to the servlet's output stream.*

(5) ***Page*** *is the instance of the JSP page's servlet processing the current request. Not typically used by JSP page authors.*

6) ***PageContext*** *is the context for the JSP page itself. It provides a single API to manage the various scoped attributes. This API is used extensively when implementing JSP custom tag handlers.*

(7) ***Request*** *provides access to HTTP request data, as well as providing a context for associating request-specific data.*

(8) ***Response*** *enables direct access to the HTTPServletResponse object and is very rarely used by JSP authors.*

(9) ***Session*** *is perhaps the most commonly used of the state management contexts. It is useful in starting a user's information when he accesses the web application over several requests.*

Q. 336 Can you prevent caching of the page; if yes, how?

ANS. You can use Microsoft Internet Information Server (IIS) to easily mark highly volatile or sensitive pages using the following script at the extreme beginning of the specific Active Server Pages (ASP) pages:-

```
<% Response.CacheControl = "no-cache" %>
<% Response.AddHeader "Pragma", "no-cache" %>
<% Response.Expires = -1 %>
```

Q. 337 Why should we use beans?

ANS. Although it is true that beans are merely Java classes that are written in a standard format, there are several advantages to their use. With beans in general, visual manipulation tools and other programs can automatically discover information about classes that follow this format and can create and manipulate the classes without the user having to explicitly write any code. In JSP in particular, use of JavaBeans components provides three advantages over scriptlets and JSP expressions that refer to normal Java classes:-

(1) No Java syntax: By using beans, page authors can manipulate Java objects using only XML-compatible syntax, that is to say, no parentheses, semicolons or curly braces.

(2) Simpler Object Sharing: When you use the JSP bean constructs, you can much more easily share objects among multiple pages or between requests than if you use the equivalent explicit Java code.

(3) Convenient correspondence between request parameters and object properties: The JSP bean constructs greatly simplify the process of reading request parameters, converting from strings, and putting the results inside objects.

Q. 338 Enumerate the various 'scopes' in a JSP.

ANS. The various scopes in a JSP are enumerated below for your reference:-

(1) *PageScope (<jsp:useBean ... scope="page" />:* This is the default value, i.e., you get the same behavior even if you omit the scope attribute entirely. This default scope implies that in addition to being bound to a local variable, the bean object should be placed in the *PageContext* object for the duration of the current request. Storing the object like this ensures that the servlet code can access it by calling the *getAttribute* method on the predefined *pageContext* variable. Since every page and every request has a different *PageContext* object, using scope="*page*" or omitting scope implies that the bean is not shared and thus a new bean will be created for each request.

(2) *RequestScope (<jsp:useBean ... scope="request" />):* This value implies that in addition to being bound to a local variable, the bean object should be placed in the *HttpServletRequest* object for the duration of the current requestwhere it is retrievable through the *getAttribute* method.

(3) *SessionScope (<jsp:useBean ... scope="session" />):* This value implies that in addition to being bound to a local variable, the bean will be stored in the *HttpSession* object associated with the current request where it can be retrieved through the *getAttribute* method. Thus, this scope lets JSP pages easily perform session tracking.

(4) *ApplicationScope (<jsp:useBean ... scope="application" />):* This value implies that in addition to being bound to a local variable, the bean will be stored in the *ServletContext* available through the predefined application variable or by a call to *getServletContext*. The *ServletContext* is shared by all servlets and JSP pages in the Web application. Values in the *ServletContext* can be retrieved through the *getAttribute* method.

Q. 339 Bring out the need for the MVC (Model View Controller) architecture.

ANS. Servlets are great when your application requires a lot of real programming to accomplish its task. Servlets can manipulate HTTP status codes and headers, use cookies, track sessions, save information between requests, compress pages, access databases, generate JPEG images on-the-fly, and perform many other tasks efficiently and flexibly. But, generating HTML with servlets can be tedious and can yield a result that is hard to modify. That's where JSP comes in. It allows you to write the HTML code in the normal manner, even using HTML-specific tools and putting your Web content developers to work on your JSP documents. JSP expressions, scriptlets, and declarations let you insert simple Java code into the servlet that results from the

JSP page and directives let you control the overall layout of the page. For more complex requirements, you can wrap Java code inside beans or even define your own JSP tags.

This all looks great. We seem to have everything. But, still something is amiss. The assumption behind a JSP document is that it provides a single overall presentation. What if you want to give totally different results depending on the data that you receive? Scripting expressions, beans, and custom tags, although extremely powerful and flexible, do not overcome the limitation that the JSP page defines a relatively fixed, top-level page appearance. Similarly, what if you need complex reasoning just to find out the type of data that applies to the current situation? JSP is poor at this type of business logic.

The solution is to use both servlets and JSP. In this approach, known as the Model view controller (MVC) or Model 2 architecture, you let each technology concentrate on what it excels at. The original request is handled by a servlet. The servlet invokes the business logic and data access code and creates beans to represent the results (that is to say, the *model*). Then, the servlet decides what JavaServer Page is appropriate to present the particular results and forwards the request there (the JavaServer Page is the *view*). The servlet decides what business logic code applies and which JSP page should present the results (the servlet is the *controller*).

Q. 340 Elucidate the MVC (Model View Controller) Frameworks.

ANS. The key desire behind the MVC approach is the desire to separate the code that creates and manipulates the data from the code that presents the data. The basic tools needed to implement this presentation-layer separation are standard in the servlet API. However, in very complex applications, a more elaborate MVC framework is sometimes beneficial. The most popular of these frameworks is Apache Struts discussed at length in one of the following chapters.

Although Struts is useful and widely used, you should not feel that you must use Struts in order to apply the MVC approach. For simple and moderately complex applications, implementing MVC from scratch with *RequestDispatcher* is straightforward and flexible. There is no need to get intimidated; in many situations, the basic approach is the best for the entire lifetime of your application. Even if you decide to use Struts or another MVC framework later, you will recoup much of your investment since most of your work will also apply to the elaborate frameworks.

Q. 341 How do you go about implementing MVC with RequestDispatcher?

ANS. The most important point about MVC is the idea of separating the business logic and data access layers from the presentation layer. The syntax is quite simple and the steps required to implement MVC with *RequestDispatcher* are brought out succinctly below for your reference:-

(1) *Define beans to represent the data :* Beans are just Java objects that follow a few simple conventions. The first step is to define beans to represent the results that will be presented to the user.

(2) *Use a servlet to handle requests :* In most cases, the servlet reads request parameters.

(3) *Populate the beans :* The servlet invokes business logic (application specific code) or data-access code to obtain the results. These results are placed in the beans defined in step 1.

(4) *Store the bean in the request, session, or servlet context* : The servlet calls *setAttribute* on the request, session, or servlet context objects to store a reference to the beans that represent the results of the request.

(5) *Forward the request to a JSP page* : The servlet determines which JSP page is appropriate to the situation and uses the *forward* method of *RequestDispatcher* to transfer control to that JSP page.

(6) *Extract the data from the beans* : The JSP page accesses beans with *jsp:useBean* and a scope matching the location of step 4. The page then uses *jsp:getProperty* to output the bean properties. The JSP page doesn't create/modify the bean. It just extracts and displays data that the servlet created.

Q. 342 How do you go about securing Web applications?

ANS. There are two major aspects to securing Web applications:-

(1) *Preventing unauthorized users from accessing sensitive data:* This process involves 'access restriction', that is, identifying which resources need protection and who should have access to them, and 'authentication', that is, identifying users to determine if they are one of the authorized ones. Simple authentication involves the user entering a username and password in an HTML form or dialog box while stronger authentication involves the use of X.509 certificates sent by the client to the server. This first aspect of Web security applies to virtually all secure applications. Even intranets at locations with physical access controls usually require some sort of user authentication.

(2) *Preventing attackers from stealing network data while it is in transit:* This process involves the use of Secure Sockets Layer (SSL) to encrypt the traffic between the browser and the server. This capability is generally reserved for particular sensitive applications or for particularly sensitive pages within a larger application. After all, unless the attackers are on your local subnet, it is exceedingly difficult for them to gain access to your network traffic.

These two security aspects are mostly independent. The approaches to access restriction are the same regardless of whether or not you use SSL. With the exception of client certificates (which apply only to SSL), the approaches to authentication are also identical whether or not you use SSL.

Within the Web application framework, there are two general approaches to this type of security:-

(1) *Declarative Security:* With declarative security, none of the individual servlets or JSP pages need any security-aware code. Instead, both of the major security aspects are handled by the server.

To prevent unauthorized access, you use the Web application deployment descriptor (*web.xml*) to declare that certain URLs need protection, and which categories of users should have access to them. You also designate the authentication method that the server should use to identify users. At request time, the server automatically prompts users for usernames and passwords when they try to access restricted resources, automatically checks the results against a predefined set of usernames and passwords, and automatically keeps track of which users have been authenticated previously. This process is completely transparent to the servlets and JSP pages.

To safeguard network data, you use the deployment descriptor to stipulate that certain URLs should only be accessible with SSL. If users try to use a regular HTTP connection to access one of these URLs, the server automatically redirects them to the HTTPS (SSL) equivalent.

(2) *Programmatic Security:* With programmatic security, protected servlets and JSP pages at least partially manage their own security. To prevent unauthorized access, each servlet or JSP page must either authenticate the user or verify that the user has been authenticated previously. To safeguard network data, each servlet or JSP page has to check the network protocol used to access it. If users try to use a regular HTTP connection to access some of these URLs, the servlet or JSP page must manually redirect them to the HTTPS (SSL) equivalent.

Q. 343 Outline the steps involved in Form-based authentication.

ANS. Eight basic steps are involved in Form-based authentication:-

(1) *Set up usernames, passwords, and roles:* In this step, you designate a list of users and associate each with a password and one or more abstract roles (e.g., normal user or administrator).This is a completely server-specific process.

(2) *Tell the server that you are using form-based authentication; designate the locations of the login and login-failure page:* This process uses the *web.xml login-config* element with an *auth-method* subelement of *FORM* and a form-*login-config* subelement that gives the location of the two pages.

(3) *Create a login page:* This page must have a form with an *ACTION* of *j_security_check*, a *METHOD* of *POST*, a text field named *j_username*, and a password field named *j_password*.

(4) *Create a page to report failed login attempts:* This page can simply say something like *"username and password not found"* and perhaps give a link back to the login page.

(5) *Specify which URLs should be password protected:* For this step, you use the *security-constraint* element of *web.xml*. This element, in turn, uses *web-resource-collection* and *auth-constraint* subelements. The first of these (*web-resource-collection*) designates the URL patterns to which access should be restricted, and the second (*auth-constraint*) specifies the abstract roles that should have access to the resources at the given URLs.

(6) *List all possible abstract roles (types of users) that will be granted access to any resource:* Each abstract role is declared using the *security-role* element. The *security-role* element contains the required *role-name* element, which contains the name of the abstract role.

(7) *Specify which URLs should be available only with SSL:* If your server supports SSL, you can stipulate that certain resources are available only through encrypted HTTPS (SSL) connections. You use the *user-data-constraint* subelement of *security-constraint* for this purpose.

(8) *Turn off the invoker servlet:* Security settings are based on URLs; so, you protect servlets by listing their URLs within *web-resource-collection* element. The servlet URLs, in turn, are normally defined with the *url-pattern* element of *servlet-mapping*. However, many servers also have a default servlet URL of the form http://host/webAppPrefix/servlet/ServletName. If you have this capability enabled, there are now two URLs that can invoke each servlet: the URL registered in *servlet-mapping* and the default (invoker servlet) URL. Remembering to protect both addresses is too hard. Instead, disable the invoker servlet, either globally for your server, or by mapping the /servlet/* pattern within your Web application.

Q. 344 Give a brief description of the steps involved in creating servlet and JSP filters.

ANS. Creating a basic servlet and JSP filter involves five steps:-

(1) *Create a class that implements the Filter interface:* Your class will need three methods: *doFilter, init, and destroy*. The *doFilter* method contains the main filtering code (step 2), the *init* method performs setup operations, and the *destroy* method does the cleanup operations.

(2) *Put the filtering behavior in the doFilter method:* The first argument to the *doFilter* method is a *ServletRequest* object. This object gives your filter full access to the incoming information, including form data, cookies, and HTTP request headers. The second argument is a *ServletResponse*; it is mostly ignored in simple filters. The final argument is a *FilterChain*; it is used to invoke the servlet, JSP page, or the next filter in the chain as described in the next step.

(3) *Call the doFilter method of the FilterChain object:* The *doFilter* method of the *Filter* interface takes a *FilterChain* object as one of its arguments. When you call the *doFilter* method of that object, the next associated filter is invoked. If no other filter is associated with the servlet or JSP page, then the servlet or JSP page itself is invoked.

(4) *Register the filter with the appropriate servlets and JSP pages:* Use the *filter* and *filter-mapping* elements in the deployment descriptor (*web.xml*).

(5) *Disable the invoker servlet:* Prevent users from bypassing filter settings by using default servlet URLs.

Q. 345 List the event listeners that respond to Web application life-cycle events.

ANS. There are eight kinds of event listeners that respond to Web application life-cycle events:-

(1) *Servlet context listeners:* These listeners are notified when the servlet context (i.e., the Web Application) is initialized and destroyed.

(2) *Servlet context attribute listeners:* These listeners are notified when attributes are added to, removed from, or replaced in the servlet context.

(3) *Session listeners:* These listeners are notified when session objects are created, invalidated, or timed out.

(4) *Session attribute listeners:* These listeners are notified when attributes are added to, removed from, or replaced in any session.

(5) *Session migration listeners:* These listeners are notified when the session objects are serialized and deserialized by the container. Usually, the serialization and deserialization of session objects occurs when the container migrates the session objects from one machine to another.

(6) *Session object binding listeners:* These listeners are notified when the implementing object is added or removed from the session object.

(7) *Request listeners*: These listeners are notified when request objects are initialized and destroyed.

(8) *Request attribute listeners:* These listeners are notified when attributes are added to, removed from, or replaced in any request.

Q. 346 Give the full form of EL as related to JSP.

ANS. Expression Language.

Q. 347 What do you understand by JSTL. Describe it briefly.

ANS. JSTL is the JSP Standard Tag Library. It provides many useful tag libraries and has been universally accepted by the Java community. The most commonly used JSTL tag library is the core library, which contains the following tags: *out, if, forEach, forTokens, choose, when, otherwise, set, remove, import, url, param, redirect,* and *catch*.

Q. 348 Discuss any one of the JSTL tags briefly.

ANS. Although any of the aforementioned tags can be discussed, here we shall only elucidate the c:set tag.

The c:set tag is used either for setting a scoped attribute or updating and creating bean properties and map values. The following are some of the common forms in which the c:set tag is used:-

```
<c:set var= "attributeName" value= "someValue" />
<c:set target= "map" property= "elementKey" value= "elementValue" />
<c:set target= "bean" property= "name">Arunesh Goyal</ c:set>
```

You may note that the c:set tag doesn't specify the *value* attribute.

Q. 349 What areas does the JSTL cover?

ANS. A particular set of tags has been collected into the JSP Standard Tag Library (JSTL) which is distributed along with the JSP framework. It covers the following areas:-

- *Assigning to variables;*
- Writing to output stream;
- Catching exceptions;
- Conditionals;
- Iterations;
- URL construction;
- String formatting;
- SQL queries; and,
- XML manipulation.

7

EJB

Q. 350 What do you understand by EJB? Elaborate.

ANS. Enterprise JavaBeans (EJB) is a server-side component framework that simplifies the process of building enterprise-class distributed component applications in Java. By using EJB, you can write scalable, reliable, and secure applications without writing your own complex distributed component framework. EJB is about rapid application development for the server side; you can quickly and easily construct server-side components in Java by leveraging a prewritten distributed infrastructure provided by the industry. EJB is designed to support application portability and reusability across any vendor's enterprise middleware services.

In short, EJB is a standard for developing and deploying server-side distributed components in Java. It defines an agreement (contract) between components and application servers that enables any component to run in any compliant application server. The three main advantages of EJB are:-

(1) It is a ubiquitous industry standard;

(2) Portability is possible; and,

(3) Rapid application development.

Q. 351 Why has EJB supported only Java thus far?

ANS. The EJB framework has supported only Java thus far, unlike the .NET framework that supports multiple languages. The reason for this is not far to seek. Java is one of the best-suited languages for building distributed components for the following reasons:-

(1) Interface/implementation separation: We need a language that supports a clean separation between the interface and implementation mainly to keep the component upgrades and maintenance to a minimum. Java supports this separation at a syntactic level through the *interface* and *class* keywords.

(2) Safe and secure: The Java architecture is much safer than traditional programming languages. In Java, if a thread dies, the application stays up. Pointers are not an issue since the language never exposes them to the programmer. Memory leaks occur much less often. Java also has a rich library set, so that Java is not just syntax of a language

but a whole set of prewritten, debugged libraries that enable developers to avoid reinventing the wheel in a buggy way. This safety is extremely important for mission-critical applications.

(3) Cross-platform: Java runs on any platform. There is a Java Virtual Machine (JVM) for all platforms. Vendors provide support for their application servers across all the platforms most of the time. This means that EJB applications could be deployed on all these platforms. This is valuable for customers who have invested in a variety of hardware platforms, such as Intel, AMD X32-X64, SPARC, and mainframes, as well as operating systems including various flavous of UNIX, Windows, and so on, in their data centers.

Q. 352 What kind of problems is EJB suitable for?

ANS. Specifically, EJB is used to help write logic that solves *business* problems. Typically, EJB components (enterprise beans) can perform any of the following tasks:-

(1) *Perform business logic:* Examples include computing taxes on a shopping cart, ensuring that the manager has authority to approve the purchase order, or sending an order confirmation e-mail using the *JavaMail API.*

(2) *Access a database:* Examples include submitting an order for books, transferring money between two bank accounts, or calling a stored procedure to retrieve a helpdesk ticket in a customer service application. Enterprise beans can achieve database access using many techniques, one of which is *Java Database Connectivity (JDBC) API.*

(3) *Integrate with other systems:* Examples include calling a highly transactional *CICS* legacy system written in C that computes the risk exposure for a new insurance customer, using a legacy VSAM (Virtual Storage Access Method) data store, or accessing *SAP R/3*. Enterprise beans can be integrated with other applications in multiple ways, one of which is the *Java EE Connector Architecture.*

Q. 353 Give three examples of EJB clients.

ANS. (1) *Application clients:* Application clients execute on a user's desktop either within an Internet browser environment as an applet or alone. They connect through the network to EJB components that live on a server.

(2) *Dynamically generated Web pages*

(3) *Web service clients*

Q. 354 How is distributed computing said to be the foundation of EJB? Elaborate.

ANS. EJB enables development and deployment of distributed components. A distributed component also referred to as a distributed object or remote object is callable from a remote system, i.e. not only it can be called from an in-process client but also from an out-of-process client that might be located on a different system on the network. A remote invocation of a method on a distributed object follows a common process that is similar across all distributed component technologies. The main steps involved in this remote invocation process are:-

(1) The client calls a *stub*, which is a *client-side proxy object*. This stub is responsible for masking network communications from the client.

(2) The stub calls over the network to a skeleton, which is a server-side proxy object. The skeleton masks network communications from the distributed object.

(3) The skeleton delegates the call to the appropriate implementation object. This object serves the call and does the work, and returns control to the skeleton, which returns it to the stub, which finally returns control to the client.

Figure 7 depicts the method invocation on a remote object. The key point here is that both the stub and the server-side implementation object implement the same interface (called the *remote interface*).

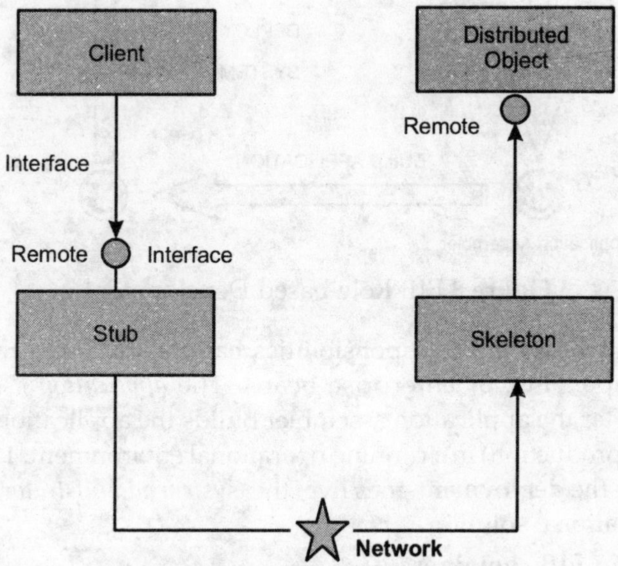

Figure 7 Remote Method Invocation

Q. 355 Enumerate the EJB middleware services.

ANS. EJB performs the middleware services in two ways, viz. implicitly and explicitly. We shall not go into the details of these but just enumerate the basic EJB middleware services as:-

(1) *Transaction management*
(2) *Persistence*
(3) *Messaging*
(4) *Security*
(5) *Clustering*

Q. 356 Explain the role-based EJB application life cycle.

ANS. An EJB application life cycle involves three phases:-

(1) Development
(2) Deployment
(3) Administration

Depending upon the size and scale of the application, the activities related to each of these phases/roles can range from simple to complex. EJB role-based development is elaborated in Figure 8.

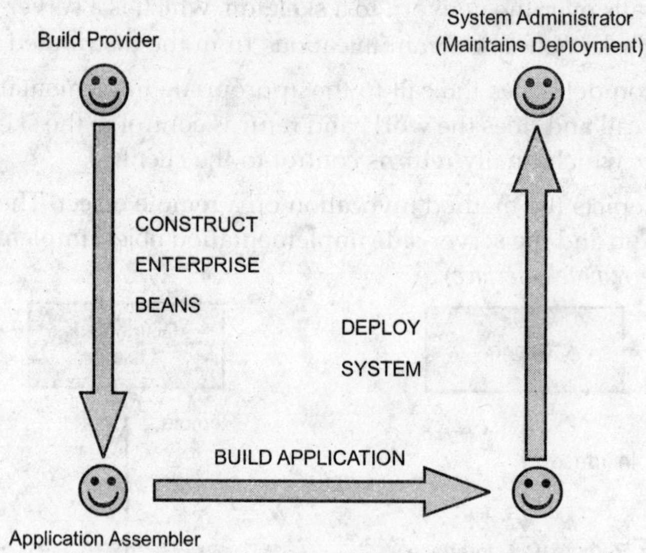

Figure 8 EJB Role-based Development

We now briefly touch upon the responsibilities handled by these roles. The *bean provider* supplies business components, or enterprise beans. The *application assembler* is the overall application architect. After the application assembler builds the application, the application must be *deployed* (and go into production) in a running operational environment. This is the responsibility of an *EJB deployer*. Once the deployment goes live, the *'system administrator'* takes over to oversee the stability of the operational solution.

Q. 357 Elucidate an EJB container.

ANS. An EJB container is the piece of software that implements the EJB specification. The reason for being called a container is that it provides an environment within which EJB components live and breathe. In other words, it provides containment to the EJB components.

An EJB container is responsible for managing your enterprise bean. The most important responsibility of the container is to provide a secure, transactional, distributed environment in which enterprise beans can execute. Enumerated in the following list are just a few of the many services that are made available by the bean container:-

(1) *Transaction management*
(2) Security
(3) Resource and life cycle management
(4) Remote accessibility
(5) Support for concurrent requests
(6) Clustering and load-balancing

Q. 358 What do you mean by isolation levels? Enumerate the various levels of isolation.

ANS. Isolation level can be defined as the degree to which operations on data by a certain transaction are affected by concurrent transactions, i.e. other transactions running at the same time. It also implies the degree to which operations on data by a transaction can affect data in concurrent transactions.

The various levels of isolations are enumerated as under:-

(1) *Dirty Reads:* A dirty read will occur when the first transaction reads uncommitted changes made by a second transaction. If the second transaction is rolled back, the data read by the first transaction would be invalid because the rollback reverses the changes. The first transaction won't be aware that the data it has read has become invalid.

(2) *Repeatable Reads:* A repeatable read occurs when the data is guaranteed to look the same if read again during the same transaction. Repeatable reads can be guaranteed in one of two ways – either the data read is locked against changes or the data read is a snapshot that doesn't reflect changes. If the data is locked, then it cannot be changed by any other transaction until the current transaction ends. If the data is a snapshot, then other transactions can change the data, but these changes won't be seen by this transaction if the read is repeated.

(3) *Phantom Reads:* Phantom reads occur when new records inserted into the database are detectable by transactions that started prior to the insert. Queries will include records added by other transactions after their transaction has started.

Q. 359 What do you mean by Heuristic decisions? Elaborate in brief.

ANS. Transactions are usually controlled by a transaction manager across multiple databases and servers. The transaction manager controls the transaction, based on the results of a poll against the resources (databases and other servers), it decides whether all the updates should be committed or rolled back.

A heuristic decision is when one of the resources makes a decision to commit or roll back by itself, without permission from the transaction manager. Once a heuristic decision has been made, the atomicity of the transaction is lost and possible data integrity errors can occur.

Q. 360 Enumerate and explain the various transaction types in EJB.

ANS. The various transaction attributes/types are enumerated as under:-

(1) *Not Supported:* This attribute means that when a method on a bean with this transaction attribute is called, the transaction gets suspended until the method is completed. This means that the transaction scope is not propagated to the Not Supported bean or any of the method calls it makes. Once the method in the Not Supported bean is done, the original transaction resumes its execution.

(2) *Supports:* Invoking a bean with this attribute will include it in the current transaction scope, i.e. if the bean or client that invokes the Supports bean is part of a transaction scope, the Supports bean and all beans accessed by that bean become part of the original transaction. However, the Supports bean doesn't have to be part of a transaction and can interact with clients and beans that are not included in a transaction scope.

(3) *Required:* When a bean's transaction attribute is set as Required, it means that the bean method must be invoked within the scope of a transaction. If the calling client or bean is part of a transaction, the Required bean is automatically included in its original transaction scope. However, if the calling client or bean is not involved in a transaction,

the Required bean starts its own new transaction. The new transaction's scope covers only the Required bean and all beans accessed by that bean. Once the method invoked on the Required bean is done, the new transaction's scope ends.

(4) *Requires New:* When a bean's transaction attribute is set as Requires New, it means that a new transaction is always started. Regardless of whether the calling client or bean is part of a transaction, a method with the Requires New attribute begins a new transaction when invoked. If the calling client is already involved in a transaction, that transaction is suspended until the Requires New bean's method call returns. The new transaction's scope only covers the Requires New bean and all beans accessed by that bean. Once the method invoked on the Requires New bean is done, the new transaction's scope ends and the original transaction resumes.

(5) *Mandatory:* When a bean's transaction attribute is set to Mandatory, it means that the bean method must always be made part of the transaction scope of the calling client. If the calling client or bean is not part of a transaction, the invocation will fail, throwing a *javax.transaction.TransactionRequiredException.*

(6) *Never (EJB* 1.1 only): When a bean's transaction attribute is set to Never, it means that the bean method must never be invoked within the scope of a transaction. If the calling client or bean is part of a transaction, the Never bean will throw a *RemoteException.* If, however, the calling client or bean is not involved in a transaction, the Never bean will execute normally without a transaction.

(7) *Bean Managed (EJB* 1.0 only): When a bean's transaction attribute is set to Bean Managed, it means that the bean or method doesn't have its transactional context implicitly managed by the EJB server. Instead, the developer can use the Java Transaction API (JPA) to explicitly manage transactions.

Q. 361 What do you mean by Re-entrant? Elaborate in brief.

ANS. The re-entrant element in a deployment descriptor of an EJB declares that the bean either allows loopbacks (re-entrant invocations) or not. This element can have one of the two values – True or False. True implies that the bean allows loopbacks; False implies that the bean throws an exception in case a loopback occurs. Beans are not re-entrant by default. When a bean is declared as re-entrant, it means that a method that is downstream in the sequence of method calls will call back the bean. This is not advisable.

Q. 362 How can you commit transactions over multiple databases?

ANS. A protocol called 2-phase commit is used. This will commit the transaction only after updates have gone through on all the different database instances.

Q. 363 Elucidate the different types of beans.

ANS. Enterprise JavaBeans are categorized into various types. Depending on the design requirements, you can use the suitable bean type:-

(1) *Session beans:* Session beans model business processes. They are like *verbs* because they perform actions. The action could be anything such as adding numbers, accessing a database, calling a legacy system, or calling other enterprise beans. Examples include a pricing engine, a workflow engine, a catalog service, a credit card authorization service, or a stock-trading service. Session beans are further divided into two categories

– *stateful* session beans and *stateless* session beans. As their names suggest, *stateful session beans* maintain state, encapsulated within the bean instance, across multiple client requests, whereas *stateless session beans* are not tasked with retaining the state across multiple client requests.

(2) *Message-driven beans* (MDBs): Message-driven beans are similar to session beans in that they perform actions. The difference is that you can call message-driven beans only implicitly by sending *messages* to those beans, i.e. there is no direct way of invoking a method on the message-driven bean. Examples of MDBs include beans that receive stock trade messages such as trade acknowledgement messages, credit card authorization messages, or messages within a given workflow or a business process where interactions are loosely coupled. These MDBs can, in turn, call the invoked methods directly on other EJBs or indirectly by sending a message to be received by another MDB.

(3) *Entity beans*: Entity beans model business data. They are like *nouns* because they are data objects, that is, Java objects that cache database information. Examples include a product, an order, an employee, a credit card, or a stock.

Note : Session beans can harness entity beans to accomplish business transactions.

Q. 364 Illustrate Lifecycle Diagrams of Session Beans.

ANS.

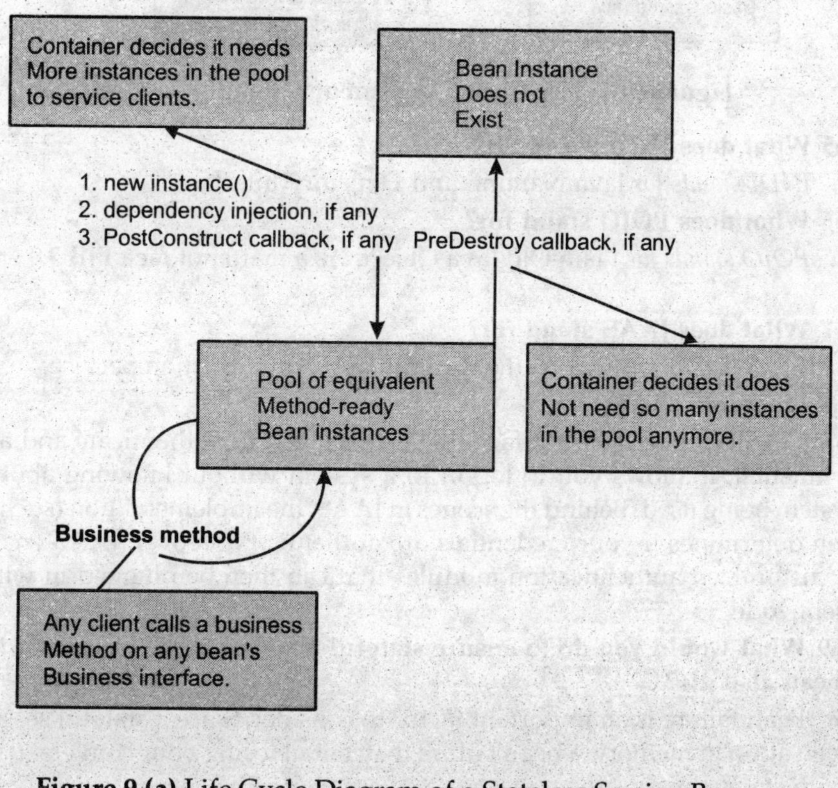

Figure 9 (a) Life Cycle Diagram of a Stateless Session Bean

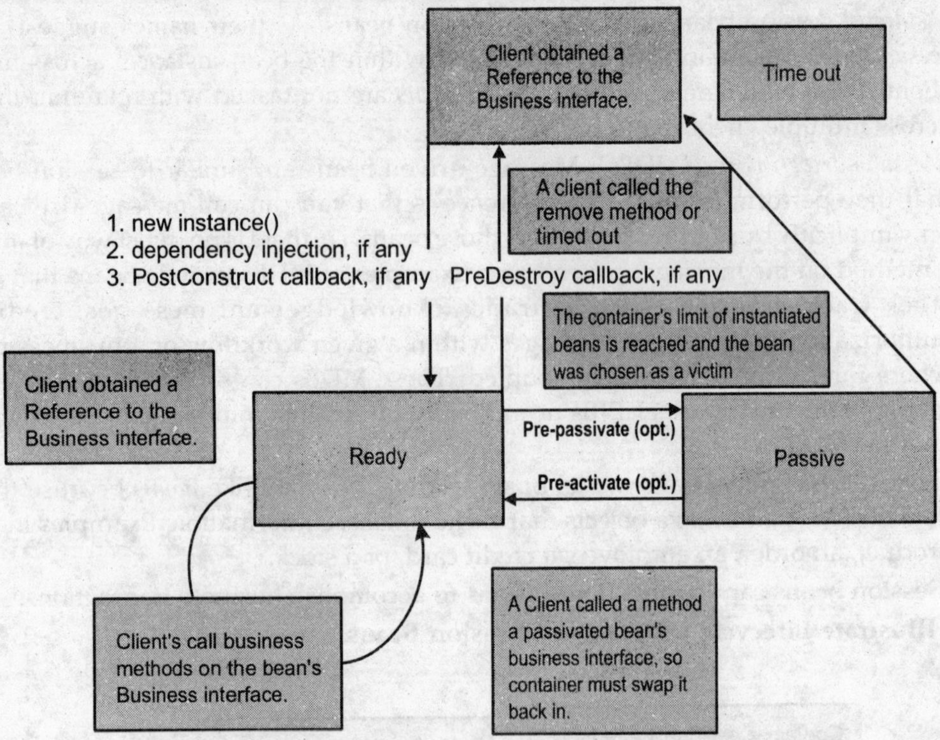

Figure 9 (b) Life Cycle Diagram of a Stateful Session Bean

Q. 365 What does JNDI stand for?

ANS. *JNDI stands for* Java Naming and Directory Interface.

Q. 366 What does POJO stand for?

ANS. *POJO stands for* Plain Old Java Object. As a matter of fact, EJB 3.0 entities are, in fact, *POJOs*.

Q. 367 What does JAAS stand for?

ANS. *JAAS stands for* Java Authentication and Authorization Service.

Q. 368 Elucidate JAAS.

ANS. *JAAS* is a portable interface that enables you to authenticate and authorize users in Java. In a nutshell, it allows you to log in to a system without knowing about the underlying security system being used. Behind the scenes in JAAS, the implementation (such as an application server) then determines if your credentials are authentic. Moreover, JAAS enables you to write your own customized authentication modules that can then be plugged in without the need to change client code.

Q. 369 What would you do to ensure stateful bean recovery in case of its failure? Can a stateless bean also die?

ANS. Bean failure is an important factor to consider. Since a stateful session bean caches a client conversation in memory, a bean failure may entail losing your conversation. This was not a problem with statelessness – there was no conversation to be lost.

Losing a conversation can have a devastating impact. If you have large conversations that span time, you have lost important work. Here are some of the guidelines you can use while designing your stateful beans to enable them to handle stateful recovery:-

- *Keep your conversations short;*
- *If the performance is feasible, consider checkpointing stateful conversations yourself to minimize the impact of bean failure (such as by using entities);*
- *Write smart client code that anticipates a bean failure and reestablishes the conversational state with a fresh stateful session bean.*

Q. 370 What is an entity? Elaborate.

ANS. In multi-tier enterprise applications, you will find typically two different kinds of objects:-

(1) *Application logic components:* These components provide methods that perform common tasks which might include the following:

- *Computing the price of an order*
- *Billing a customer's credit card*
- *Computing the inverse of a matrix*

Session beans model these application logic components very well.

(2) *Persistent data objects:* These are objects that can be rendered into persistent storage by a persistent mechanism. These kinds of objects represent 'data' – simple/complex information that you would like saved. Examples in this case include:

- *Bank account information, such as account number and balance*
- *Human resources data, such as names, departments, and salaries of employees*
- *Lead-tracking information, such as names, addresses, and phone numbers of prospective customers that you want to keep track of over time*

You may note that these objects represent people, places, and things (they are nouns). They are well suited to handling long-lived business data. Such persistent objects are called 'entities' in the new Java specification. These entities are plain old Java objects (POJOs) that are persisted to durable storage such as a database or legacy system. As elaborated above, entities store data as fields such as bank account numbers and bank account balances. They also have methods associated with them such as getAccountNumber() and getBalance().

Q. 371 Distinguish between entities and session beans.

ANS. The big differences between entities and session beans are that:-

- *Entities have a client*-visible, persistent 'identity' (the primary key) that is distinct from their object reference;
- *Entities have persistent client*-visible state;
- *Entities are not remotely accessible;*
- An entity's lifetime may be completely independent of an application's lifetime.

In fact, entities are in-memory Java representation of persistent data that:

(1) Is loaded from storage and has its field populated with the stored data;

(2) Can be modified in-memory to change the values of data;

(3) Can be saved back, thus updating the database data.

Q. 372 Elucidate the Entity Life-Cycle.

ANS.

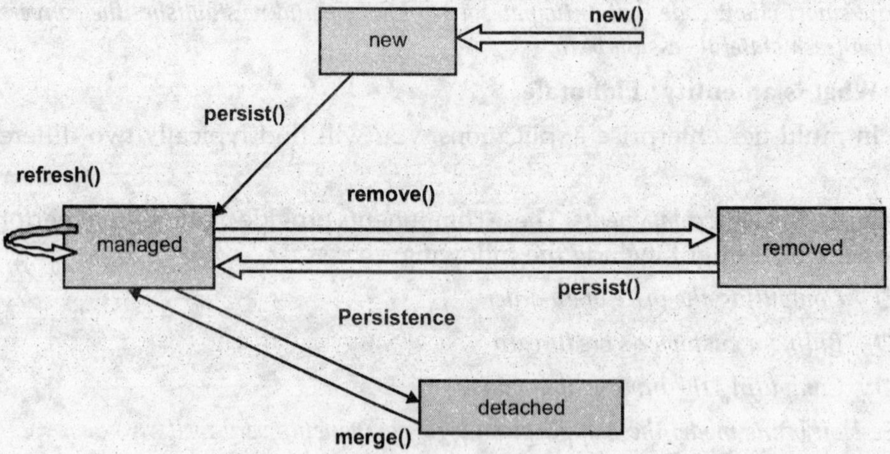

Figure 10 Entity Life Cycle

The life of an entity instance has two main aspects: its relationship to a specific persistence context, and the synchronization of its state with the database. The *EntityManager* (the *EntityManager* is the interface that lets you access the entities in your application's persistence context) distinguishes between four states in the life cycle of an entity (Figure 10 shows these four states and the transitions between them as *EntityManager* operations are called):-

- *new:* The entity instance was created in memory but is not yet associated with either a persistent identity in the database or a persistence context. Changes in the entity state are not synchronized with the database at this stage.
- *managed:* The entity has a persistent identity in the database and is currently associated with a persistent context. Changes to the identity will be synchronized with the database when transactions are committed or when synchronization is explicitly triggered using *the flush()* operation.
- *detached:* The identity does have a persistent identity but is not or is no longer associated with the persistence context.
- *removed:* The identity is currently associated with a persistence context but has been scheduled for removal from the database.

Q. 373 What are Java RMI-IIOP and JNDI in the context of EJB?

ANS. EJB depends upon Java RMI-IIOP and JNDI. While RMI-IIOP is the networking protocol used in EJB and is a must for interoperability with non-EJB applications such as legacy applications written in C++ or COBOL, JNDI is how beans (and their clients) look up other beans and external resources by name when dependency injection is not available or is insufficient.

Q. 374 Elucidate Java RMI-IIOP.

ANS. Java RMI (which stands for Java Remote Method Invocation) is a mechanism for performing simple but powerful networking. Using RMI, you can write distributed objects in Java, enabling objects to communicate in memory, across Java virtual Machines and physical devices. Java RMI-IIOP (which stands for Java RMI over the Internet Inter-ORB Protocol) is J2EE's de facto mechanism for providing networking services relying on the CORBA network protocol IIOP. The main advantage of IIOP over plain RMI's native transport protocol JRMP (Java Remote Method Protocol) is that IIOP lets your code interoperate remotely with any application on any platform that uses CORBA (Common Request Broker Architecture). It is also more mature than JRMP.

Q. 375 Elucidate RPC and RMI. How does RMI score over RPC?

ANS. A Remote Procedure Call (RPC) is a procedural invocation from a process on one machine to a process on another machine. RPCs enable traditional procedures to reside on multiple machines yet still remain in communication. They provide a simple way to perform cross-process or cross-machine networking.

A Remote Method Invocation (RMI) in Java takes the RPC concept one step further and allows for distributed 'object' communications. RMI enables you to invoke not procedures, but methods, on objects remotely. You can build your networked code as full objects. This yields the benefits of object-oriented programming, such as inheritance, encapsulation, and polymorphism.

Q. 376 Elucidate JNDI.

ANS. The Java Naming and Directory Interface (JNDI) is a Java API that provides a standard interface for locating users, machines, networks, objects, and services by name, e.g. you can use JNDI to locate a printer on your corporate intranet. You can also use it to locate a Java object or a database. JNDI is used in EJB, RMI-IIOP, JDBC, and more. It is the standard Java way of looking up things by name over the network and is also used to manage an enterprise bean's environment.

Q. 377 What do you understand by a naming service? Explain giving a suitable example.

ANS. *To understand JNDI, you must first get familiar with a naming service.* A naming service is an entity that performs the following tasks:-

- *It associates names with objects:* We call this *'binding'* names to objects. This is similar to a telephone company's associating a person's name with a specific residence's telephone number.
- *It provides a facility to find an object based on a name:* We call this looking up an object, or *'resolving'* a name. This is similar to a telephone operator finding a person's telephone number based on that person's name.

Naming services are everywhere in computing. When you want to locate a machine on a network, the *Domain Name System (DNS)* is used to translate a machine name to an IP (Internet Protocol) address.

Q. 378 Expiain the underlying need for using JNDI.

ANS. JNDI is a system for Java-based clients to interact with naming and directory systems. JNDI is a 'bridge' over naming and directory services, a beast that provides one common interface to disparate directories. All directory operations are done through the JNDI interface, providing a common framework. The following surveys the advantages that JNDI has to offer:-

- *You need to learn only a single API to access all sorts of directory service information such as security credentials, phone numbers, electronic and postal mail addresses, application preferences, network addresses, machine configurations, and more.*
- *JNDI insulates the application from protocol and implementation details.*
- *You can use JNDI to read and write whole Java objects from directories.*
- *You can link different types of directories, such as an LDAP directory with an NDS directory, and have the combination appear to be one large, federated directory. The federated directory appears to the client to be one contiguous directory.*

In J2EE, you can use JNDI for many purposes inclusive of the following:-

- *Using JNDI to acquire a reference to the Java Transaction API (JTA) User-Transaction interface;*
- *Using JNDI to connect to resource factories, such as JDBC drivers or Java Message Service (JMS) drivers;*
- *Using JNDI for clients and for beans to look up other beans.*

Q. 379 List at least four JNDI operations.

ANS. After acquiring the initial context, you could begin to execute JNDI operations such as reading or writing data to and from the JNDI tree by using the other API calls available in JNDI. Here is a brief list of available operations that you can call on the context (although only four operations have been asked for, I am giving the complete list; you can choose any four):-

- *list() retrieves a list of bindings available in the current context;*
- *lookup() resolves a name binding in the context, meaning that the operation returns the object bound to a given name in the context;*
- *rename() gives a context a new name, such as renaming c:\temp to c:\tmp;*
- *createSubcontext() creates a subcontext from the current context, such as creating c:\foo\bar from the folder c:\foo;*
- *destroySubcontext() destroys a subcontext from the current context, such as destroying c:foo\bar from the folder c:\foo;*
- *bind() creates a new name binding in the current context;*
- *rebind() is the same operation as bind() except that it forces a bind even if there is already something in the JNDI tree with the same name.*

Q. 380 How are annotations useful for EJB?

ANS. For EJBs, annotations are an alternative to the sometimes tedious and error-prone task of specifying the required metadata in XML descriptor files. The most prominent example of this technique is the popular *Xdoclet* tool that can, for example, be used to generate EJB deployment descriptor files in XML from EJB-specific source code comments provided by developers. The main point to remember about the *Javadoc/Xdoclet* approach is that the metadata is placed in comments. This means that it is not processed by the Java compiler.

Q. 381 Outline the pros and cons of Java annotations.

ANS. The metadata facility in Java defines an annotation language that is part of the language itself. This has the following advantages when compared with the *Xdoclet* approach:-

- *Ease of use:* Annotations are checked and compiled by the Java language compiler, so no external tool is required.
- *Portability:* Because the metadata facility is standardized, annotations are as portable as the rest of the code.
- *Type Checking:* Annotations are instances of 'annotation types', which are compiled in their own class files.
- *Runtime Reflection:* Annotations on a class can be kept in a class file and retained for runtime access.

However, the Java annotation facility in its current form also has its shortcomings:-

- Unlike interface classes and exceptions, annotation types cannot form an inheritance hierarchy.
- Annotation member types are restricted to primitive types, String, Class, enum types, annotation types, and arrays of the preceding types.
- To annotate 'existing' code, you must have access to the source code.
- Many developers have expressed their dislike of a syntax that leads to source code cluttered with @-signs. Of course, it is a matter of taste.

Q. 382 The above problem mentioned the more general criticism. What about the pros and cons of annotations with regard to EJBs?

ANS. From the EJBs point of view, following are the pros of annotations:-

- *Keeping the code and the metadata that describes it in sync is much easier with annotations directly on the source code;*
- *Compile-time checking on typed source code annotations helps you catch errors earlier than the XML compiler because it cannot detect semantic mismatches with the Java code. This must be checked by additional verifiers at or before deployment time.*

As for the cons, the one main argument against using annotations for EJBs is the following:-

To work with the metadata for beans that you didn't write yourself, you would still need access to the source code. Adding metadata to beans that come in an *EJB-jar* file without code is not going to work well unless you are allowed to disassemble the code, which is usually not much fun. Fortunately, the EJB specification defines how annotations and XML descriptors can be *'combined'*: the specification requires that containers give descriptor files precedence over source code annotations. Thus, you can always overrule and redefine the metadata that comes embedded in a *.jar* file. In a process that requires different individuals to incrementally modify metadata, you should still consider using external XML descriptor files rather than annotations embedded in the source code.

■

8

STRUTS

Q. 383 What is Struts?

ANS. Struts is the premier framework for building Java-based Web applications. Using the Model-View-Controller (MVC) design pattern, Struts solves many of the problems associated with developing high-performance, business-oriented Web applications that use Java servlets and JavaServer Pages.

Although the Model-View-Controller architecture is a powerful means of organizing code, developing such code can be a painstaking process. This is where Struts comes in. Struts is a Web application framework that streamlines the building of Web applications based on the MVC design principles. But, what does it mean? Is Struts an MVC Web application that you just add on or extend? Is Struts just some libraries? Actually, Struts is a little bit of both. Struts provides the foundation, or framework, for building MVC-oriented application along with libraries and utilities for making MVC development faster and easier.

Q. 384 Describe the advantages of using Struts by taking up a suitable analogy.

ANS. Consider the following analogy. If you were to create a GUI application in Java, you wouldn't write a text field widget and a drop-down widget yourself. You would instead use Java's swing API that already has standardized, fully functional code that provides these controls. Not only are the Swing controls ready-to-use, but they are also understood by all Java programmers.

Struts provides the same type of advantages. Struts supplies a standard way of implementing an MVC application, the Struts code is tried and true, and the techniques required to use Struts are well known and documented.

*Besides, Struts is open source and information for signing up to be a member of the Struts users mailing list can be found on the Struts Web site at http://*struts.apache.org/.

Q. 385 What are the basic components of Struts?

ANS. The Struts framework is a rich collection of Java libraries and can be broken down into the following major pieces/components:-

(1) Base framework which provides core MVC functionality

(2) JSP tag libraries which enable JSP authors to use HTML-like tags to represent functionality that is defined by a Java class

(3) Tiles plugin or framework which is a rich JSP templating framework that facilitates the reuse of presentation (HTML) code

(4) Validator plugin or framework which provides a rich framework for performing data validation on both the sever side and the client side (browser).

Q. 386 According to you, is Struts an MVC framework, a collection of utilities, or a set of JSP custom tag libraries?

ANS. All three viewpoints are legitimate. The answer depends upon what you are going to use it for. However, the most common way of looking at Struts is an MVC framework.

Q. 387 What are the steps involved in installing Struts?

ANS. Basically, the following three steps are involved in installing and configuring Struts:-

(1) *Downloading the Struts code:* You can get the latest release build at **http://struts.apache.org/downloads.html**. You can get the source code, example applications, or the documentation, but all that is absolutely required is the struts-blank Web application.

(2) *Updating your CLASSPATH:* To compile your Struts-based Web application, add struts-core-1.3.5.jar to the CLASSPATH used by your compiler or IDE.

(3) *Bookmarking the Struts documentation:* You can access the documentation online at **http://struts.apache.org/1.x/learning.html.** Alternatively, you can download a copy of the documentation for local access.

Q. 388 Explain the Struts flow of control.

ANS.

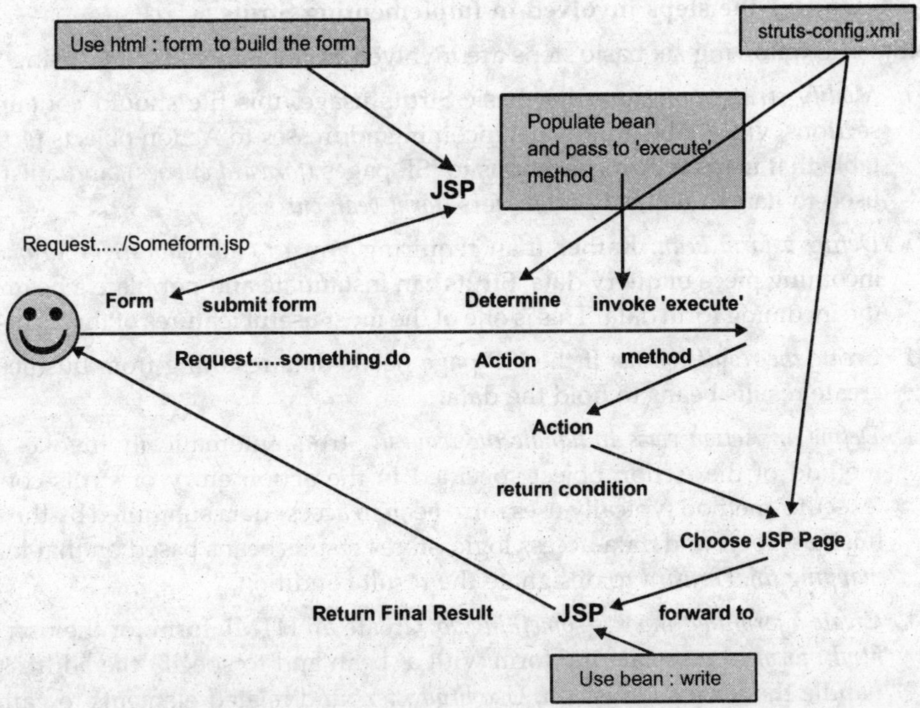

Figure 11 Flow of Control in the Struts Framework

The Struts flow of control is summarized as follows:-

(1) *The user requests a form:* The input form is built with the Struts *html : tags*. These tags associate a bean with the form so that you can pre-populate the form with values from your application, so that you can redisplay incorrectly filled out forms, and so that Struts knows where to store the request parameters when the form is submitted.

(2) *The form is submitted to a URL of the form something.do:* The form contains an ACTION ending in *something.do*. The Struts system receives the request, where an action mapping in struts-config.xml associates the address with an Action object.

(3) *The execute method of the Action object is invoked:* One of the arguments to 'execute' is a form bean that is automatically created and whose properties are automatically populated with the incoming form data. Once it examines the user input data in the bean, the 'execute' method invokes business logic and data-access logic, placing the results in normal beans stored in the request, session or application scope. Finally, the 'execute' method uses *mapping.findForward* to return various conditions that are mapped by struts-config.xml to JSP pages.

(4) *Struts forwards the request to the appropriate JSP Page: Struts* normally invokes the results page with *RequestDispatcher.forward*, although *request.sendRedirect* is occasionally used (e.g., with session-scoped data). In most real applications, the results page uses *bean : write* or the JSP 2.0 EL to output bean properties.

Q. 389 Outline the steps involved in implementing Struts.

ANS. The following six basic steps are involved in implementing and using Struts:-

(1) *Modify struts-config.xml:* For basic Struts usage, this file should contain three main sections, viz. a table that maps incoming addresses to Action objects (*action entries*), a table that maps return conditions to JSP pages (*forward entries*), and a list of the beans used to handle request parameters (*form-bean entries*).

(2) *Define a form bean:* Rather than requiring you to call *request.getParameter* for each incoming piece of query data, Struts can instantiate and populate a bean representing the incoming form data. This is one of the most useful features of the Struts framework.

(3) *Create the results beans:* If the JSP page needs data resulting from business logic, then create results beans to hold the data.

(4) *Define an Action class to handle the request:* Struts automatically invokes the 'execute' method of the Action object specified in the action entry of struts-config.xml. The 'execute' method typically uses form bean to access data submitted by the user, invokes business logic and data-access logic, stores results beans based on that logic, and calls *mapping.findForward* to designate the result condition.

(5) *Create a form that invokes something.do:* Create an HTML form for the user's input. Use *html : form* to associate the form with a bean and to specify the address that should handle the form submission. Use *html : text* and related elements to gather user data and to associate bean properties with the input elements.

(6) *Display the results in a JSP page:* Write a JSP page to display the results. Depending upon the user input and business logic, you could have more than one possible results page. Use *bean : write* or the JSP EL to output bean properties.

Q. 390 How and why do you lay out pages with Tiles?

ANS. Many Web sites contain pages with a common header, footer and menu. If you would like to build your site with a common look and feel, starting with Struts Tiles is an excellent choice. With the Tiles framework, you create a common page layout for your site, and then, based on the layout, use Struts *tiles : tags* to include JSP fragments and Strings for the main pages of the site. The Tiles approach is much more powerful than the traditional *jsp : include* for including files in a JSP page. In fact, some developers use Struts just for the sake of the Tiles capability as the servlet/JSP community has very few equivalents.

We outline three main reasons for using Tiles:-

(1) *Reuse (not rewrite) repeated sections of pages:* For similar content, you need only sections once and then use Tiles to easily add those sections to your JSP pages.

(2) *Simplify the creation of similar pages:* With templates, you can easily lay out similar pages in your site. Then, with the layout template, provide specific content for the layout pieces.

(3) *Increase flexibility and ease of maintenance:* With Tiles, you get a lot more flexibility than with the traditional *<jsp:include .../>* tag. Plus, the supporting elements for Tiles (such as handling relative URLS, inheritance etc.) eases the overall maintenance of the site.

The four basic steps required for using Tiles are enumerated as follows:-

(1) *Sketch out the desired page layout*

(2) *Make a template file that represents the layout using tiles : insert wherever a layout piece should go and tiles : getAsString wherever changeable text goes*

(3) *Create JSP pages that define the layout pieces*

(4) *Create JSP pages that populate the layout using tiles : insert to refer to the layout from step 1 and tiles : put to specify the layout pieces that apply to each specific page*

Q. 391 How and why do you use the Struts Validation framework?

ANS. Probably the most tedious and time-consuming part of developing a Web site is validation of the input data. There is no easy way of getting around it – you have to check for missing or poorly formatted input values. Unfortunately, the servlet and JSP APIs provide no mechanism for easily validating input data. To the rescue come the Struts Validation framework. This framework is incredibly flexible and easy to use, supporting both client-side and server-side validation. For validating form fields, Struts gives you the following options:-

(1) *Do validation in the Action:* This is the most powerful and flexible approach. Validation in the Action has access to business logic, databases, and so on. However, this validation may require repetition of code in multiple Actions and requires you to write the validation rues yourself. Also, you need to manually map conditions back to the input page.

(2) *Do validation in the form bean:* You can do validation in individual setter methods – not really validation, but useful to modify values. Better, you can use the 'validate' method in *ActionForm*. This approach does not require repetition of code in multiple Actions, but still requires you to write the validation rules.

Based on the return value from 'validate', Struts can automatically redisplay the input page.

(3) *Use automatic validator:* Automatic validation is the most powerful approach. The Struts Validation framework includes many rules for automatically checking the input values (missing data, phone number format, e-mail format, etc.). In addition, the automatic validator can incorporate client-side JavaScript for field validation.

Q. 392 Distinguish between manual and automatic validation.

ANS. We briefly discuss the differences between manual and automatic validation:-

- *Manual Validation:* Manual validation of input fields is the most flexible. You have full access to beans, to business logic, and to the application database. Unfortunately, manual validation often results in repeated logic and often runs only on the server. If you also do client-side validation, then most likely, you are writing lots of tedious JavaScript code embedded in JSP code. This approach violates the Struts strategy of placing as much as possible in editable files versus in code that must be compiled.
- *Automatic Validation:* Automatic validation typically consolidates the amount of validation code needed and lets you use standard validation rules. Also, automatic validation runs on the server, but can optionally include JavaScript that runs on the client. With automatic validation in Struts, instead of building code that requires compilation, you can easily describe the validation rules in XML files.

Q. 393 Distinguish between client-side and server-side validation. Should you validate data on the server or the client?

ANS. *A common question for any new Web developer is – "Should I validate data on the client or the server?" For security reasons alone, you must always validate the data on the server – a hacker (or the user) can deliberately or accidentally bypass your input forms completely (especially JavaScript validation on the client).* We briefly discuss the differences between client-side and server-side validation:-

- *Client-side Validation:* For client-side validation, JavaScript code verifies the format of input fields. If any fields are bad, a dialog box can warn the user of any illegal values. If the input is bad, JavaScript can block the submission to the server. Client-side validation with JavaScript tends to be very fast. The validation does not require a trip to the server. However, there are limitations. You cannot do validation that requires application logic, such as talking to the database server. Finally, with client-side validation, you need to consider the possibility of the user deliberately or accidentally bypassing JavaScript (i.e., turning it off).
- *Server-side Validation:* For server-side validation, Java code on the server can validate the fields. Most likely, server-side validation performs similar checks as client-side validation, but can invoke stronger application logic for additional checks. Instead of

a pop-up dialog box, you can display warning messages back on the input form. Unfortunately, server-side validation is slower, but you really have no choice here. You must do server-side validation regardless of whether or not you do client-side validation.

Q. 394 What do you understand by properties files? What are the advantages of using properties files in the Struts framework?

ANS. In the simplest terms, properties files are nothing more than text files containing name-value pairs, or rather, key-message pairs. By using *bean : message* from the Struts tag library, you can easily retrieve your properties files and display them on your JSP pages.

Nearly, all Struts developers use properties files to simplify development of their Web applications. We summarize two greatest advantages of using properties files as follows:-

(1) *Centralized updates:* If the application uses a message in several JSP pages, with properties files you can easily update a message with a single change. This capability is consistent with the Struts philosophy of making as many changes in the configuration files, not in the Java or JSP code.

(2) *Internationalization (I18N):* If you use messages pervasively in your JSP pages, you can internationalize your application by having multiple properties files corresponding to the locale (as with standard I18N in Java). Simply create a file for each language that requires support. For instance, to support English, Japanese, and Spanish (Mexico dialect), you would create the following properties files, respectively:

MessageResouces.properties

MessageResouces_ja.properties

MessageResouces_es_mx.properties

(In the chapter on internationalization, we cover I18N in more detail)

■

9

WEB SERVICES & XML

Q. 395 Elucidate UDDI.

ANS. The Universal Description, Discovery, and Integration is a database of web services providers that is accessible from within a program and supplies information about the web services available from the provider including information about interfaces to web services. The web services community centers around a group of web-based registries that contain information about each member, their web services, and the application programming interfaces used to access those services. This group of registries is referred to as the *Universal Description, Discovery, and Integration (UDDI)*. A UDDI entry is called a *tModel* and contains:-

(1) *The name of the business*

(2) *Contact information*

(3) *Industry codes*

(4) *Product classification*

(5) *A description of the web service*

(6) *Requirements for rights to access the web service*

(7) *Technical reference to the interface and properties*

Q. 396 Elucidate JAXR.

ANS. The keystone of web services is the XML registry that is the repository for information about availability of web services and information necessary to access web services. The XML registry is the mechanism for organizations to make available web services to other organizations and top avail themselves of another organization's web services. Two important XML registry standards are UDDI (refer previous problem) and the Java API for XML registries (JAXR) that is used to access an XML registry. The JAXR architecture is organized into two groups – the JAXR client and the JAXR provider. The JAXR client is a Java program that accesses information contained in an XML registry by interacting with a JAXR provider. A JAXR provider implements the RegistryService interface giving a JAXR client registry access. There are two packages that are necessary to implement JAXR: the *javax.xml.registry* package contains the interface to access the registry while the *javax.xml.registry.infomodel* package contains interfaces that define registry objects and how those objects are interrelated.

Q. 397 Elucidate SOA. Are SOA and EJB mutually exclusive?

ANS. At the core of Service-oriented architecture (SOA) lies the concept of *service*. A simplistic definition of service is a group of related components that carry out a given business process function, e.g. transferring funds between banks or booking an itinerary. An SOA, thus, is a paradigm focusing on development of services rather than piecemeal components such that these services provide a higher level of abstraction from a functional standpoint.

It is, of course, essential for EJB developers and architects to understand that SOA and EJB are not mutually exclusive but rather are symbiotic. You can write robust SOA architectures using EJB. You might even be called upon to implement SOA projects using EJB.

Q. 398 Are SOA and Web Services the same? Elaborate.

ANS. The terms Web Services and SOA are often used interchangeably and wrongly so. SOA is a paradigm as elaborated above. There are many possible ways of building software so that it implements salient features of SOA (mainly coarse granularity and loose coupling). One such way is Web Services. Web Services are a group of XML technologies that can be used for implementing SOA. Core Web Service technologies – mainly SOAP and WSDL – form the basis of most of these Web Service implementations today.

Q. 399 Elucidate SOAP.

ANS. Simple Object Access Protocol (SOAP) is an XML-based application-level protocol intended for exchanging information in a distributed network. SOAP supports both the models of distributed computing: RPC as well as document-style messaging. RPC style SOAP allows remote invocation of operations. The RPC in-out parameters and return values of these operations are serialized into XML, whereas in document-style SOAP, because an operation's input and output are XML fragments, serialization of parameters and return values to XML is not needed.

Although most of the Web Service applications use SOAP over HTTP today, the standard does not preclude using SOAP over other Internet protocols, such as Simple Mail Transfer Protocol (SMTP). The latest version of SOAP, viz. SOAP 1.2, is a World Wide Web Consortium (W3C) Recommendation.

Q. 400 Elucidate WSDL.

ANS. Web Service Description Language (WSDL) is an XML-based metadata standard that is used to describe the service interface as well as service binding information. For RPC style services, a WSDL service interface consists of the supported operations, the input-output parameters that these operations accept, and their return values. For document-style services, the service interface description contains the XML schema fragments for the input-output messages of the service operations, whereas the service binding description specifies communication protocols, ports, the service URL, and other such binding information. Now, the latest version of WSDL, viz. WSDL 2.0, is well on its way to becoming a W3C standard.

The backbone of web services is communication used to transmit between web service providers to an XML registry and from an XML registry to a web services consumer. The Web Service Description Language (WSDL) is a standard used to describe network services used to facilitate the interaction between web services providers and consumers. Organizations that either publish web services or consume web services must be able to communicate with each other using an agreed upon protocol. Protocols supported by an organization are described using WSDL.

WSDL standardizes XML elements that describe a collection of communication endpoints. WSDL defines a network service using seven XML elements, viz. type, message, operation, port type, binding, port, and service. WSDL has binding extensions for popular protocols and message formats that are positioned on top of the network service definition. These include SOAP 1.1, HTTP GET/POST, and MIME.

Q. 401 Explain service-oriented architecture with Web services.

ANS. Web services are a way of building a Service-Oriented Architecture (SOA). SOA is an architectural approach to structuring large-scale, distributed systems that integrate heterogeneous applications behind 'service' interfaces. Figure 12 shows the basic model of a service lookup in a Service-Oriented Architecture as supported by Web services technologies:-

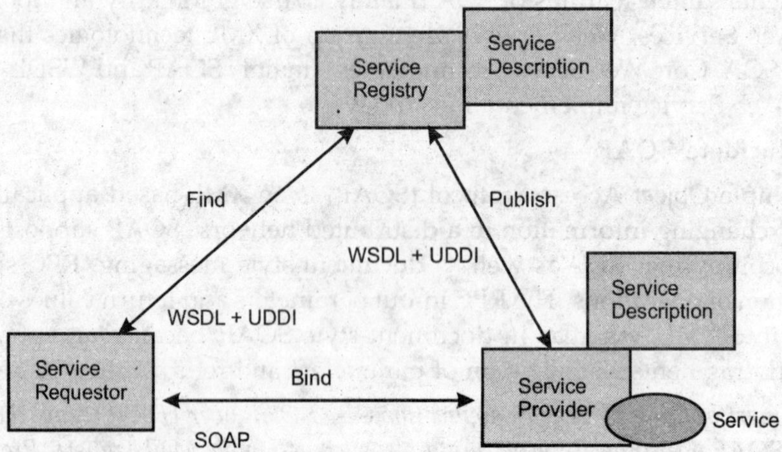

Figure 12 Service-oriented Architecture with Web services

- *A service provider creates an abstract service definition that can 'publish' in a service registry. With Web services, the description is a Web Services Description Language (WSDL) file, and the registry follows the Universal Description, Discovery, and Integration (UDDI) standard.*
- *A service requestor can find the service description, possibly using a set of selection criteria to query the registry.*
- *If a suitable description is found, the requestor can bind to and use the service.*

Q. 402 Can you explain the concept of Web services in the form of an equation?

ANS. The set of de facto standards that make up Web services today can be summarized in the form of the following simple equation:-

Web Services = WSDL + SOAP + UDDI

Q. 403 Elucidate JMS.

ANS. The Java Message Service (JMS) is a messaging standard, designed to eliminate many of the disadvantages MOM (Message-Oriented Middleware) products have faced over the past few years. JMS has two parts: an API, for which you write code to send/receive messages, and a Service Provider Interface (SPI) where you plug in JMS providers. A JMS provider knows how to talk to a specific MOM implementation.

Q. 404 What is an Object-Relational (OR) mapping? Elaborate.

ANS. The simplest way to persist objects in Java is to use Java's native serialization API that lets you write objects to files. Another popular way to store Java objects is to use a traditional relational database management system (RDBMS) such as Oracle, DB2, Microsoft SQL Server etc. Rather than serialize an object as a complete bit blob, we would decompose each object into its constituent parts and store each part separately. For instance, for a bank account object, the bank account number could be stored in one relational database field and the bank account balance in another field. When you save your Java objects, you would use JDBC to 'map' the object data into a relational database. When you want to load your objects from the database, you would instantiate an object from that class, read the data in from the database, and then populate that object instance's field with the relational data read in. This is shown in Figure 13.

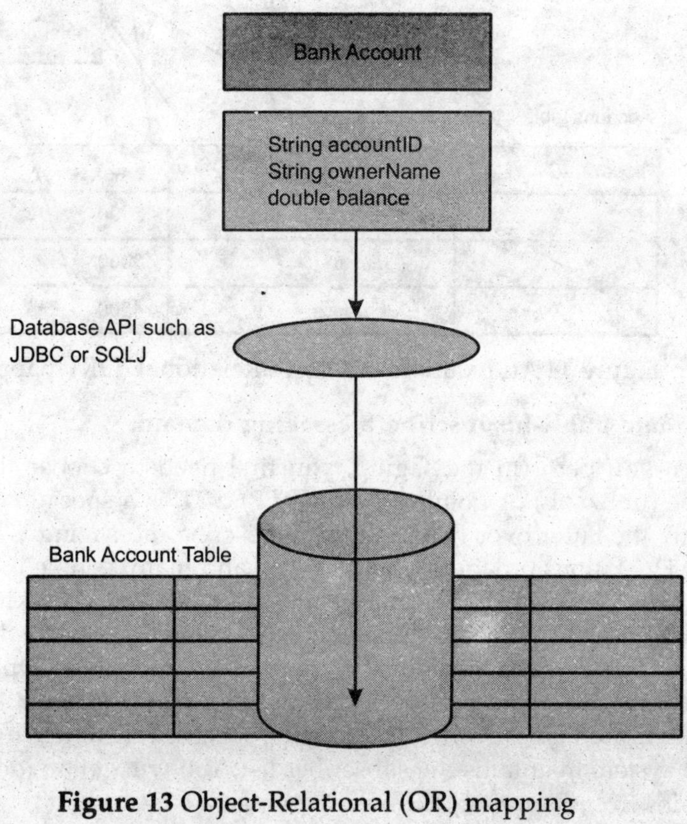

Figure 13 Object-Relational (OR) mapping

This mapping of objects to relational databases is a technology called object-relational mapping. It is the act of converting and unconverting in-memory objects to relational data. An object-relational (OR) mapper may map your objects to any kind of relational database schema.

For instance, a simple object-relational mapping engine might map a Java class to a SQL table definition. An instance of that class would map to a row in that table, while fields in that instance would map to individual cells in that row. This is shown in Figure 14.

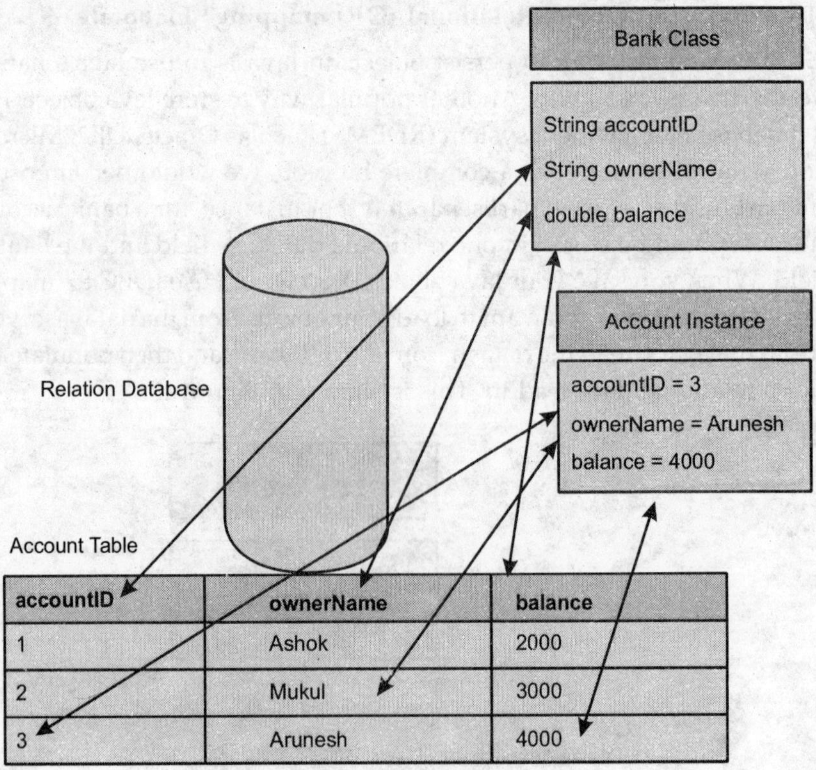

Figure 14 An Example of Object-Relational (OR) mapping

Q. 405 Elucidate publish/subscribe messaging domain.

ANS. When you perform messaging, you first need to choose the messaging domain: publish/subscribe (pub/sub) or point-to-point (PTP). PTP is a special case of pub/sub. So, we shall describe only the latter over here. Publish/subscribe messaging is analogous to watching television: many TV stations broadcast their signals, and many people listen to their broadcasts. Thus, with pub/sub, you can have 'many' message producers talking to 'many' message consumers. In this sense, the pub/sub domain is an implementation of a distributed event-driven processing model. Subscribers (listeners) register their interest in a particular event 'topic'. Publishers (event sources) create messages (events) that are distributed to all of the subscribers (listeners). Producers aren't hard-coded to know the specific consumers in receiving its messages; rather, the MOM system maintains the subscriber list. You will get an idea of pub/sub vs. P-T-P messaging domains from Figure 15.

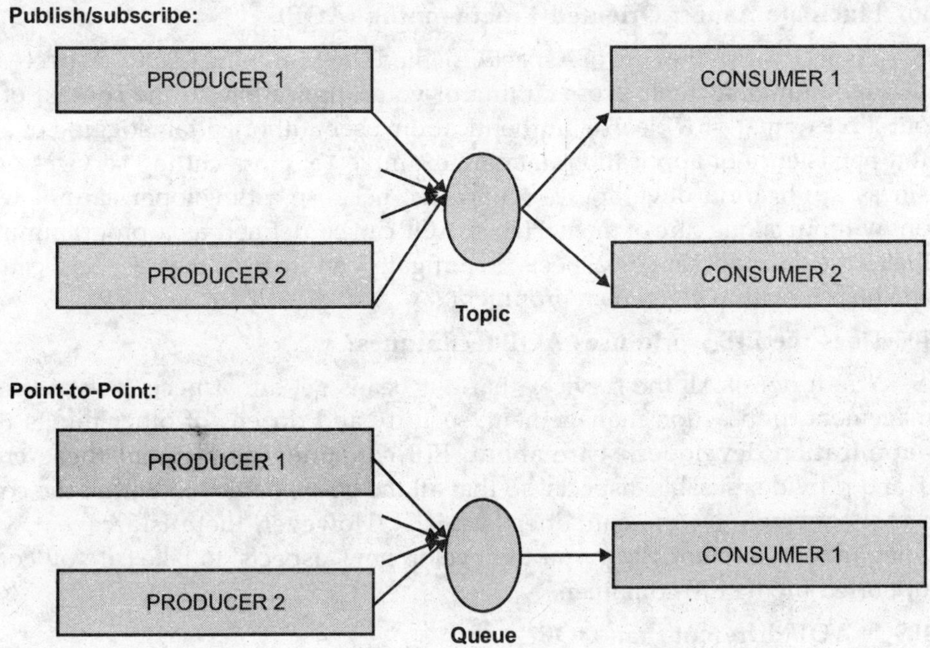

Figure 15 Publish/subscribe Versus Point-to-Point Messaging domains

Q. 406 What criteria would you employ while choosing between servlets and stateless session beans as Web service endpoints?

ANS. Here are some guidelines that should help you in choosing between servlets and stateless session beans as Web service endpoints.

Use a servlet as Web service endpoint if:

- The business logic of the service is within a Web tier since in this case both the endpoint and Web service's business implementation will reside in the same tier.
- You need a lightweight Web service container, viz. servlet container.
- You need to execute some logic that resides on the Web tier before invoking Web services.
- You do not mind writing logic for synchronizing multithreaded access to your service. This is required since the servlet container does not synchronize concurrent requests to the servlet instance and hence, in this case, to your Web service endpoint.

Use a stateless session bean as Web service endpoint if:

- The business logic of the service is within an EJB tier since in this case both the endpoint and Web service's business implementation will reside in the same tier.
- You need the Web service implementation to avail themselves of the transaction- and component-level security services from the container.
- You need to execute some logic that resides on the EJB tier before invoking Web services.
- You want the container to take care of synchronizing concurrent access to your service.

Q. 407 Elucidate Aspect-Oriented Programming (AOP).

ANS. 'Aspect' forms the core of Aspect-Oriented Programming (AOP). Aspects are reusable services that are quintessentially cross-cutting of your application. In the context of a business application, services that provide user authentication, user authorization, logging of access to the system, and persistence of application data are examples of cross-cutting services or 'concerns' for a business application developer – 'concerns' because a developer cannot write robust applications without taking care of them. Hence, AOP can be defined as a programming platform that facilitates the development of 'aspects' to mitigate 'concerns' so that 'aspects' can be 'reused' by all living objects within a given environment.

Q. 408 Does the EJB world uses AOP techniques?

ANS. Yes! It does!! All the services that our beans get are 'aspects', e.g. persistence, life-cycle management, transaction management, security and dozens of other things that we, the business application developers, care about. EJB containers implement these cross-cutting 'concerns' and provide reusable 'aspects' so that all the beans deployed within the container can offload these 'concerns' on the container 'aspects'. However, there is a caveat, viz. the EJB programming model does not allow you to develop new 'aspects' to take care of 'concerns' that are not supported by the EJB container.

Q. 409 Is AOP different than OOP?

ANS. Yes! It is!! One of the common traits of both AOP and OOP is reusability. However, OOP instills reusability via inheritance. This works well in a vertical parent-child relationship chain. But, OOP does not work when behavior needs to be used horizontally, owing to the behavior's cross-cutting nature. Now, why should you want to reuse behavior horizontally? Since you don't want your business object, e.g. a *ShoppingCart*, to inherit the behavior pertaining to transactions, because these behaviors are unrelated; you don't want an apple to inherit grape-like qualities; rather, you want to mix apples and grapes to prepare a margarita. This is exactly where AOP comes into the picture. AOP and OOP are not competing but complementary technologies. Consider, for example, an EJB server where cross-cutting 'aspects' are provided to your object-oriented beans. To conclude, OPP and AOP coexist.

Q. 410 Elucidate XML.

ANS. XML (*Extensible Markup Language*) is a framework for defining markup languages. In contrast to HTML (*HyperText Markup Language*), there is no fixed collection of markup tags in XML. Instead, XML lets you define your own tags, tailored and customized to the kind of information you wish to represent. Each XML language is targeted at a particular application domain, but all of them will share many common features such as they all use the same markup syntax and they all benefit from a common set of generic tools for processing documents.

Q. 411 Is XML merely an extension of HTML? Elaborate.

ANS. XML is not an extension of HTML, nor is it a replacement for HTML, which ideally should be just another XML language. However, because of a number of minor syntactical differences, HTML does not directly fit into the XML framework. As a remedy, the W3C has designed XHTML as an XML variant of HTML.

Q. 412 What are the inherent advantages in using XML?

ANS. XML has been designed with some simple but powerful principles in mind. First of all, it allows tailor-made markup for any imaginable application domain. As an additional benefit, XML is inherently internationalized and platform independent. All XML documents are written in the Unicode alphabet which leads to easy internationalization. Finally, XML is designed and intended to be the future of all structured information. This even includes information stored in relational databases, which has motivated and led to the development of the powerful query language – *XQuery*. In fact, XML was designed to bring the power of SGML (*Standard Generalized Markup Language*), which was standardized in 1986, to the Web. A major benefit of using XML is the availability of "generic tools and technologies" that surround the core XML notation.

Q. 413 When would you use XML with EJB?

ANS. Using XML with EJB is useful in the following scenarios:-

(1) For data-driven integration

(2) As a document persistence mechanism

(3) As a Web service interface

Q. 414 In the XPath data model, what is an XML tree?

ANS. In the XPath data model, an XML tree is a special kind of ordered tree whose nodes can be any of the following kinds:-

(1) Text nodes
(2) Element nodes
(3) Attribute nodes
(4) Comment nodes
(5) Processing instruction nodes
(6) Root nodes

Q. 415 Is an XML document just a tree structure, just a textual representation, or both?

ANS. An XML document can be considered both in its textual representation and as a tree structure.

Q. 416 Elucidate XPath.

ANS. XPath is a language used to navigate XML trees.

❒ *The development of several different XML technologies has identified a common need for a flexible notation for pointing into and navigating around XML documents. This has resulted in the XPath language, which is used for:*

❒ *uniqueness and scope descriptions in XML Schema;*

❒ *for pattern matching and selection in XSLT;*

❒ *for selection and iteration in XQuery; and,*

❒ *as a key component of XLink and XPointer.*

Besides, a part of XPath is able to express computations on data values, which is well exploited in XSLT and XQuery.

Q. 417 Elucidate XPointer and XLink.

ANS. XPointer and XLink provide hyperlinks in general XML documents. The XPointer language generalizes the ability to point at specific places in XML documents.

Q. 418 Elucidate XSLT.

ANS. The XSLT language is used to transform XML documents using XSL (*Extensible Stylesheet Language*) technology.

- *The XSL technology has two constituents: XSLT (XSL Transformations), which is a declarative programming language for specifying transformations between XML languages, and XSL-FO (XSL Formatting Objects, which is a particular target language suitable for specifying the physical layout.*
- *XSLT was originally developed and designed as a generalized stylesheet, intended to fit in the same niche as CSS (Cascading Stylesheets). However, it has developed into a complete programming language with many more applications. The behavior of a stylesheet may be obtained by specifying a transformation into the XHTML language, which enables rendering in a browser. But, XSLT transformations may also be used to translate between other XML languages, to extract views of XML data, and to perform query-like computations.*
- *XSLT transformations may be executed in standalone tools, but they are also supported by all modern browsers. Specifically, an XML document may contain a processing instruction that links to an external XSLT document. A browser will, then load the XSLT file, execute the corresponding transformation and present the result, which will presumably be an XHTML document.*

Q. 419 Elucidate XQuery.

ANS. XML documents naturally generalize database relations. XQuery is the corresponding generalization of SQL. There are many reasons why a merger of XML and databases is attractive. But, the main strategic advantage is that if XML is the future of WWW and XML becomes the future of databases, then in the future, the WWW will simply become one gigantic database. That's why XQuery is designed to generalize SQL, as XML generalizes database tables.

Q. 420 Evaluate XQuery vis-à-vis XSLT.

ANS. XQuery and XSLT may emulate each other but are designed for different tasks:-

- While XSLT is exceedingly good at defining complicated recursive traversals and transformations to arbitrary depths of XML documents, while XQuery must use explicit recursion for user-defined functions.
- Conversely, XQuery has more the flavor of a database programming language and allows simple solutions for simple problems, while XSLT may be more verbose.

Q. 421 Can you elucidate the relation between Web services and XML?

ANS. Web services support *service-oriented architectures* (SOA) using in particular, XML and HTTP.

- *The basic Web service standards, as already elaborated, are SOAP, WSDL and UDDI.* While SOAP is a protocol for exchanging XML documents, typically but not necessarily using HTTP, WSDL is an interface description language for Web services. Again, UDDI is a system for making clients and servers find each other. And, not surprisingly, *all three of them use an XML notation.*

Q. 422 Give one feature each of SOAP, WSDL and UDDI.

ANS. The main strengths of SOAP are support for intermediaries, fault management and RPC (*Remote Procedure Calls*) interactions. A WSDL description of a Web service describes its functionality, data encodings, communication protocols and location. UDDI allows Web services to be registered and discovered.

10

INTERNATIONALIZATION

Q. 395 Elucidate UDDI.

ANS. The Universal Description, Discovery, and Integration is a database of web services providers that is accessible from within a program and supplies information about the web services available from the provider including information about interfaces to web services. The web services community centers around a group of web-based registries that contain information about each member, their web services, and the application programming interfaces used to access those services. This group of registries is referred to as the *Universal Description, Discovery, and Integration (UDDI)*. A UDDI entry is called a *tModel* and contains:-

Q. 423 What do you mean by internationalization?

ANS. *Internationalization*, also known as *I18N*, encompasses tailoring content specific to locales based on their different languages, currencies, and formatting conventions. Due to international globalization has arisen the need for software that can adapt to the conventions and languages used by customers in different countries.

The acronym I18N is sometimes used in place of the word internationalization since it is such a long word to type. I18N represents the first letter i, followed by 18 characters, and then the final letter n.

Q. 424 What is Java's built-in internationalization support?

ANS. Java's built-in internationalization support is centered on three main classes. The following table (Table 1) lists each class and its description:-

Class	*Description*
Java.util.Locale	*Encapsulates the language, country and variant for a specific locale*
Java.util.ResourceBundle	*Encapsulates locale-specific resources*
Java.text.MessageFormat	*Provides methods for creating locale-specific formatted messages*

Table 1 Understanding Java's Internationalization Support

Q. 425 How do you internationalize applications using Struts?

ANS. With Struts, creating an I18N application is easy. If you are willing to pull all the titles, labels and text messages from a properties file, then you can easily I18N your application. Just create a properties file for each language (locale) you would like to support.

- *Struts attempts to use a properties file that corresponds to the browser language setting.* When requesting a page, the browser sends an Accept-Language request header, listing the language preferences. If no corresponding language (locale) is found, then Struts uses the default properties file.
- *Default properties file:* To establish a default properties file, use the message-resource element in struts-config.xml. Thus, when you say:

  <*message*-resources parameter= "someName" ...>
- *The file,* WEB-INF/classes/someName.properties, is loaded and treated as the default language file.
- *Locale-specific properties file:* Based on the languages accepted by the browser, Struts automatically looks for specialized files corresponding to the locale. A locale-specific file has the same name as the default properties file, but is augmented with local information, e.g. someName_es.properties (Spanish locale) or someName_fr.properties (French locale). Entries from a more specific file override entries from the default file. The locale can also be set explicitly (e.g., based on the incoming checkbox value) in an Action with *setLocale.*

Once you have created a locale-specific properties file, you will want to test it in your Web application. To test the new properties file, change the language settings in the browser. For Internet Explorer, for instance, select Tools from the menu, then Internet Options, then Languages. Click the Add button to select other languages for the browser. To change the language preference order, use the Move Up button.

Now, we present an example where we internationalize for English, Spanish and French. All we need to do is to create two new properties files (refer chapter 8 on Struts for more on properties files), *MessageResources_es.properties* for the Spanish locale and *MessageResources_fr.properties* for the French locale. The assumption is that the original file, *MessageResources.properties,* supports the English locale. The two new locale files need to contain all the same messages as *MessageResources.properties* but translated to the appropriate language. The keys remain the same. This change is all that is required to internationalize the application for Spanish and French – there are no changes to any configuration files or code!

■

11

JNI

Q. 426 What are native methods? What purpose do they serve?

ANS. Although it is rare, occasionally you may want to call a subroutine that is written in a language other than Java. Typically, such a subroutine exists as executable code for the CPU and environment in which you are working – that is, native code. For instance, you may want to call a native code subroutine to achieve faster execution time, or, you may want to use a specialized, third-party library, such as a statistical package. Such subroutines are called native methods.

Q. 427 Java programs are compiled to bytecode, which is then interpreted (or compiled on-the-fly) by the Java run-time system, so how is it possible to call a native method from within your Java program?

ANS. Java provides the *native* keyword, which is used to declare native code methods. Once declared, these methods can be called from inside your Java program just as you call any other Java method.

Q. 428 How do you declare a native method?

ANS. To declare a native method, precede the method with the 'native' modifier, but do not define any body, i.e. content, for the method, e.g.

public native void my_method();

Q. 429 *What are the problems faced with native methods? Or, why should the use of native methods be restricted?*

ANS. Native methods seem to offer great promise since they enable you to gain access to an existing base of library routines. Moreover, they offer the possibility of faster run-time execution. However, the use of native methods should be restricted since they render your Java program non-portable and pose significant security risks elaborated as under:-

- *Potential Security Risk:* Since a native method executes actual machine code, it can gain access to any part of the host system, i.e. native code is not confined to the Java execution environment. This could allow a virus infection, for instance. It is for this reason that applets cannot use native methods. Also, the loading of DLLs can be restricted, and their loading is subject to the approval of the security manager.

- *Loss of Portability:* Since the native code is contained in a DLL, it must be present on the machine that is executing the Java program. Furthermore, since each native method is dependent on the CPU and operating system, each DLL is inherently non-portable. Thus, a Java application that uses native methods will be able to run only on the machine for which a compatible DLL has been installed.

Q. 430 Can applets use native methods? Why or why not?

ANS. Since a native method poses potential security risk such as a virus infection (refer previous problem), applets cannot use native methods at all.

Q. 431 What do you understand by JNI?

ANS. After you declare a native method, you must write the native method and follow a rather complex series of steps to link it with your Java code. Most native methods are written in C. The mechanism used to integrate C code with a Java program is known as the *Java Native Interface (JNI).*

Q. 432 Illustrate the use of JNI with a suitable example.

ANS. Consider the following *native* method called *my_method():*

```
// A simple example using a native method
public class MyNative
{
    int i;
    public static void main(String args[])
    {
        MyNative mn = new MyNative();
        mn.i = 100;
        System.out.println("Before native method, mn.i = " + mn.i);
        mn.my_method();        // call a native method
        System.out.println("After native method, mn.i = " + mn.i);
    }
    // DECLARE NATIVE METHOD
    public native void my_method();
    // LOAD DLL that contains static method
    static
    {
        System.loadLibrary("MyNative");
    }
}
```

The 'static' block is used to load the DLL which contains the native implementation of *my_method()*. The library is loaded by the *loadLibrary()* method which is part of the *System* class.

The compilation of the above program produces *MyNative.class*. Next, you must use *javah.exe* (included in JDK) to produce *MyNative.h* as follows:

javah –jni MyNative

This command produces *MyNative.h* which must be included in the C file that implements *my_method()*. The output produced by this command is machine generated and is as follows:-

```
/* Do not edit this file – it is machine generated */
#include <jni.h>
/* Header for class MyNative */
#ifndef _Included_MyNative
#define _included_MyNative
#ifdef _ _cplusplus
extern "C"
{
    #endif
    /* Class: MyNative * Method: my_method * Signature: ()V */
    JNIEXPORT void JNICALL Java_MyNative_my_method (JNIEnv *, jobject);
    #ifdef _ _cplusplus
}
#endif
#endif
```

Pay special attention to the following line which defines the prototype of the *my_method()* function that you will create:-

*JNIEXPORT void JNICALL Java_MyNative_my_method (JNIEnv *, jobject);*

Note that the name of the function is *Java_MyNative_my_method()*. You must use this as the name of the native function that you implement, i.e. instead of creating a C function called *my_method()*, you will create one called *Java_MyNative_my_method()*.

After having produced the necessary header file, you can write your implementation of *my_method()* and store it in a file named *MyNative.c:*

```
{
/* This file contains the C version of my_method() */
#include <jni.h>
#include "MyNative.h"
#include <stdio.h>
JNIEXPORT void JNICALL Java_MyNative_my_method (JNIEnv *env, jobject obj)
{
```

```
    jclass cls;
    jfieldID fid;
    jint      i;
    printf("Start\n");
    cls = (*env)->GetObjectClass(env, obj);
    fid = (*env)->GetFieldID(env, cls, "i", "I");
    if (fid == 0)
    {
        printf("couldn't get field id\n");
        return;
    }
        /* get i */
        i = (env)->GetIntField(env, obj, fid);
        printf("i = %d\n", i);
        /* update i */
        (*env)->SetIntField(env, obj, fid, 10 * i);
    printf("End");
}
```

Note that this file includes *jni.h,* which contains interfacing information. This file is provided by your Java compiler. The header file *MyNative.h* was created by *javah* earlier.

In this function, the *GetObjectClass()* method is used to obtain a C structure that has information about the class *MyNative.* The *GetFieldID()* method returns a C structure with information about the field named "i" for the class. *GetIntField()* retrieves the original value of that field. *SetIntField()* stores an updated value in that field.

After creating *MyNative.c,* you must compile it and create a DLL. To achieve this by using the Microsoft C/C++ compiler, use the following command line (you might have to specify the path to *jni.h* and its subordinate *jni_md.h*):-

```
Cl/LD MyNative.c
```

This produces a file called *MyNative.dll*; once this done, you can execute the Java program producing the following output:-

```
Before native method, mn.i = 100
Start
i = 100
End
After native method, mn.i = 1000
```

■

12

ARCHITECTURE
(including Design Patterns)

Q. 433 What was the underlying need for J2EE? Elaborate.

ANS. With the onset of web-centric applications that grew more dependent than ever on server-side technologies such as middleware, information technology departments of corporations needed a sustainable way to develop applications and related middleware that were both portable as well as scalable. These applications needed to be designed to handle thousands of users simultaneously 24 hours a day, seven days a week, without any downtime. One of the major challenges to building such a complex application is to be able to design and test it.

J2EE simplifies the creation of enterprise-wide application, since functionality is encapsulated in components of J2EE. This enables designers and programmers to organize the application into functionality that is distributed across the server-side components built using J2EE. Furthermore, J2EE is a versatile technology since application components built using J2EE are able to communicate with each other behind the scenes using standard communication methods such as HTTP, SSL, HTML, XML, RMI, and IIOP.

All J2EE programs are written in Java enabling a corporation to use its existing staff of Java programmers to create programs that work at each layer of the multi-tier infrastructure. J2EE contains all the interfaces and libraries to handle multithreading and synchronization as well. Java Beans, Java Servlets and JavaServer Pages are core components of J2EE. In addition, J2EE consists of seven more standard services, all of which increase its usefulness and contribution to the industry.

Q. 434 Explain and elaborate the J2EE multi-tier architecture.

ANS. J2EE is a four-tier architecture (refer Figure 16) consisting of the Client Tier (also referred to as the Presentation or Application Tier), Web Tier, Enterprise JavaBeans Tier (also referred to as Business Tier), and the Enterprise Information Systems Tier. Each tier is focused on providing a specific type of functionality to an application. It's important to delineate between functionality and physical location. Two or more tiers can physically reside on the same Java Virtual Machine (JVM) although each tier provides a different type of functionality to a J2EE application.

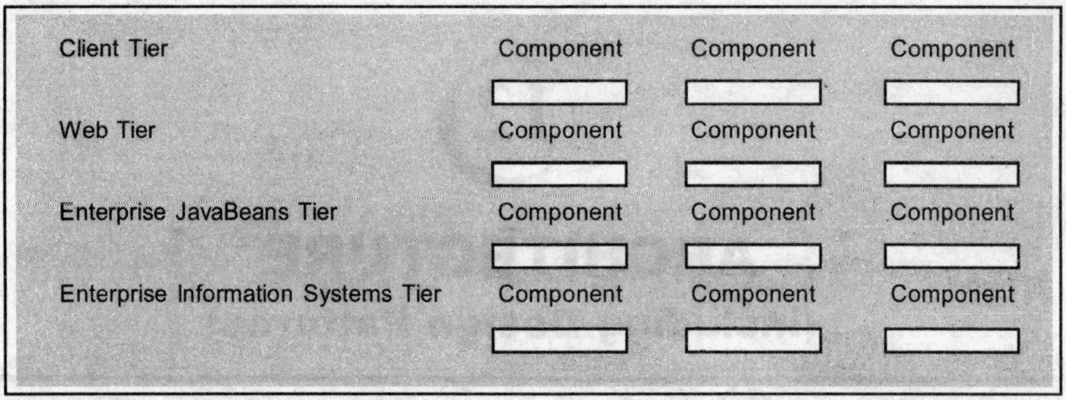

Figure 16 J2EE consists of four tiers each of which provides specific functionality to an application

And, since the J2EE multi-tier architecture is functionally centric, a J2EE application accesses only tiers whose functionality is required by the J2EE application. It's also important to disassociate a J2EE API with a particular tier, i.e. some APIs (that is, XML API) and J2EE components can be used on more than one tier while others APIS (that is, Enterprise JavaBeans API) are associated with a particular tier.

The Client Tier consists of programs that interact with the user. These programs prompt the user for input and then convert the users' response into requests that are forwarded to software on a component that processes the request and returns results to the client program. The Web Tier provides Internet functionality to a J2EE application. Components that operate on the Web Tier use HTTP to receive requests from and send responses to clients that could reside on any tier (a client being any component which initiates a request). The Enterprise JavaBeans Tier contains the business logic for J2EE applications. It's here that where one or more Enterprise JavaBeans reside, each encoded with business rules that are called upon indirectly by clients.

Although an Enterprise JavaBean can access components on any tier, typically an Enterprise JavaBean accesses components and resources such as DBMS on the Enterprise Information System (EIS) Tier. The EIS links a J2EE application to resources and legacy systems that are available on the corporate backbone network. It's on the EIS where a J2EE application directly or indirectly interfaces with a variety of technologies including DBMS and mainframes which are part of the mission-critical systems that keep the corporation operational. Components that work on the EIS communicate to resources using CORBA or Java connectors, referred to as J2EE Connector Extensions.

Q. 435 What do you understand by design patterns?

ANS. By design patterns, we mean certain standard solutions for certain common problems which occur while designing a software system, e.g. whenever we want to restrict an application to create only one instance of a class, we make use of the Singleton Design Pattern.

Q. 436 Elucidate the Singleton Design Pattern.

ANS. As already mentioned in the previous question, the Singleton Design Pattern is made use of whenever we need to design a class which can just one instance. The *Singleton* design pattern is a very useful from the software engineering point of view.

The rules for creating the Singleton class are:-

(1) Constructor should be protected (it could be made private to prevent inheritance).

(2) Declare a static "self" pointer to hold a reference to the single instance of the class when it is created and initialize it to null.

(3) Declare a static "instance" function which creates and returns the newly created instance of the class when the static "self" pointer is null, otherwise it returns the previously created instance.

(4) Declare a protected destructor that deletes the "self" pointer.

Q. 437 What do you understand by design principles.

ANS. Design principles provide certain rules that an Object Oriented software designer should keep in mind during the software design phase in order that:-

(i) each module/class is zero or less dependent on other modules/classes; and,

(ii) each module/class is less effected by frequent requirement changes.

Q. 438 What is the Open Closed Principle (OCP)?

ANS. The OCP states that – "A module should be open for extension, but closed for modification".

Q. 439 What is the Liskov Substitution Principle (LSP)?

ANS. The LSP states that – "Subclasses should be substitutable for their superclasses; derived classes should be substitutable for their base classes". Thus, a user of a base class should continue to function properly even if a derivative of that super class is passed to it.

Q. 440 How would you go about writing a singleton in EJB?

ANS. As already elaborated, a singleton is a very useful design pattern in software engineering. In a nutshell, a singleton is a single instantiation of a class with one global point of access. You would normally create a singleton in Java by using the 'static' keyword when defining a class.

However, one restriction of EJB is that you cannot use static fields in your beans. This precludes the use of the singleton design pattern. But, if you still have to use a singleton, here are a couple of strategies:-

(1) Limit the pool size

(2) Use RMI-IIOP and JNDI

Q. 441 Explain briefly the JNDI architecture.

ANS. JNDI is made up of two halves: thee client API and the Service Provider Interface (SPI). The client API allows your Java code to perform directory operations. This API is uniform for all types of directories. You will spend most of the time using the client API. The JNDI SPI is a framework for JNDI implementers: an interface that implementations of naming and directory services can be plugged into. The SPI is the converse of the API: while the API allows clients to code to a single unified interface, the SPI allows naming and directory service vendors to fit their particular proprietary protocols into the system, as shown in Figure 17. This allows client code to leverage proprietary naming and directory services in Java while maintaining a high level of code portability.

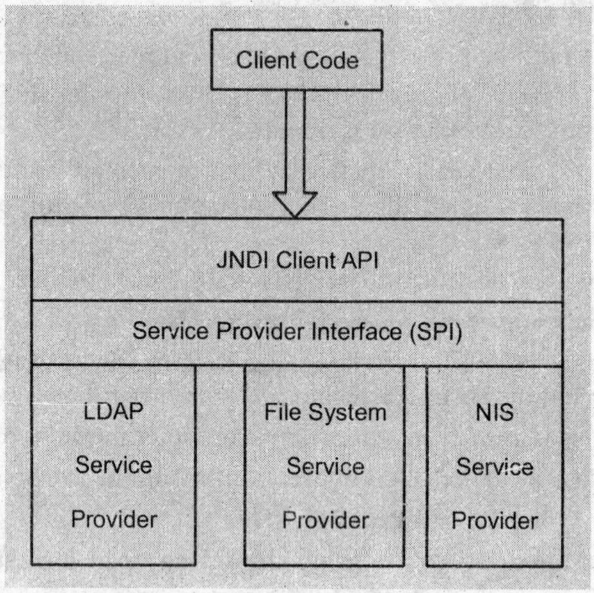

Figure 17 The JNDI Architecture

Q. 442 Can you elaborate on the similarities between JNDI architecture and JDBC?

ANS. The JNDI architecture is somewhat like the Java Database Connectivity (JDBC) package in that:-

- *In JDBC, one uniform client API performs database operations.* In JNDI, naming and directory service clients invoke a unified API for performing naming and directory operations.
- *In JDBC, relational database vendors provide JDBC drivers to access their particular databases.* In JNDI, directory vendors provide service providers to access their specific directories. These providers are aware of specific directory protocols, and they plug in to the JNDI SPI.

Q. 443 What do you understand by "design patterns" in general? Elucidate.

ANS. Design patterns offer simple and elegant solutions to specific problems in object-oriented software design such as Java, C++, Smalltalk, and so on. They capture solutions that have developed and evolved over time. They reflect untold redesign and recoding as developers have struggled for greater reuse and flexibility in their software. Design patterns capture these solutions in a succinct and easily applied form. In other words, "design patterns" make it easier to reuse successful designs and architectures. Simply put, they help a designer get a design "right" faster!

Q. 444 What are the types of design patterns? Enumerate with suitable examples.

ANS. There are, in general, three kinds of design patterns:-

(1) *Creational, e.g.* Abstract Factory, Factory Method, Singleton, Builder and Prototype.

(2) *Structural, e.g.* Façade, Adapter, Bridge, Composite, Decorator, Flyweight and Proxy.

(3) *Behavioral*, e.g. Chain of Responsibility, Command, Interpreter, Iterator, Mediator, Momento, Observer, State, Strategy, Template Method and Visitor.

Q. 445 Elaborate on the following design patterns as regards their applicability and consequences:

(a) **Abstract Factory Creational Pattern;**

(b) **Factory Method Creational Pattern;**

(c) **Singleton Creational Pattern; and,**

(d) **Façade Structural Pattern**

ANS. ***Applicability***

(a) The Abstract Factory pattern should be used when:

- ❒ A system is independent of how its products are created, composed, and represented;
- ❒ A system is configured with one of multiple families of products;

  A family of related product objects is designed to be used together, and you need to enforce this constraint; and,
- ❒ You want to provide a class library of products, and you want to reveal just their interfaces, not their implementations.

(b) The Factory Method pattern should be used when:

- ❒ A class cannot anticipate the class of objects it must create;
- ❒ A class wants its subclasses to specify the objects it creates; and,
- ❒ Classes delegate responsibility to one of several helper subclasses, and you want to localize the knowledge of which helper subclass is the delegate.

(c) The Singleton creational pattern should be used when:

- ❒ There must be exactly one instance of a class, and it must be accessible to clients from a well-known access point; and,
- ❒ When the sole instance should be extensible by subclassing, and clients should be able to use an extended instance without modifying their code.

(d) Use the Façade structural pattern when:

- ❒ You want to provide a simple interface to a complex subsystem;
- ❒ There are many dependencies between clients and the implementation classes of an abstraction; and,
- ❒ You want to layer your subsystems. Use a façade to define an entry point to each subsystem level.

Consequences

(a) The Abstract Factory pattern has the following benefits and liabilities:

- ❒ It isolates concrete classes;
- ❒ It makes exchanging product families easy;

- It promotes consistency among products; and
- Supporting new kinds of products is difficult.

(b) The Factory Method pattern has the following consequences:

- Provides hooks for subclasses; and,
- Connects parallel class hierarchies.

(c) The Singleton pattern has several benefits:

- Controls access to sole instance;
- It creates reduced namespace;
- Permits refinement of operations and representation;
- Permits a variable number of instances; and
- More flexible than class operations.

(d) The Façade pattern has the following consequences:

- It shields clients from subsystem components, thereby reducing the number of objects that clients deal with and making the subsystem easier to use;
- It promotes weak coupling between the subsystem and its clients; and,
- It doesn't prevent applications from using subsystem classes if they need to. Thus, you can choose between ease of use and generality.

Q. 446 What is JAXB?

ANS. JAXB (*Java Architecture for XML Binding*) is a popular data binding framework. It supports most of XML Schema, excluding wildcards, notations, redefinitions, keys, and substitution groups. And, the binding is customizable.

Q. 447 Elucidate the Model-View-Controller (MVC) pattern.

ANS. Web applications when seen as collections of JSP pages (or servlets) that the client navigates between refer to a design known as the *Model 1* approach. For larger applications, this architecture is too ad hoc. Instead, it is recommended to use the *Model 2* approach, which is an instance of the *Model-View-Controller* (*MVC*) design pattern that dates back to GUI (Graphical User Interface) applications in the early Smalltalk-80 system.

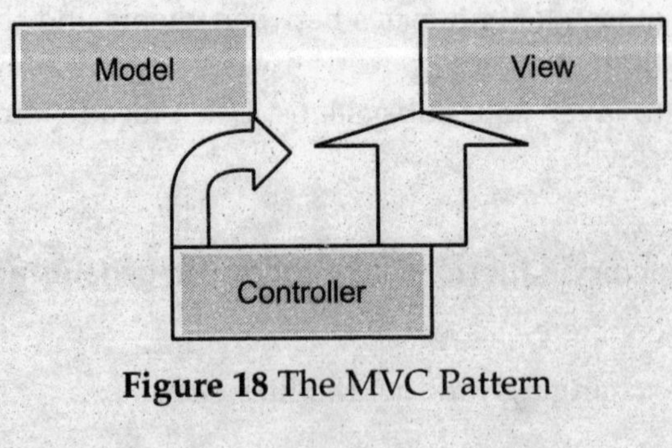

Figure 18 The MVC Pattern

- The MVC pattern distributes an application into three main parts: *model, view,* and *controller.*
- The *model* encapsulates the data and accompanying operations (the *business logic*), and is typically programmed as Java classes, perhaps with an underlying database.
- The *view* is typically a collection of JSP pages that interact with the model to present various data to the client.
- The *controller* is written as a single servlet that handles all interactions with the client, updates the model, and selects appropriate views as responses.
- The MVC pattern is often illustrated by the above general picture (Figure 18) wherein, the arrows indicate method invocations.

■

13

UML

Q. 448 What do you understand by an Object Model?

ANS. In Object Oriented Programming, all real world things are modeled as a collection of Objects with relationships amongst them. This representation is known as the Object Model. This model plays the same role in software development that sitemaps, elevations and blueprints play in the construction of skyscrapers.

Q. 449 What do you understand by UML?

ANS. UML or Unified Modeling Language, as it is called, is used for designing object models in software development and applications. The language helps to specify, visualize, and document the models of software systems.

Q. 450 Enumerate the various UML diagrams.

ANS. In general, UML defines twelve types of diagrams which can be classified into three categories:-

(i) *Structural: Class diagrams, Object diagrams, Component* diagrams, and Deployment diagrams;

(ii) Behavioral: Use Case diagrams (very handy to have in requirements gathering), Sequence diagrams, Activity diagrams, and Collaboration diagrams; and,

(iii) Model Management diagrams inclusive of Packages, Subsystems, and Models.

Q. 451 What does an UML class element comprise of?

ANS. An UML class element comprises class_name, attributes/data, and methods. (note that class_name cannot be blank or empty while attributes and methods can be)

Figure 19 A UML Class Element

Q. 452 Enumerate the various relationships between classes in UML.

ANS. In general, UML defines five types of relationships between classes:-

(i) Association;

(ii) Aggregation;

(iii) Composition;

(iv) Inheritance/Generalization; and,

(v) Realization

Q. 453 *(a)* **Who is an actor? Explain with the help of suitable examples wherever necessary.**

(b) **What are Use Cases? Explain with reference to the case of a vending machine.**

(c) **What are Use Case Diagrams? Explain with reference to the Use Case in (b).**

(d) **What guidelines would you suggest for use case models? Elaborate.**

ANS. *(a)* An *actor* is a external user of a system – an object or set of objects that communicates directly with the system but that is not part of the system. Each actor represents those objects that behave in a particular way towards the system, e.g. *customer* and *repair technician* are different actors of a vending machine. Similarly, for a travel agency system, actors might include *traveler, agent*, and *airline.* And, for a computer database system, actors might include *user* and *administrator*. Actors can be persons, devices, and other systems – anything that interacts directly with the system. An object can be bound to multiple actors if it has different facets to its behavior, e.g. Varun, Arun, and Mukesh may be customers of a vending machine; Arun may also be a repair technician for the vending machine.

(b)

Buy a Beverage: The vending machine delivers a beverage after a customer selects and pays for it.

#Perform Scheduled Maintenance: A repair technician performs the periodic -service on the vending machine necessary to keep it in good condition.

#Make Repairs: A repair technician performs the unexpected service on the vending machine necessary to repair a problem in its operation.

#Load Items: A stock clerk adds items into the vending machine to replenish its stock of beverages.

Figure 20 Use case summaries for a vending machine

The various interactions of actors with a system are quantized into use cases. A *use case* is a coherent piece of functionality that a system can provide by interacting with actors, e.g. a *customer* actor can "buy a beverage" from a vending machine. The customer inserts money into the machine, makes a selection, and finally receives the beverage. Similarly, a *repair technician* can perform "scheduled maintenance" on the vending machine. Figure 20 summarizes several use cases for a vending machine. Each use case involves one or more actors as well as the system itself.

A use case involves a sequence of messages among the system and its actors, e.g. in the "buy a beverage" use case, the customer first inserts a coin and the vending machine indicates the amount deposited. This can be repeated several times over. Then, the customer pushes a button to indicate a selection; and, the vending machine dispenses the beverage and issues change, if necessary.

(c)

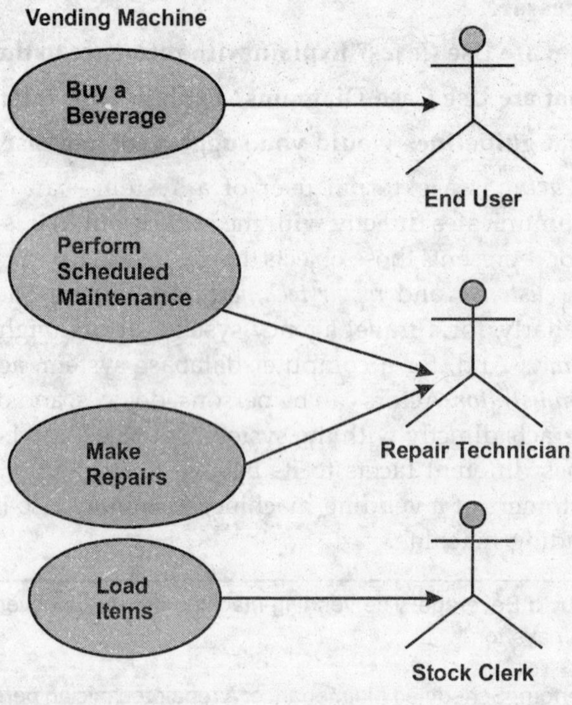

Figure 21 Use case Diagram for a vending machine

A system involves a set of use cases and a set of actors. Each use case represents a slice of functionality the system provides. The set of use cases shows the complete functionality of the system at some level of detail. Similarly, each actor represents one kind of object for which the system can perform behavior. The set of actors represents the complete set of objects that the system can serve. Objects accumulate behavior from all the systems with which they interact as actors.

The UML has a graphical notation (use case diagrams) for summarizing use cases and Figure 21 shows an example. A rectangle contains the use cases for a system with the actors listed on the outside. The name of the system may be written near a side of the rectangle. A name within an ellipse denotes a use case. A "stick man" icon denotes an actor, with the name being placed below or adjacent to the icon. Solid lines connect use cases to participating corresponding actors. In the figure, the actor *repair technician* participates in two use cases, the others in one each. Multiple actors can participate in a use case, even though the example has only one actor per use case.

(d) The main purpose of a system is almost always found in use cases, with the traditional requirements lists supplying additional implementation constraints. Here are some guidelines for constructing use case models:-

(1) *First determine the system boundary:* It is impossible to identify use cases or actors if the system boundary is vague or unclear.

(2) *Ensure that the actors are focused:* Each actor should have a single, coherent purpose. If a real-world object embodies multiple purposes, capture them with separate actors, e.g. the owner of a personal computer may install software, set up a database, and send email. These functions differ greatly in their impact on the computer system and the potential for system damage. They might be broken into three actors, viz. *system administrator, database administrator*, and *computer user*. Remember that an actor is defined w.r.t a system, not as a free-standing concept.

(3) *Each use case must provide value to users:* A use case should represent a complete transaction that provides value to users and should not be defined too narrowly, e.g. "dial a telephone number" is not a good use case for a telephone system. This is because it does not represent a complete transaction of value by itself; it is merely part of the use case "make telephone call". The latter use case involves placing the call, talking, and terminating the call. By dealing with complete use cases, we focus on the functionality provided by the system, rather than jumping into implementation decisions. The details come later. Often there is more than one way to implement desired functionality.

(4) *Relate use cases and actors:* Every use case should have at least one actor, and every actor should participate in at least one use case. A use case may involve several actors, and an actor may participate in several use cases.

(5) *Remember that use cases are informal:* It is important not to be obsessed by formalism in specifying use cases. They are not intended as a formal mechanism but as a way to identify and organize system functionality from a user-centric point of view. It is acceptable if use cases are a bit loose at first. Detail can come later as use cases are expanded and mapped into implementations.

(6) *Use cases can be structured:* For many applications, the individual use cases are completely distinct. For large systems, use cases can be built out of smaller fragments using relationships (refer next question in this context).

Q. 454 (a) What do you understand by Use Case Relationships? Explain with the help of suitable examples wherever necessary.

(b) What guidelines would you suggest for use case relationships? Elaborate.

ANS. *(a)* Independent use cases suffice for simple applications. However, it can be helpful to structure use cases for large applications. Complex use cases can be built from smaller pieces with the *include*, *extend*, and *generalization* relationships:-

(1) *Include Relationship:* The *include* relationship incorporates one use case within the behavior of another use case. An included use case is like a subroutine – it represents behavior that would otherwise have to be described repeatedly. Often the fragment is a meaningful unit of behavior for the actors, although this is not required. The included use case may or may not be usable on its own.

The UML notation for an include relationship is a dashed arrow from the source (including) use case to the target (included) use case with the keyword <<include>> annotating the arrow. Figure 22 shows an example from an online stock brokerage system. Part of establishing a secure session is validating the user password. In addition, the stock brokerage system validates the password for each stock trade. Use cases "secure session" and "make trade" both include use case "validate password".

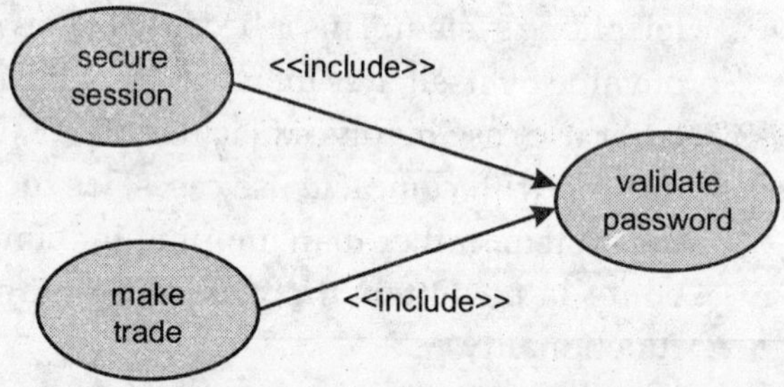

Figure 22 Use case Inclusion

(2) *Extend Relationship:* The *extend* relationship adds incremental behavior to a use case. It is like an include relationship looked at from the opposite direction, in which the extension adds itself to the base, rather than the base explicitly incorporating the extension. It represents the frequent situation in which some initial capability is defined, and later features are added modularly, e.g. a stock brokerage system might have the base use case "trade stocks", which permits a customer to purchase stocks for cash on hand in the account. The

extension use case "margin trading" would add the ability to make a loan on purchase stocks when the account doesn't contain enough cash.

Figure 23 shows the base use case "trade stocks" for the said system. The UML notation for an extend relationship is a dashed arrow from the extension use case to the base use case with the keyword <<*extend*>> annotating the arrow.

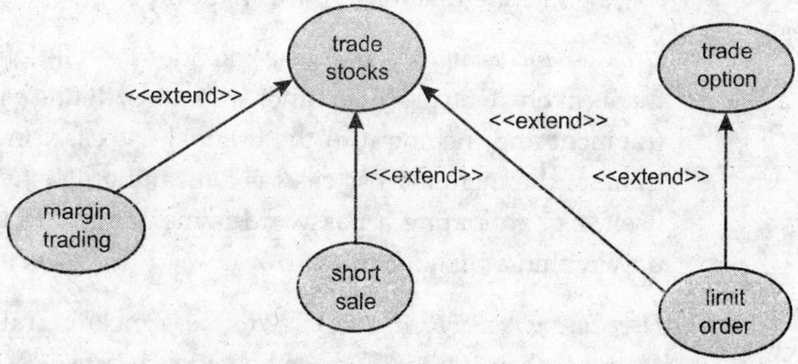

Figure 23 Use case Extension

(3) *Generalization: Generalization* can show specific variations on a general use case, analogous to generalization among classes. A parent use case represents a general behavior sequence. Child use cases specialize the parent by inserting additional steps or by refining steps. The UML indicates generalization by an arrow with its tail on the child use case and a triangular arrowhead on the parent use case, e.g. an online brokerage system (Figure 24) might specialize the general use case "make trade" into the child use cases "trade bonds", "trade stocks", and "trade options". The parent use case contains steps that are performed for any kind of trade, such as entering the password. Each child use case contains the additional steps particular to a specific kind of trade, such as entering the expiration date of an option.

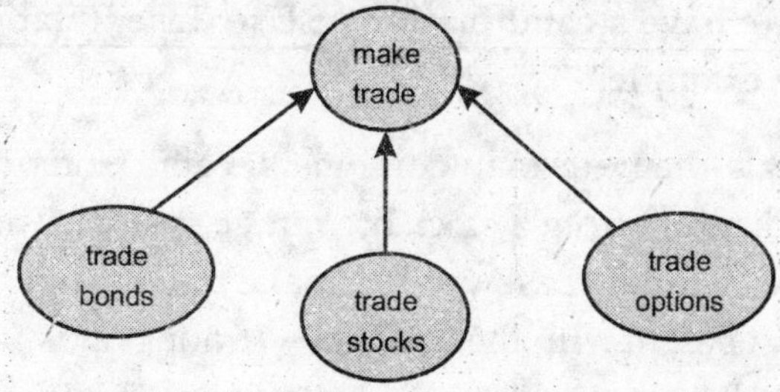

Figure 24 Use case Generalization

(*b*) One of the basic guidelines for use case relationships is not to carry them to extremes and lapse into programming. There can be many ways to implement requirements and you should not commit to an approach before fully understanding the problem. Here are some additional guidelines:-

(1) *Use Case generalization:* If a use case comes in several variations, model the common behavior with an abstract use case and then specialize each of the variations. Don't use generalizations simply to share a behavior fragment; use the include relationship for that purpose.

(2) *Use Case inclusion:* If a use case includes a well-defined behavior fragment that is likely to be useful in other situations, define a use case for the behavior fragment and include it in the original use case. In most cases, you should think of the included use case as a meaningful activity but not as an end in itself, e.g. validating a password is meaningful to users but has a purpose only within a broader context.

(3) *Use Case extension:* If you can define a meaningful use case with optional features, then model the base behavior as a use case and add features with the extend relationship. This permits the system to be tested and debugged without the extensions, which can be added later. Use the extend relationship when a system might be deployed in different configurations, some with the additional features and some without them.

(4) *Include Relationship vs. Extend Relationship:* The include relationship and the extend relationship can both factor behavior into smaller pieces. The include relationship, however implies that the included behavior is a necessary part of a configured system (even if the behavior is not executed every time), whereas the extend relationship implies that a system without the added behavior would be meaningful (even if there is no intention to configure it that way).

Q. 455 Can we have a combination of Use Case Relationships? If yes, elaborate with the help of a suitable example.

ANS. A single diagram may combine several kinds of use case relationships. Figure 25 shows a use case diagram from a stock brokerage system. The "secure session" use case includes the behavior of the "validate password", "make trade", and "manage account" use cases. "Make trade" is an abstract parent with the children – "trade bonds", "trade stocks", and "trade options". Use case "make trade" also includes the behavior of "validate password". The brokerage system validates the password per session and additionally for every trade.

The use case "margin trading" extends both "trade bonds" and "trade stocks" – a customer may purchase stocks and bonds on margin, but not options. Use case "limit order" extends abstract use case "make trade" – limit orders apply to trading bonds, stocks, and options. We assume that a "short sale" is only permitted for stocks and not for bonds or options.

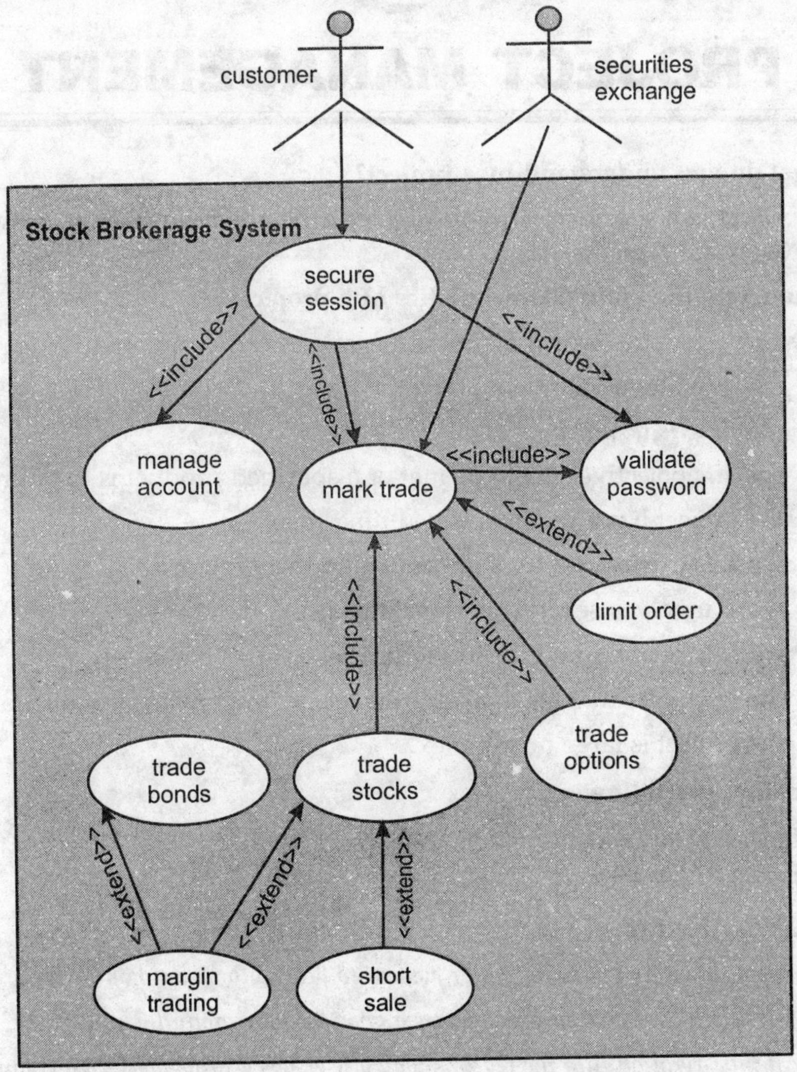

Figure 25 Use case Relationships (Combinations)

Note that the customer actor connects only to one secure session per use case. The brokerage system invokes all the other use cases indirectly by inclusion, specialization, or extension. The *securities exchange* actor connects to the "make trade" use case. This actor does not initiate a use case but is invoked during execution.

■

14

PROJECT MANAGEMENT

Q. 456 What do you understand by a project?

ANS. A project is a specific plan or design or a planned undertaking towards achieving some specific objective(s) / goal(s).

Q. 457 Enumerate the main characteristics of a project.

ANS. The characteristics which distinguish projects can be summarized as follows:-

(1) *non*-routine tasks are involved;

(2) *planning is required;*

(3) specific objectives are to be met or a specified product is to be created;

(4) the project has a predetermined time span;

(5) work is carried out for someone other than yourself;

(6) work involves several specializations;

(7) work is carried out in several phases;

(8) the resources that are available for use on the project are constrained;

(9) the project is large or complex.

Q. 458 Consider the following:

(i) Producing an edition of a newspaper;

(ii) Putting a robot vehicle on Mars to search for signs of life;

(iii) Getting married;

(iv) Amending a financial computer system to deal with a common European currency;

(v) A research project into what makes a good human-computer interface;

(vi) An investigation into the reasons why a user has a problem with a computer system;

(vii) A second-year programming assignment for a computing student;

viii) Writing an operating system for a new computer;

(ix) Installing a new version of a word processing package in an organization;

Some of the above would appear to merit the description 'project' more than the others. Put them into an order that most closely matches your ideas of what constitutes a project. For each entry in the ordered list, describe the difference between it and the one above which makes it less worthy of the term 'project'.

ANS. The order you put these projects in is, of course, to a large degree subjective. Here is one example of a possible ordering:-

(1) *Putting a robot vehicle on Mars to search for signs of life:* Almost everybody would put this first. The huge scale of the task, the relative novelty of the project, all the different specializations involved and the international nature of the project make it special. Note that the successful achievement of the project from the engineering point of view is the safe landing of the robot, not the discovery of signs of life.

(2) *Writing an operating system for a new computer:* This is a prime example of a software development project.

(3) *Amending a financial computer system to deal with a common European currency:* This project is modifying an existing system rather than creating a new one from scratch. Many software projects have this characteristic and it does not make them any less a software project.

(4) *Installing a new version of a word processing package in an organization:* Although no software is being produced/modified, many of the stages that are associated with software projects will be involved and the techniques of software project management would be appropriate.

(5) *Investigation into the reasons why a user has a problem with a computer system:* This will have many of the stages common to software projects, although the precise nature of the end result is uncertain at the outset. It could be that the user needs some simple remedial training. On the other hand, it could turn out to be quite a considerable software modification task.

(6) *Getting married:* There could be lots of arguments about this one! Some will be reluctant to give high rating to this because of its personal nature. The degree to which this is 'project-like' will depend very much upon the cultural milieu in which it takes place. Very often it requires a high degree of planning, involves lots of different people and, for most people, is a non-routine operation.

(7) *A research project into what makes a good human-computer interface:* Compared to some of the projects above, the objectives of the research project are more open-ended and the idea of a specific client for the end-product may be less well defined. Research projects are in some ways special cases and the approach to their planning needs a rather different approach, which is outside the scope of the normal 'project management' course.

(8) *Producing an edition of a newspaper:* In some ways this has all the characteristics of a project. There are lots of different people with lots of different specializations whose work needs to be coordinated in order to produce an end-product under very tight time constraints. What argues against this as a typical project is that it is repeated. After a while, everyone knows what he/she needs to do and most of the problems that arise are familiar and the procedures to deal with them are well defined.

(9) *A second-year programming assignment for a computing student:* This is not being done for a customer, although it could be argued that the tutor responsible for setting and assessing the assignment is, in effect, a surrogate client. Not all the stages of a normal project will be gone through in this case.

Q. 459 Enumerate the activities covered by software project management.

ANS. Usually there are three successive processes that bring a new system into being:-

(1) Feasibility Study

(2) Planning

(3) Project execution

The complete set of activities under software project management can be outlined as follows:-

- Requirements analysis
- Architecture design
- Detailed design
- Coding & Testing (individual software units)
- Integration
- Qualification testing (complete system)
- Installation
- Acceptance support (resolving of new problems, correction of any new bugs, extension, improvement and maintenance)

Q. 460 What are the problems generally faced by software projects? Enumerate at least ten.

ANS. Following is an exhaustive list of the problems frequently faced by software projects (you can enumerate any ten):-

- Poor estimates and plans;
- Lack of quality standards and measures;
- Lack of guidance about making organizational decisions;
- Lack of techniques to make progress visible;
- Poor role definition (who does what?);
- Incorrect success criteria;
- Inadequate specification of work;
- Management ignorance;
- Lack of knowledge of application area;
- Lack of up-to-date documentation;
- Preceding activities not completed on time – including late delivery of equipment;
- Lack of communication between users and technicians;
- Duplication of work;

- Lack of commitment – especially when a project is tied to one person who then moves;
- Narrow scope of technical expertise;
- Changing statutory requirements;
- Changing software environment;
- Deadline pressure;
- Lack of quality control;
- Remote management;
- Lack of training.

Q. 461 What does the mnemonic SMART stand for as regards the objectives of a project.

ANS. S – *Specific*

M – *Measurable*

A – *Achievable*

R – *Relevant*

T – *Time constrained*

Thus, the objectives of a project must be so well defined as to be specific, measurable, achievable, relevant and time constrained.

Q. 462 Bearing in mind the above discussion of objectives, comment on the appropriateness of each of the following 'objectives' for software developers:

(i) To implement the new application on time and within budget;

(ii) To implement the new software application with the fewest possible software errors that might lead to operational failures;

(iii) To design a system that is user-friendly;

(iv) To produce full documentation for the new system.

ANS. Among the comments and queries that could be made in each case are:-

(i) Has the actual time and amount of the budget been specified somewhere? Deadline and budget constraints normally have to be set against the scope and the quality of the functions to be delivered, e.g. if the deadline were not achieved, would the customer rather have the full set of functionality at a later date, or an essential subset of the function on the deadline date?

(ii) "The fewest possible software errors" is not precise. Removing errors requires effort and hence money. Can developers spend as much money and time as they like if this reduces errors?

(iii) What does "user-friendly" really mean? How is it measured? Normally 'ease of use' is measured by the time it takes for beginners to become proficient in carrying out standard operations.

(iv) What does "full documentation" mean? A list of all types of documents to be produced, perhaps with an indication of the content layout, would be more useful.

Q. 463 How would you go about initiating a new software project? Elaborate.

ANS. The first step in initiating a new software project is triggered by the creation of an agreed *project mandate*. Ideally this should be a formal document describing:-

(1) The new services or capabilities the project should deliver;

(2) How the organization will be improved by the use of the new services or capabilities;

(3) How the project fits with corporate goals and any other initiatives.

At this point, a *project director* ought to be appointed to provide initial leadership for the project. To be successful, the project needs a champion who is in a prominent position within the organization. This will signal the seriousness with which the organization takes the project. The project director is likely to come from the *sponsoring group* who have identified the need for a project and have initiated its progress.

A *project brief* is now produced which would be the equivalent of a feasibility study for the project. It will have sections setting out:-

(1) A preliminary *vision statement* which describes the new capacity that the organization seeks (it is 'preliminary' as it will later be elaborated);

(2) The *benefits* that the project should create – including when they are likely to be generated and how they might be measured;

(3) Risks and issues;

(4) Estimated costs, timescales and effort.

The project brief should have given the sponsoring group enough information to decide whether it's worth moving to a more detailed definition of the project. This next stage will involve a lot of detailed planning work and would justify the setting up of a small team. At this point a *project manager* who would have day-to-day responsibility for running the project could well be appointed. The project manager is likely to be someone with considerable project management experience.

This group can now take the vision statement outlined in the project brief and refine/expand it. It should describe in detail the new capabilities that the project will endow the organization with. If estimates for costs, performance, and service levels can't be provided, the there should at least be an indication of how they might be measured. For example, the headings under which costs will be incurred can be recorded. Similarly, for performance, one might be able to say that repeat business will be increased, even if the precise size of the increase can't be provided.

The achievement of the improved capabilities described in the vision statement can only come about when changes have been made to the structure and operations of the organization. These are detailed in the *blueprint*. This should contain:-

(1) Business models outlining the new processes required;

(2) Organizational structure – indicating the numbers of staff required in the new system and the skills they will need;

(3) The information systems, equipment and other non-staff resources that will be needed;

(4) Data and information requirements;

(5) Costs, performance and service level requirements.

Q. 464 What do you understand by cost-benefit analysis? Can all benefits and costs be quantified and valued? Elaborate.

ANS. The standard way of evaluating the economic benefits of any project is cost-benefit analysis, comprising two steps:-

(1) *Identifying and estimating all of the costs and benefits of carrying out the project and operating the delivered application:* These include the development costs, the setup costs, the operating costs and the benefits that are expected to accrue from the new system. Where the proposed system is replacing an existing one, these estimates should reflect the change in costs and benefits due to the new system. A new sales order processing system, for example, could not claim to benefit an organization by the total value of sales – only by the increase due to the use of the new system.

(2) *Expressing these costs and benefits in common units:* You need to evaluate the net benefit, that is, the difference between the total benefit and the total cost of creating and operating the system. To do this, you must express each cost and each benefit in some common unit, that is, as money.

Most direct costs are relatively easy to identify and quantify in approximate monetary terms. In this context, it is helpful to categorize costs according to where they originate in the life of the project:-

- *Development costs:* Include the salaries and other employment costs of the staff involved in the development project and all associated costs.
- *Setup costs:* Include the costs of putting the system into place. These consist mainly of the costs of any new hardware and ancillary equipment but will also include costs of the conversion, recruitment and staff training.

  Operational costs: Consist of the costs of operating the system once it has been installed.
- *Benefits, on the other hand, are often quite difficult to quantify in monetary* terms even once they have been identified. In general, benefits can be:-
- *Quantified and valued* – that is, a direct financial benefit is experienced;

  Quantified but not valued – for example, a decrease in number of customer complaints;
- *Identified but not easily quantified* – for example, public approval of the organization in the locality where it is based.

Q. 465 IIT, Delhi is considering the replacement of the existing payroll service, operated by a third party, with a tailored, off-the-shelf computer-based system. List some of the costs it might consider under the headings of:

(i) *Development costs*

(ii) *Setup costs*

(iii) *Operational costs*

List some of the benefits under the headings:

(i) Quantified and valued benefits

(ii) Quantified but not valued benefits

(iii) Identified but not easily quantified benefits

For each cost or benefit, explain how, in principle, it might be measured in monetary terms.

ANS.

Category	*Cost*
Development costs	Software purchase – software cost plus selection and purchasing cost; Project team employment costs
Setup costs	Training – costs of trainers and operational time lost while training; Staff recruitment; Computer hardware and other equipment which might have a residual value at end of projected life; Accommodation – any new/refurbished accommodation and furniture required to house new system; Initial system supplies – purchase of stationery, disks and other consumables
Operational costs	Operations staff – full employment costs; Stationery – purchase and storage; Maintenance and standby – contract or estimation of occurrence costs; Accommodation including heating, power, insurance etc.

Table 2 Costs for the IIT, Delhi payroll system

Category	*Benefit*
Quantified and valued benefits	Savings on local authority fees; Later payment – increased interest income through paying salaries later in the month
Quantified but not valued benefits	Improved accuracy – the number of errors needing to be corrected each month
Identified but not quantified benefits	Improved management information – this should lead to improved decision making but it is very difficult to quantify the potential benefits

Table 3 Benefits for the IIT, Delhi payroll system

Table 2 and Table 3 list costs and benefits, respectively, for the proposed IIT, Delhi payroll system. They are not comprehensive but illustrate some of the types of items that you should have listed.

{

These items (such as insurance), and some other elements, might show corresponding savings or costs through no longer being required. For example, although new office furniture might be required for the new system, the existing furniture might be redeployed / sold.

}

Q. 466 What do you understand by Parkinson's Law and Brooks' Law regarding effort estimation?

ANS. According to Parkinson's Law, Work Expands to Fill the Time Available, so that given an easy target, the staff will work less hard.

According to Brooks' Law, The effort required to implement a project will go up disproportionately with the number of staff assigned to the project. As the project team grows in size, so will the effort that has to go into management, coordination and communication. This has given rise, in extreme cases, to the notion of Brooks' Law: "putting more people on a late job makes it later!" If there is an over-estimate of the effort required then this could lead to more staff being allocated than are needed and increase in managerial overheads. This is more likely to be of significance with large projects.

Q. 467 How are effort, system size and productivity rate related to each other?

ANS.

Effort = (System Size) x (Productivity Rate)

Q. 468 What do you understand by COCOMO as regards software effort estimation?

ANS. Boehm's COCOMO (*COnstructive COst MOdel*) is often referred to in the literature ON SOFTWARE PROJECT MANAGEMENT, PARTICULARLY, in connection with software estimating. The term COCOMO refers to a group of models. Boehm originally based his models in the late 1970s on a study of 63 projects. Of these only seven were business systems and so the models could be used with applications other than information systems. The basic model was built around the equation

$$\textbf{Effort} = \textbf{c(size)}^{k}$$

where *effort* was measured in *pm* or the number of 'person-months' consisting of units of 152 working hours, *size* was measured in *kdsi*, thousands of delivered source code instructions, and *c* and *k* were constants.

Q. 469 What do you understand by risk? How would you assess it?

ANS. Risk is an uncertain event or condition that, if it occurs, has a positive or negative effect on a project's initiatives. It can also be looked as the chance of exposure to the adverse consequences of future events. People may use different terms but the key elements of a risk follow:-

(1) *It relates to the future:* Risk planning involves speculating about future events. The future is inherently uncertain. Some things which seem obvious when a particular project is over, e.g. that the costs were under-estimated or that a new technology was overly difficult to use, might not have been so obvious during planning.

(2) *It involves cause and effect:* For example, a 'cost-over-run' might be identified as a risk, but the simple description of 'cost-over-run' gives the consequence of some adverse event, but doesn't say what caused it. Was it, for example, an inaccurate estimate of effort, the use of untrained staff, or a poor specification? A good definition of a specific risk identifies a situation (or *hazard*), such as 'inexperienced staff', and a particular type of negative outcome, such as 'lower productivity'.

A common problem with risk identification, particularly for the more anxious, is that a list of risks is potentially endless. Some way is therefore needed of distinguishing the more damaging and likely risks. This can be done by assessing or estimating the risk exposure for each risk using the formula

risk exposure = (potential damage) x (probability of occurrence)

Q. 470 Match the following causes (a – d) to their possible effects (i – iv). The relationships are not necessarily one-to-one. Explain the reason(s) for each match.

Causes

(a) *Staff inexperience*

(b) *Lack of top management commitment*

(c) *New technology*

(d) *Users uncertain of their requirements*

Effects

(i) *Testing takes longer than planned*

(ii) *Planned effort and time for activities exceeded*

(iii) *Project scope increases*

(iv) *Time delays in getting changes to plans agreed*

ANS. There is not one correct answer to this. An example of a possible answer is provided below:-

(a) *i & ii.* Staff inexperience leads to code that has many errors in it and which therefore needs additional testing time. Inexperienced staff will take longer to carry out development in any case.

(b) *iv.* If top management do not have a strong commitment to the project they will not act with a sense of urgency.

(c) *ii.* New technology takes time to get used to.

(d) *iii.* If users are uncertain of their requirements then they are likely to identify new requirements as the project progresses.

Q. 471 Give the full forms of PERT and CPM.

ANS. PERT – *Program Evaluation and Review Technique*

CPM – *Critical Path Method*

Q. 472 Enumerate the three principles of 'Taylorism' as regards organizational behavior.

ANS. F.W. Taylor, the father of 'scientific management' of which organizational behavior is a part, had three basic objectives:-

(1) To select the best people for the job;

(2) To instruct them in the best methods;

(3) To give incentives in the form of higher wages to the best workers.

'Taylorism' is often considered crude and mechanistic. However, a concern for identifying the best practice remains valid even today.

Q. 473 Enunciate Theory X and Theory Y regarding human behavior and management as proposed by McGregor.

ANS. The cash-oriented or *instrumental* view of work by some managers can be contrasted with a more rounded vision of people in their place of work. The two attitudes were labeled Theory X and Theory Y by Donald McGregor.

Theory X holds that:-

- The average human has an innate dislike of work;
- There is therefore a need for coercion, direction and control;

People tend to avoid responsibility.

Theory Y, on the other hand, holds that:-

- Work is as natural as rest or play;
- External control and coercion are not the only ways of bringing about effort directed towards an organization's ends;
- Commitment to objectives is a function of the rewards associated with their achievement;
- The average human can learn to accept and further seek responsibility;
- The capacity to exercise imagination and other creative qualities is widely distributed.
- One way of judging whether a manager espouses Theory X or Theory Y is to observe how staff react when the boss is absent: if there is no discernible change then this is *Theory Y* environment; if everyone visibly relaxes, it is a *Theory X* environment.

Q. 474 According to Maslow's Hierarchy of Needs Theory of Motivation, where does the need for 'self-actualization' stand?

ANS. According to Maslow's theory, as the lower level of needs is satisfied, there emerges a higher level of needs. The basic needs are food, shelter and personal safety. The highest level need, according to Maslow, is the need for 'self-actualization', the feeling that you are completely fulfilling your potential.

Q. 475 What do you understand by Herzberg's two-factor theory about job satisfaction?

ANS. Research into job satisfaction by Herzberg and his associates found two sets of factors about a job:-

(1) *Hygiene or maintenance factors,* which can make you dissatisfied if they are not right, e.g. the level of pay or the working conditions;

(2) *Motivators,* which make you feel that the job is worthwhile, like a sense of achievement or the challenge of the work itself.

Q. 476 What is your personal motivational factor?

ANS. (This question is a catch/trap and must be answered very carefully. We give the ideal answer. You can juxtapose it according to your background). I personally feel that apart from a good salary and hygienic working conditions, the job should give me a keen sense of satisfaction that I am doing something worthy. I like to take up challenges and would ultimately like to tap my full working talent and potential.

Q. 477 Distinguish between structured and unstructured decisions.

ANS. Decisions can be categorized as being:-

(1) *Structured:* generally relatively simple, routine decisions where rules can be applied in a fairly straightforward way (involving no risk and uncertainty normally), or

(2) *Unstructured:* much more complex and often requiring a degree of creativity (involving a fair amount of risk and uncertainty at times).

Q. 478 On what does the style of leadership depend upon?

ANS. Leadership is based on the idea of authority or power although leaders do not necessarily have much formal authority. Power may come either from the person's position (*positional* power) or from the person's individual qualities (*personal* power), or may be a mixture of the two.

Positional power has been further analyzed into:-

- *Coercive power, the ability to force someone to do something by threatening punishment;*
- *Connection power, which is based on having access to those who have power;*
- *Legitimate power, which is based on a person's title conferring a special status;*
- *Reward power, where the holder can give rewards to those who carry out task to his/her satisfaction.*

Personal power, on the other hand, can be further analyzed into:-

- *Expert power, which comes from being a person who is able to do a specialized task;*
- *Information power, where the holder has exclusive access to information;*
- *Referent power, which is based on the personal attractiveness of the leader.*

Q. 479 What is your personal preferred style of leadership?

ANS. (This question is a catch/trap and must be answered very carefully. We give the ideal answer. You can juxtapose it according to your own background and preferences). I personally like to lead by example and thereby, motivation. I would rarely use coercive or connection powers although I am not averse to legitimate and reward powers. I would frequently like to lead by expert power of carrying out my specialized tasks and duties.

Q. 480 What do you understand by egoless programming?

ANS. In the early days of computer development, managers tended to think of the software developers as communing mysteriously with the machine. The tendency was for programmers to see programs as being an extension of themselves and to feel over-protective towards them. The effects of this on the maintainability of the programs can well nigh be imagined.

Gerald Weinberg made the then revolutionary suggestion that programmers and programming team leaders should read other people's programs. Programs would become, in effect, the common property of the programming group and thus, programming would become *"egoless"*. Peer code reviews are based on this idea. Weinberg's ideal programming team was a decentralized group freely communicating within itself.

Q. 481 What causes stress in general? Is stress always a negative factor towards the quality of work? Elucidate.

Ans. Projects are about overcoming obstacles and achieving objectives. Almost by definition, both the project manager and team members will be under pressure. But, some amount of pressure is actually 'healthy'. Boredom can render many a job soul-destroying. Beyond a certain level of pressure, however, the quality of work decreases and health can be affected.

Stress can be caused due to many reasons. It may be caused by role ambiguity when staff does not have a clear idea of the objectives that their work is supposed to be fulfilling, what is expected of them by others, and the precise scope of their responsibilities. The project manager could clearly be at fault in these instances.

Role conflict can also heighten stress. This is where the person is torn between the demands of two different roles, e.g. the parent of young children might be torn between the need to look after a sick child and the need to attend an important meeting to win new business.

As the deadline approaches and the staff is faced with some unexpected situation/problem they might have to work overtime to meet the deadline as well as take care of the unnecessary crisis due to the new problem resulting in cases of stress at times.

Good project management can reduce the reliance on overtime by the more realistic assessment of effort and elapsed time needed, based on careful recording and analysis of the performance of previous projects. Good planning and control can also help to reduce the 'unexpected' problems generating unnecessary crises.

■

15

THE SOFTWARE DEVELOPMENT PROCESS

Q. 482 Outline the steps involved in software development process.

ANS. Software development has a sequence of well-defined stages, each with a distinct purpose, input, and output:-

- *System conception:* Conceive an application and formulate tentative requirements.
- *Analysis:* Deeply understand the requirements by constructing models. The goal of 'analysis' is "what needs to be done" rather than "how it is done". You must first understand the problem before attempting a solution.
- *System design:* Devise a high-level strategy – the architecture – for solving the application program. Establish policies to guide the subsequent class design.
- *Class design:* Augment and adjust the real-world models from analysis so that they are amenable to computer implementation. Determine algorithms for realizing the operations.
- *Implementation:* Translate the design into programming code and database structures.
- *Testing:* Ensure that the application is suitable for actual use and that it truly satisfies the requirements.
- *Training:* Help users master the new application.
- *Deployment:* Place the application in the field and gracefully cut over from legacy applications.
- *Maintenance:* Preserve the long-term viability of the application.
- *The entire process is seamless.* You continually elaborate and optimize models as your focus shifts from analysis to design to implementation.

Q. 483 Elaborate the software development life-cycle.

ANS. An OO approach to software development supports multiple life-cycle styles. You can use a waterfall approach performing the phases of analysis, design and implementation in strict sequence for the entire system. However, we typically recommend an iterative development strategy. We summarize the distinction as follows:-

(1) *Waterfall Development:* The waterfall approach dictates that developers perform the software development stages in a rigid linear sequence with no backtracking.

Developers first capture requirements, then construct an analysis model, then perform a system design, then prepare a class design, followed by implementation, testing and deployment. Each stage is completed in its entirety before the next stage is begun.

*The waterfall approach is suitable for well-*understood applications with predictable outputs from analysis and design, but such applications seldom occur. A waterfall approach also does not deliver a useful system until completion. This makes it difficult to assess progress and correct a project that has gone awry.

(2) *Iterative Development:* Iterative development is more flexible. First you develop the nucleus of a system – analyzing, designing, implementing and delivering working code. Then you grow the scope of the system, adding properties and behavior to existing objects, as well as adding new kinds of objects. There are multiple iterations as the system evolves to the final deliverable.

Each and every iteration includes a full complement of stages: analysis, design, implementation and testing. This is unlike the strict sequence of the waterfall method. Some parts may be completed early, while other, less crucial parts are completed later. Each iteration ultimately yields an executable system that can be integrated and tested. You can accurately gauge progress and make adjustments to your plans based on feedback from the early iterations. If there is a problem, you can move backward to an earlier stage for rework.

Iterative development is the best choice for most applications because it gracefully responds to change and minimizes risk of failure. This is due to the fact that management and business users get early feedback about progress.

Q. 484 Outline the steps involved in feasibility study.

ANS. The steps involved in feasibility study can be enumerated as under:-

A. Form the systems team;
B. Develop generalized flowcharts, data flow diagrams referred to as DFD's etc;
C. Find system candidates;
D. Carry out a preliminary survey and a thorough investigation while evaluating each of these candidates;
E. Follow it up with a detailed extensive study of each one of these candidate solutions;
F. Undertake a cost-benefit analysis;
G. Weigh cost with performance characteristics; and
H. Finally, select the "BEST" candidate system based on the above criteria.

Q. 485 What does the systems design entail?

ANS. Systems design entails the following:-

A. It covers detailed specifications of the "BEST" solution selected in the 'Systems Analysis' phase;
B. These specifications include programming requirements meant for the system developers / project team;
C. It also includes input, output, database, and file considerations.

Q. 486 What are the characteristics of a good SRS (Software Requirement Specifications)?

ANS. Characteristics of a good SRS (software Requirement Specifications) include the following:-

A. Correct / Robust
B. Complete
C. Unambiguous
D. Verifiable
E. Consistent
F. Modifiable
G. Traceable
H. Ranked in order of stability/importance/priority

Q. 487 How is a request for a new system reviewed and selected?

ANS. Generally, many more requests for system development projects are generated/ received than the business/firm/organization can pursue. A decision has to be made as to which projects to approve and which to reject (or, perhaps solve by other means/methods). This decision is made in a number of different ways and by various members of the concerned organization with the system analyst not being the final arbiter/decision-maker.

The project proposal submitted by users/analysts etc. to the project selection committee is a critical element in launching the systems study. Although the form of such a request varies from organization to organization, there is a broad agreement on the kind of information that should be provided in this request. This information is as follows:-

A. What is the problem?
B. What is the detailed description of the problem?
C. How significant is the problem?
D. What is the solution in the opinion of the user?
E. How will the new information system help in solving the problem?
F. Besides the person who has made the request, who are the people in the know-how of the problem? How could these people be contacted?

The project selection committee reviews the proposals carefully and finally selects those that are most beneficial to the organization. Since the information given in the project request form is usually inadequate to take decisions in this respect, a preliminary investigation is often required to gather further details about the system project envisaged in such project proposals/ forms.

There are requests for projects from a number of different sources. All of them cannot be selected for further investigation. We must be very clear as to which of them solves an existing system problem or could help in its improvement. We have to also consider the motives behind the suggestion of a new system project. Any project that has emerged merely for enhancing anyone's personal reputation or is politically motivated must be rejected outright. Such a project can never succeed as it is ill conceived and hence, it will not eventually be accepted by the end-users.

Again, as we know that different subsystems of a system are interdependent and interrelated, so, any change in one of the subsystems can affect the others adversely. Therefore, any project for one subsystem/department cannot be taken up in isolation from the rest of the subsystems/ departments of the organizational system.

After these broad considerations, we must also take into account the following five specific/ particular criteria for selecting a project:

(1) *Management's backing*- The first and foremost criterion is backing from the management since nothing can be done without its endorsement. They are the people who will finance the project and hence, their green signal to the project is a must.

(2) *Appropriate timing*- The timing of the project is another important factor in project selection. The project must be appropriately so timed as to suit the organization, the analyst, and all the personnel involved in it.

(3) *Improvement in goal fulfillment*- The third criterion for project selection is to take into account if it betters or deters the chances of attainment of organizational aims/goals. The project should get the nod only if it does improve these chances.

(4) *Practical in terms of resources*-The fourth factor to be considered is whether the project is practically sound / worthwhile to invest in from the point of view of the resources available in the organization.

(5) *Prioritization*-We also must not forget that when we are committing to one project, we are making the resources committed to it unavailable for other projects. So, even if a project seems to be okay from the point of view of the previous four criteria, we cannot give it top priority in case there are better projects available. In other words, we must appropriately prioritize the projects and then, proceed in order from the first project having the highest priority down to the last project that has been accorded the lowest priority.

Usually, a steering committee is formed consisting of system analyst(s), users, computer staff personnel, managers of the various departments, members from the management etc. to discuss proposals and evaluate them. Generally, several levels of management are involved in this committee. So, it can have detailed information about the day-to-day operations in the organization. The committee is usually headed by a senior executive such as the Director, Chairman etc. who have all the knowledge of the organizational long term plans at their command.

Once this committee approves a system project, the system analyst can proceed with its development. Of course, the committee or its sub-committee continues to monitor and periodically review the progress of the project from time to time.

When, a committee is formed, it must choose certain criteria for a preliminary survey and a feasibility study. In this regard, two important questions come to mind at once:

A. What data is to be included in the feasibility study?

B. How many alternative solutions should be chosen / presented?

The committee should also select a format for taking decisions. Such possible criteria may include the following:

A. Estimated time to implement the system alternative;

B. The tangible/intangible savings;

C. Benefit of each alternative to the users;

D. The proportion of user demands/needs met by each alternative solution;

E. Total cost that the organization shall incur for carrying out each alternative;

F. Operational and maintenance cost of each alternative;

G. Effect of each alternative on the existing system;

H. The technology component- do we need any additional hardware/software?

I. Chances of failure of the new system i.e., the risk factor/uncertainty level associated with it.

The final phase of project review and selection involves identifying the"BEST" solution (generally, computer based) meeting the end-user requirements. Its main objective is to define the most suitable alternative solution in terms of Information System components. These components might include the following:

A. Methods by which inputs and outputs shall be implemented. For instance, an information requirement could be implemented as a terminal screen display or a printed report.

B. Roles and duties/functions of the end-users in the system e.g., how will job description be affected/changed?

C. Information system methods/procedures, e.g. an on-line versus a batch processing system.

D. Computer equipment/hardware required to implement the alternative solutions.

E. Software/computer programs that need to be developed or purchased in order to implement the alternative solutions.

F. Files and databases that need to be defined / described, built, and coded for each of the alternative solutions.

G. Internal controls that need to be installed to ensure the security and reliability of the solutions.

Q. 488 How would you handle an infeasible project?

ANS. Not all requested projects are desirable or feasible. Some organizations receive so many project requests from employees etc. that only a few of them can be pursued. But, projects that are both desirable and feasible should be put into a schedule.

In some cases, development can start immediately although systems people/staff are busy doing other ongoing projects. In such cases, the management decides as to which of the projects are the most important ones and schedules them accordingly. Many business organizations develop information system plans very carefully just as they plan for new products, new manufacturing units, or plant expansion.

After a project request has been approved, its cost, priority, completion time, and personnel requirements are estimated and used to find out where to add it to any existing project scheduling list. The findings are reported to the management with recommendations outlining the acceptance or rejection of the proposal.

Finally, this discussion cannot be complete without a word about infeasible projects. Such system projects are either dumped straight away or solved by other means, if possible. Another point is that a project that is infeasible under the present circumstances may become feasible in due course of time. So, projects that seem to have this potential must be kept carefully in a separate list and filed accordingly.

Q. 489 Suppose you are the systems analyst. How would you arrive at feasible solutions from the candidate solutions?

ANS. A very important task of the systems analyst is to decide on project goals, quantify them, and obtain consensus of the users on them. Several guidelines can be given for arriving at these goals. Some of them are given as follows:

A. Find out any deficiency in the existing/current system by pinpointing any missing functions, unsatisfactory performance, or excessive cost of operations;

B. Set goals to get rid of these drawbacks;

C. Try to quantify these goals;

D. Understand once for all that these goals have to be met within the limitations/ constraints of the organization;

E. Break down these goals into parts i.e., sub-goals;

F. Convey these goals to all the concerned people and win their approval/consensus; and,

G. Last but not the least, set goals not only to remove lacunae but also to compete effectively in the open market.

During the feasibility phase, broad alternative candidate solutions to the problems in the existing system are examined in detail, especially their cost-benefit. These broad solutions usually constitute the following:

A. Specifications of the information offered by the new system

B. Description of what will be taken care of manually and which features/procedures shall be computerized?

C. Specifications of any new equipment and/or expansion of any existing equipment, if required.

These broad alternative solutions are further shortlisted on the basis of their technical, operational, and economic feasibilities. The technical grounds judge if the required technology is available/within reach and whether it is useable. On the operational front, we have to answer questions like - whether the proposed solution can fit into the scheme of things well enough, that is to say, whether it is in line with the existing system and whether the system would be able to provide right information at the right time to the end-users. Finally, economic feasibility ascertains if enough financial resources are at our command to carry out or implement the proposed solution and whether the expenditure incurred is justifiable, that is to say, whether it is recoverable either in terms of savings or better user satisfaction. To answer the second part of this last query, a cost-benefit analysis is in order.

The culmination of the feasibility study is a feasibility report addressed to the organizational management. This report tells/informs the management in a simple non-technical language things like:

A. What the proposed new system shall achieve?

B. Who shall be the personnel involved in operating this new system?

C. What organizational changes shall be required for the successful implementation of this system?

D. What is its estimated cost?

E. What are its likely benefits, once installed?

The feasibility report evaluates the impact of the proposed changes on the area(s) under consideration or in question. This report generally consists of the following sections:

A. Cover letter;

B. Table of Contents;

C. Overview;

D. Detailed findings;

E. Economic justification for the change;

F. Recommendations & Conclusions; and,

G. Appendices, if any.

The report can be written or presented orally. The suggested outline for an oral presentation is Table 4.

This oral presentation can also serve as a guideline for a written presentation/report. The length/duration of the presentation is an important aspect/point to be kept in mind. It should neither be too short nor too lengthy so as to become dull and boring. Keep your audience interested all the while. This shall certainly go a long way in securing the management's approval for the project proposal.

(A) Introduction:

(i) Introduce self and the topic;

(ii) Describe current system briefly:

	(a) Why it is unable to solve the problem(s)? (b) User dissatisfaction; (iii) Describe in brief the scope and goals etc. of the proposed system.
(B) Body of the Presentation:	(i) Weaknesses of the present/current system; (ii) How the proposed system intends to solve the problem(s)? (iii) Specify savings, benefits accruing from proposed system (sell your idea); (iv) Use visual aids, if possible; (v) Implementation plan/schedule; (vi) Personnel required.
(C) Conclusions:	(i) Summary of the proposal; (ii) Recommendations/objectives (restate); (iii) Benefits & savings (tell again to have impact); (iv) Solicit apprcval for project from top management.
(D) Query Session: Answer any doubts raised in a convincing manner.	

Table 4 Feasibility Report Presentation

Q. 490 Suppose you have to design an on-line human-computer interface. How would you go about doing it?

ANS. Twenty-three types of on-line computer interaction have been used depending on the particular application, format, and ease of use. Another factor to weigh is the cost and difficulty of programming each such type of input/interaction:

1. The first type of dialogue is a 'simple query', there being no elaborate conversation. The terminal operator keys in a number/symbol and retrieves the data e.g., an inventory part number produces a display showing the quantity of that part on hand and an order along with its reorder point.
2. 'Mnemonics' are memory aids; since most terminal users are unfamiliar with programming, we can construct abbreviations that have natural meaning to the user. This requires keying in less than the full text. An example can be *"RSRV"* to reserve a room.
3. 'English-language-entry' can be helpful for the novice user but can lead to a great deal of typing e.g., *LOCATE EXPERIMENTS FOR GUINEA-PIGS SINCE 2002.*
4. Sometimes, the application justifies the use of a 'programming - like language'. In certain cases, for instance, the user shall already be familiar with programming or he shall use the system so much that it makes sense to learn the language.

5. 'Function keys' are very popular and represent an example of what we call "action codes". Only a single key has to be pressed in order to indicate what the machine is supposed to do e.g., most of the software packages currently in vogue like MS-Word, MS-Excel etc. use the 'F2' function key for the *"HELP"* action.

6. The above approach can be extended to 'multiple-action codes' since in a complex system, there might not be enough single character codes or function keys. For instance, a common such example is the pressing of the Ctrl, Alt, and Del keys simultaneously in order to reboot the computer.

7. In some systems, it is helpful to 'build a record' on the screen as the user enters data. Consider adding a new customer to a file. In this case, we can start with the name and address. This data would remain visible on the screen even as additional parts of the record would be entered such as type of customer, credit terms etc.

8. 'Scrolling' techniques are often used to add information continuously to the bottom of the screen while the oldest information retrieved is larger than what can fit on a single display screen. With this type of display, it is helpful to have a 'move-up' and a 'move-down' command so that the terminal user can use the system like a scroll.

9. Some systems feature 'simple instructions' to the operator such as to enter certain data elements. Often, the instruction contains the acceptable answers such as *"Enter Y for Yes, N for No"*.

10. The above mentioned technique can be extended to provide 'multiple instructions' to the operator. One screen asks the user at the terminal to enter more than one piece of data. It is helpful to design this kind of a dialogue in order that the user does not have to follow a pre-determined set order for data entry.

11. 'Menu selection' is one of the most popular types of input for an on-line system. This approach works only if there is a limited set of valid operator answers to a question asked by the program. An example can be:

"Please indicate the student's level of education:

A. *B.A.*

B. *B.Sc.*

C. *M.A.*

D. *M.Sc.*

E. *M.C.A.*

F. *Ph.D."*

The user would only have to enter the character of his choice, e.g. 'E' for an *M.C.A.* educational level.

12. If there are too many items on the menu for one screen, one can list all that shall fit in. The last entry is a continuation to the next screen that has more choices for this question.

13. If there are more choices, say in thousands, the menu selection becomes more like a telephone directory. The choices can be arranged alphabetically, and the user could direct the system to approximately the right location, for example to the *"I's"*.
14. The menu can also be expanded to provide for several questions and selections on the same screen forming a multi-part menu.
15. Menus can be arranged so that the user chooses more than one answer and completes a series of questions using the same display.
16. Some systems use a displayed-format approach to interaction. Here, the system gives the format like *"Enter Date DD/MM/YYYY"*. The user types over the *"DD/MM/YYYY"* characters with the appropriate data. This operation is akin to fill-in-the-blanks form, but one writes over the blanks and erases the format during data entry.
17. An alternative approach to the above is to have the program state the *sequence* in which the data must be entered but not the exact format.
18. To provide flexibility, the program might give the user the choice of several alternative formats/forms for the data to be entered.
19. The techniques above quite naturally lead to the idea of *form filling* in which the program presents the outline of the form to be completed by the user.
20. Sometimes, entire lines are overwritten in response to a question.
21. Sometimes, when the operator is making changes or there are many standard default options for the information entered, the user is presented with a display of the completed data. The operator then uses the cursor to move to any field of data he wishes to change and makes the appropriate changes.
22. *'Text editing'* is a very specialized type of dialogue. Often, the user is actually running a text-editing program with its own complex command language.
23. Finally, we have the *'hybrid technique'* involving really interactive communication with the program. In this approach, the conversation is partly initiated by the user and partly by the program.

Personal computer software packages have established new standards for interaction. A good example of this type of interface can be found with electronic spreadsheet systems such as LOTUS 1-2-3. Clearly, there are many forms of interactive dialogue; the choice depends upon the nature of application, the volume of interaction involved, and the type of computer system being used.

In addition to these general design considerations, the user should be given courteous error messages and must have the opportunity to rekey data that are in error.

Messages should be polite and explain the error to the user. It might also be advisable to give no explanation unless the user types a question mark or presses some other key after receiving an error message. This way, the user already familiar with the system can avoid tedious error messages really meant/designed for someone with lesser experience.

Q. 491 Suppose you have to design the documentation for a new system. How would you go about doing it?

ANS. Documentation is a term used to describe all the instructions, programs, narratives, that is, virtually anything written about an information system. Documentation serves several purposes; first, during systems design, it is the evolving product developed by the design team and users; after installation, it is the basis for making changes to the system. The quality of documentation determines how much flexibility the computer department has in being responsive to user requests. Finally, good documentation serves to reduce the conflict between users and the computer department, since a well-documented system is easier for users to understand. Good documentation means that an adequate reference is available when problems arise, and this information helps users learn how to solve their problems with the system.

Some of the best documentation of any type available today comes with software packages, especially for personal computers. As the market is so large and also as the users are not expected to be experts, developers of personal computer packages must provide for an easy user interface and a package that can be used without training. For good ideas on how one can create good user documentation and how to prepare users for training as well as reference, we can consult the popular software manuals. Some of the simple word-processing systems like Ms-Word can be used without a manual. Rather, the command 'Menu' serves as a guide and a help in this case. The electronic spreadsheet packages like Ms-Excel also have good on-line interactive and reference documentation. Although not very exciting, good documentation makes a large difference in case of use and in reducing frustration for the users.

Systems documentation is an important part of systems testing. All design and test documentation must be finalized and kept in a library for future reference. The library is the central location for the maintenance of the new system. The formal organization and language of the documentation should be in accordance with the system standards.

Many structured approaches to design include the production of documentation as a part of the design process itself. This documentation aids communication among those on the design team; it represents the current conceptualization of a new system or the understanding of an existing system. The librarian is that member of the design team who is responsible for maintaining documentation.

During design, another approach purpose of documentation is one of control; that is, providing a record of what has been developed and of changes. It is vitally important to be sure that all parts of a system affected by a change are considered and that those responsible for the components of the system affected by the change are notified. For instance, if a file format or the contents of a file are altered, what program modules and what programmers are affected?

Control is also the ability to retrieve past test runs and old versions of programs or files. This type of documentation builds up an excellent database for making future estimates of how long it would take to develop a similar system. The librarian must keep and maintain a copy of all the runs and progress reports so that a complete description of the project activities can be found easily.

Table 5 outlines some of the most essential elements of design documentation. Many of the documents in this table shall be used for other purposes in a slightly modified form. Probably the most important document is the 'table of contents' that serves as a directory and a dictionary to the manual files containing all the other information describing the system. The 'table of contents' must be hierarchical, and parts of it may be distributed elsewhere. For instance, the 'main table of contents' points to the location of the input/output specification and at the beginning of the file of input/output specifications, another directory points, in particular, to each respective input/ output.

Table of Contents

- Survey
- Feasibility Study
- Existing Systems Documentation
- Specifications for New System
    - Input / Output
    - File Versions
    - Logical Specifications
    - Program Modules
        - Flowcharts/Decision Tables/Pseudocode
        - Cross-references
    - Tests
    - Design
    - Data
    - Runs & Results
    - Manual Procedures
        - Flowcharts (Hierarchical)
        - Narrartives
        - Error Controls
    - Work Plans
- Progress Reports

Table 5 Components of Design Documentation

The library should contain the 'survey' and 'feasibility study' as well as other documents regarding the analysis of the existing system. It is also a natural storehouse for the detailed 'specifications' for the new system being envisaged. As items like 'system flowcharts' undergo change, the original are kept as backup copies. We can indeed keep the 'most recent document' in the working area with each page dated and a pointer to the location of all the past versions in archival storage. Another major area of the library is the actual 'programs' as they are coded. It is very important to keep and maintain copies of the input/output, file record formats, and a list of all the modules. Also, we can provide relevant cross-references between various modules wherever necessary. In database management applications, it is also desirable to keep a central library or the meta-data/data dictionary (DD) as it is referred to. This shall help to keep consistency amongst variable names cutting across the different modules and programs. This sort of 'standardization' also helps in avoiding confusion and also makes it easier to debug the programs at a later stage.

Last but not the least, there is an urgent need for good documentation 'within' the programs itself! This helps particularly in making the programs easier to understand and thereby, in their maintenance also. Moreover, there is enough reason to keep an updated record of all the test runs that shall help, somewhat in the analysis of the programs developed by the design team later on, as well as in avoiding duplication of effort and consequential time wastage. In particular, all error conditions must be carefully noted and maintained in the library.

Q. 492 Suppose you are responsible for the quality assurance of the new software developed? What factors would you bear in mind to ensure the quality of the product?

ANS. As compared to the staggering amount of software produced, unfortunately, the quality of the software has left much to be desired. As compared to the staggering amount of software produced, unfortunately, the quality of the software has left much to be desired. It has not lived up to the users' demands and objectives. That's exactly where 'quality assurance' comes into play. It ensures some sort of standardization for the software products and thereby, a degree of reliability. The concept of quality assurance comes as a welcome assurance for the user that the software he has purchased is indeed a good quality product and shall indeed fulfill whatever the software vendor has assured him of.

From the point of view of the systems life cycle, the concept of quality assurance assures us that the new system is a good quality system and shall meet the user objectives as much as possible. Several factors or attributes contribute to the quality of a system. These are broadly outlined below:

A. *Reliability*: This is the extent/degree up to which the system shall perform along expected lines over a period of time.

B. *Correctness*: This is the extent/degree up to which the system meets the users' objectives and demands as well as the requirements specifications.

C. *Efficiency*: This is indicative of the fact that the system is able to perform well with as little resources as possible.

D. *Ease of Use*: The system must be user-friendly. In other words, it must be easy to learn and operate.

E. *Error Tolerance*: This indicates that in spite of any undetected errors, the system does not breakdown. In other words, it is the degree up to which the system can tolerate/bear with the errors and run smoothly in spite of them.

F. *Accuracy*: The degree of accuracy of the outputs produced by the system such as the reports etc. is indicated by this particular attribute of quality assurance.

G. *Portability*: The system must be highly portable, that is, independent of the operating system/hardware etc. It should be able to run across a wide range of platforms without any malfunctioning.

H. *Security*: Security features must be built into the system so as to prevent unauthorized access or any fraudulent use.

I. *Audit Control*: This indicates the level up to which the system can be periodically audited and reviewed.

J. *Maintainability*: The system programs must be easy to maintain and correct in case of any errors or bugs.

K. *Expandability*: The system must be capable of being expanded / enhanced at a later stage.

Q. 493 Suppose you are one of the system designers. What factors would you bear in mind to ensure the moral and ethical quality of the product?

ANS. Before developing a new application/system, the system designers should ask themselves the following list of questions:

A. Is this application a potential threat to anyone's rights? What could go wrong? For instance, do the files contain rumors, hearsay information, or unevaluated reports on any individual?

B. Is there a natural disincentive to use the system? For instance, does it act to police the workers who contribute the data?

C. Is it difficult to use the system? For instance, can anybody fill out the forms, understand the output, enter data through a terminal etc.?

D. In how many ways could anybody, possibly, defraud the system?

E. In how many ways could anybody get around the built-in safeguards and misuse the data?

To ensure that the system is fair and complete, we must think along the lines suggested by the above queries. Every potential system must have built-in features for the security and integrity of data. Without safeguards against unauthorized access, embezzlement, and natural disasters, a system can be so vulnerable so as to threaten the very existence of the organization itself. To provide protection, we could use measures such as passwords, encryption/decryption etc. Further, we must have backup copies of the data as well as the software and disaster recovery procedures to restart the system whenever required. The strength behind system integrity and success is ethics, moral code of conduct and professional behavior.

Q. 494 Suppose you are responsible for maintenance of the new system developed. What issues would weigh on your mind while carrying out this responsibility?

ANS. Several possible arrangements for maintaining a system along with its equipment are available. Out of these, three noteworthy ones are outlined as under:

A. Maintain using own personnel.

B. Purchase equipment (including software) from an outside firm and sign a maintenance agreement referred to as AMC (Annual Maintenance Contract) with it.

C. Pay for maintenance personnel on an hourly rate as and when required as well as pay for computer parts as and when replaced.

Maintenance support is a very crucial factor for the system after it has been installed / implemented. The three key considerations involved are the warranty, suitable terms and conditions of maintenance, and the response time to attend to the complaint as and when the system breaks down. Another vital factor in systems maintenance is that whatever (hardware or software) you may buy from a vendor, it must be compatible with the existing system. For example, most of the microcomputers (PC's etc.) have "plug & play" compatibility feature that allows for easy attachment of various supporting devices so that the system can work with a variety of computer equipment.

In case the system/software has been developed in-house by an external firm/company, it must be mandatory upon that company to train the existing computer staff (or some of them) explaining the new features that have been incorporated into the system so that they can themselves take action in the event of an emergency rather than waste crucial time in calling upon the firm to come to their aid.

Finally, we come to some of the features of maintainable designs that reduce the need for maintenance and simultaneously make it possible to do essential tasks much more efficiently:-

A. Define the users' requirements during systems development more precisely/ accurately;

B. Better systems documentation;

C. More effective means of designing the processing/programming logic;

D. Better use of existing tools/techniques; and,

E. More effective and efficient way of managing the systems engineering/design process.

All the above are some of the good design practices that help to produce a system that can be maintained more effectively, more easily, and at a much lower expense/cost.

Q. 495 Suppose the company has deputed you to purchase new hardware and software. Discuss the specific and general criteria while selecting any equipment (hardware or software) from a vendor.

ANS. Some of the general considerations involved when buying any equipment (Hardware or Software) from a vendor include the following:

A. *Extent of automation* proposed, i.e. the maximum amount of computerization involved;

B. *Throughput performance* or the amount of data that can be processed by the system in a given time period;

C. *Availability* and *Quality*;

D. *Vendor Support & Reputation*: Are warranty and maintenance included? Is there a money-back guarantee? Is there a cancellation clause if the vendor fails to perform up to the standards agreed upon?

E. *Documentation:* Is sufficient documentation included to allow future modifications/ enhancements/maintenance and expandability? Is there a users' reference manual?

F. *Flexibility:* Is the software adaptable to changing user needs and requirements?

G. *Reliability:* Is the equipment reliable? Is there any backup support in case of a system crash/failure? Is there any clause for updation to any new version that may be developed in future course of time? And, if so, is there any extra charge for updates?

Now, we come to some of the specific criteria and considerations involved while buying any equipment (H/w or S/w) for an application:

A. What transactions and what data about each transaction must be handled?

B. What reports, documents, and other output are required?

C. What files and databases does the system depend upon?

D. What transaction files are needed to maintain such files databases?

E. Are there any unique features involved about the application requiring special consideration?

F. What inquiry requirements must be supported by the application?

G. What future enhancements are possible? How will they be supported?

H. What are the communication requirements of the system?

I. What are the limitations of the equipment

(H/w or S/w)?

Q. 496 Supposing that you are the systems analyst, what role would you have to play in the development of new software?

ANS. The system analyst designs the new software envisaged carefully according to the requirements listed by the user. After a careful analysis of these requirements, the analyst formulates software specifications stating input, processing functions, and algorithms/procedures to be carried out in order to produce the desired output stated by the user. The analyst must also design the data flows, controls/standards/guidelines to ensure that everything is working in the anticipated manner and must also specify actions to be taken when unexpected situations/ problems crop up. In other words, the system analyst is responsible for designing the control procedures.

While designing inputs, the analyst decides what data is to be input, media to be used for input, how the data is to be coded, the input dialogue, methods to perform input validation as also procedures to follow if any input error occurs.

Finally, the output design by the analyst entails determining what and how the information/ output is to be presented as also deciding upon the output (reports etc.) format.

Q. 497 What do you understand by Object Oriented Life Cycle Modeling? Explain and Elucidate.

ANS. A software development project can be viewed as a set of objects that interact with each other to accomplish a certain objective(s). The project goes through an evolutionary development life cycle containing objects decided at three distinct stages as elaborated below:

A. Objects decided at OOA (Object Oriented Analysis) stage;

B. Objects decided at OOD (Object Oriented Design) stage; and,

C. Objects decided at OOP (Object Oriented Programming) stage.

In object oriented analysis (OOA), we decide the objects, their behavior, and their interactions meeting the requirements of the software project.

Next, in object oriented design (OOD), we draw the hierarchies from which the objects can be created.

Finally, in object oriented programming (OOP), we implement the programs in C++, Java, or any other object oriented programming language using objects.

Q. 498 Compare and contrast the Object-Oriented and Module-Oriented approaches for Systems Design.

ANS.

S. No.	*Object Oriented Approach*	*Module Oriented Approach*
1.	System seen as a collection of objects each having a functional purpose.	System seen as a collection of data, functions, processes, and their inter-relationships.
2.	Easy maintenance at low cost.	Maintenance at high cost.
3.	Code can be reused.	Code reuse limited and infrequent.
4.	Easy implementation in large distributed systems.	Difficult to implement in distributed systems.
5.	Suitable for object oriented situations like C++, Java, CORBA, GUI, DCOM etc.	Not efficient in such cases.
6.	Leads to flexible systems.	Not as flexible.
7.	Start-up and performance costs high; Costlier manpower.	Initial and overhead costs not so high; Cheaper manpower as well.

Table 6 Comparison of Object-Oriented and Module-Oriented Approaches

Q. 499 From amongst the following multiple choice questions, select the best alternative:

(1) System analyst is:

(a) an agent of change

(b) a communicator

(c) a problem solver

(d) all of the above

ANS. (d)

(2) On-line data entry is most suitable in:

(a) entering monthly journal entries

(b) payroll master updation

(c) processing for payments of cheques in a bank

(d) none of the above

ANS. (c)

(3) The System Development phase associated with creation of test data is:

(a) system analysis

(b) system acceptance

(c) physical design

(d) logical design

ANS. (b)

(4) Prototype is a:

(a) mini-model of the existing system

(b) mini-model of the proposed system

(c) working model of the existing system

(d) none of the above

ANS. (b)

(5) Which of the following is a part of the Software Development Life Cycle?

(a) requirements analysis

(b) bench marking

(c) program specifications

(d) all of the above

ANS. (d)

(6) Entities, attributes, and relationships are associated with:

(a) logical concepts of data

(b) physical concepts of data

(c) persons of an organization

(d) none of the above

ANS. (a)

(7) File conversion is a part of:

(a) system cut-over

(b) day-to-day activity of data processing

(c) system design

(d) none of the above

ANS. (a)

(8) Software quality pertains to:

(a) reliability

(b) efficiency

(c) maintainability

(d) all of the above

ANS. (d)

(9) Objects may be viewed as:

(a) clients in a system

(b) servers in a system

(c) both (a) & (b)

(d) neither (a) nor (b)

ANS. (c)

(10) In a Unified Modeling Language (UML) diagram, an object:

(a) can't be represented

(b) is irrelevant

(c) is represented as an attribute

(d) is represented as a result of an operation

ANS. (c)

(11) The components that make up any system are known as:

(a) system boundary

(b) system description

(c) system environment

(d) all of the above

ANS. (d)

(12) A distributed data processing system:

(a) attempts to capture advantages of centralized processing

(b) attempts to capture advantages of decentralized processing

(c) allows greater flexibility

(d) provides slow access of data

(e) both (a) & (b)

(f) none of the above

ANS. (e)

(13) "Back up" refers to:

(a) delay in production of outputs

(b) accumulation of programs in memory

(c) job scheduling failures
(d) all of the above
(e) none of the above

ANS. (e)

(14) Cost of error correction is least in the stage of:

(a) requirements analysis
(b) system design
(c) evaluating the tangible factors
(d) evaluating the intangible factors
(e) both (c) & (d)
(f) all of the above
(g) none of the above

ANS. (a)

(15) An object is selected for modeling, if:

(a) its attributes are invariant during operation of the system
(b) it has numerous attributes
(c) its attributes change during operation of the system
(d) it has no attributes relevant to the system
(e) none of the above

ANS. (c)

(16) Tangible benefits, by their very nature, require:

(a) subjective evaluation
(b) feasible evaluation
(c) quantifiable evaluation
(d) none of the above

ANS. (c)

(17) A menu-driven software:

(a) helps the user to reduce errors during data entry
(b) is developed for planning meals at a restaurant
(c) contains options for the user to enter his choice
(d) all of the above
(e) none of the above

ANS. (c)

(18) While designing a report layout, which of the following should be avoided?

(a) report should be read from top to bottom
(b) report should be read from left to right
(c) the most important items must come first

(d) use of abbreviations

(e) none of the above

ANS. (e)

(19) A business accounting system includes:

(a) order entry

(b) shipping / billing

(c) sales analysis

(d) all of the above

ANS. (d)

(20) In a modern supermarket using computerized systems, which of the following would be found in use?

(a) Point-of-Sale (POS) terminal

(b) scanner

(c) bar code reader

(d) all of the above

(e) none of the above

ANS. (d)

(21) Open systems interact with the:

(a) system environment

(b) system boundary

(c) closed systems

(d) feedback

ANS. (a)

(22) Information is:

(a) data

(b) computer output

(c) manipulated input

(d) processed data

ANS. (d)

(23) The first step in Software Development Life Cycle (SDLC) is:

(a) system design

(b) database design

(c) feasibility study

(d) preliminary investigation and analysis

(e) none of the above

ANS. (d)

(24) On-line data entry is preferable to batch data entry because:

(a) it is faster

(b) it ensures better accuracy of input

(c) it reduces human effort in checking control totals, checklists etc.

(d) all of the above

(e) none of the above

ANS. (a)

(25) If the requirements analysis phase of a software development project is not conducted properly, then the:

(a) resulting system would be delivered before the deadline

(b) output reports won't be easy to decipher and make out

(c) system might fail to address the real needs of the users

(d) all of the above

ANS. (c)

(26) The detailed study / investigation of the existing system is often referred to as:

(a) system planning

(b) feasibility study

(c) system analysis

(d) none of the above

ANS. (c)

(27) System specifications are mainly concerned with:

(a) how the functions are performed

(b) what functions are to be performed

(c) both (a) & (b)

(d) neither (a) nor (b)

ANS. (c)

(28) In data processing, classifying, calculating and summarizing data pertain to:

(a) capturing of input data

(b) managing output results

(c) manipulation of data

(d) all of the above

(e) none of the above

ANS. (c)

(29) In case a data dictionary is not included in the system analysis and design of a software project, then the following task(s) can't be carried out well:

(a) over-all cost-benefit analysis

(b) bench marking of equipment to be acquired

(c) cross referencing and consistency checks of various data

(d) all of the above

(e) none of the above

ANS. (c)

(30) In a Railway Reservation System, which of the following is the most critical?

(a) Ease of programming

(b) Response time

(c) GUI

(d) none of the above

ANS. (c)

(31) Tactical information is needed to:

(a) carry out day-to-day routine operations

(b) meet government requirements

(c) perform long range planning

(d) perform short range planning

(e) none of the above

ANS. (d)

(32) Operational information is required by:

(a) middle managers

(b) line managers

(c) top managers

(d) all workers

ANS. (b)

(33) Inheritance in object modeling can be used to:

(a) generalize classes

(b) specialize classes

(c) both (a) & (b)

(d) neither (a) nor (b)

(e) create new classes

ANS. (c)

(34) Object-oriented modelling:

(i) allows easy integration of subsystems

(ii) promotes reuse of code
(iii) allows modification of some objects by other objects
(iv) allows data structures in objects to be modified by other objects

State whether:

(a) (i) & (ii) are true
(b) (i), (ii) & (iv) are true
(c) (ii), (iii) & (iv) are true
(d) (i), (ii), (iii) & (iv) are true

ANS. (a)

(35) Loss of data integrity implies that data is:

(a) outdated
(b) unsuitable for running in an integrated environment
(c) repeated
(d) inconsistent
(e) all of the above
(f) none of the above

ANS. (d)

(36) The main advantage of normalized relations in relational DBMS is that they:

(a) are highly secure
(b) occupy minimal storage
(c) do not suffer from anomalies during delete and update operations
(d) all of the above

ANS. (c)

(37) Digital signatures are used in:

(a) data communications
(b) floppy disk marking
(c) programming
(d) none of the above

ANS. (a)

(38) Which one of the following statements is incorrect?

(a) a report format file can show any object within a box
(b) a report format can show vertical lines in the report
(c) current date can be shown both in page header and footer
(d) none of the above

ANS. (d)

(39) A system design is said to be functionally modular if:

(a) system is able to handle all functions of the application

(b) system is developed through structured programming using languages like PASCAL or COBOL

(c) system makes extensive use of function keys for maximum user assistance

(d) each module performs a specific function and can be developed independently by programmers

ANS. (d)

(40) In considering the total cost associated with desired information, cost of data collection, data input and computer processing are:

(a) recurring costs

(b) one-time costs

(c) temporary costs

(d) permanent costs

(e) none of the above

ANS. (a)

(41) The present trend in data processing systems is towards:

(a) real-time processing

(b) remote processing

(c) distributed processing

(d) none of the above

ANS. (c)

(42) Whether a proposed system can provide right information for the organization's personnel or not, would fall under the study of:

(a) economic feasibility

(b) technical feasibility

(c) operational feasibility

(d) all of the above

(e) none of the above

ANS. (c)

(43) A class, in object-oriented programming, is a:

(a) template for objects of a particular type

(b) group of objects

(c) classification of objects

(d) none of the above

ANS. (a)

(44) Encapsulation in object modeling is useful because:

(a) it hides implementation details of the methods

(b) it allows improving methods of an object, independent of other parts of the system

(c) it allows for an easy design

(d) it encapsulates attributes and operations of objects

ANS. (b)

(45) In a motor car manufacturing company, following information is tactical:

(a) assessing competitor's car

(b) decision on introducing a new model

(c) computing sales tax collected

(d) scheduling production

ANS. (a)

(46) A Management Information System (MIS) is required because:

(a) the size of the organization has become too large

(b) computers are available economically

(c) it is difficult for clerks to process data

(d) timely decisions have to be taken based on available data

ANS. (d)

(47) The term used to refer to checking of outputs of a computer with the corresponding input documents is called:

(a) auditing around the computer

(b) auditing through the computer

(c) regression testing

(d) process control

ANS. (a)

(48) Bench mark is used during:

(a) computer contract

(b) software selection

(c) hardware selection

(d) both (b) & (c)

(e) neither (b) nor (c)

ANS. (d)

(49) Smart card pertains to:

(a) system project management

(b) return on investment

(c) GUI
(d) structured design
(e) none of the above

ANS. (a)

(50) A use case diagram is a classic case of:

(a) flow chart
(b) what-if analysis
(c) interaction between system and its environment
(d) gathering qualitative information
(e) none of the above

ANS. (c)

Q. 500 Illustrate the software development life cycle with the help of a suitable diagram.

ANS. Figure 26 illustrates the software development life cycle (SDLC). It is more or less self-explanatory and is left as an exercise for you.

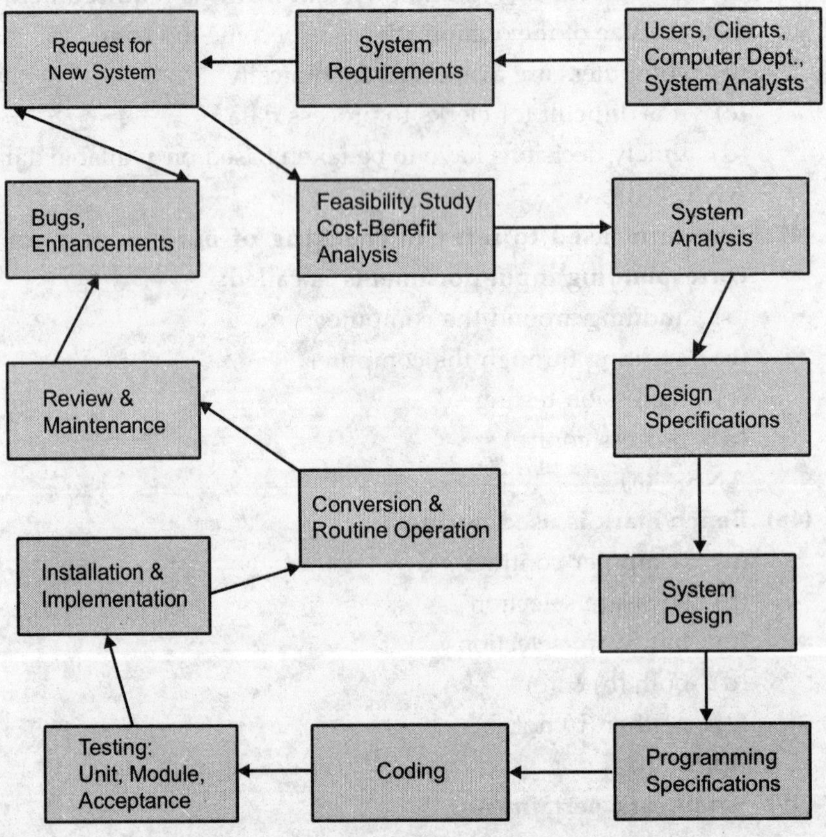

Figure 26 Software Development Life Cycle (SDLC)

16

BONUS INTERVIEW QUESTIONS ON C#.NET

Q. 501 Compare in brief C++, Java, and C#.

ANS. C++, Java, and C# share a common ancestry but differ in many ways. C# and Java are like close cousins. Both support distributed programming and both use intermediate code to achieve safety and portability. However, the details differ. Both also support run-time error checking, security and managed execution. But, the details differ a lot once more. Furthermore, unlike Java, C# provides access to pointers, a facet supported by C++. In this way, we come to see that C# combines the raw power of C++ with the type safety of Java.

Q. 502 Discuss the evolution of the various versions of C#.

ANS. Many new features have been added to C# ever since its initial version 1.0 in the year 2000, the first major revision being 2.0, followed by release 3.0, and eventually 4.0.

The most important change brought about by C# 2.0 was the revolutionary introduction of generics. LINQ (*Language Integrated Query*) and lambda expressions were the major additions made by the 3.0 release while named & optional arguments and the keyword dynamic (which relaxes type checking rules to run-time rather than at compile time) along with support for parallel programming by means of TPL (*Task Parallel Library*) and PLINQ (*Parallel* LINQ) were the major introductions made by the version 4.0 of C#.

Q. 503 Give two compelling reasons for the creation of C#.

ANS. Java answered many of the needs of the programmers but was lacking on two scores, namely:-

(a) *Mixed-language programming / Cross-language interoperability*

(b) *Full integration with the Windows platform*

C# was the result of mainly these two needs and Microsoft's overall .NET strategy in the late 1990s.

Q. 504 Mention two main points as to how C# relates to the .NET Framework.

ANS. (a) *First, C# was initially meant to program on the .NET Framework.*

(b) *Secondly, the libraries used by C# are those as defined by the .NET Framework.*

Q. 505 Distinguish between managed and unmanaged code.

ANS. A normal C# program written under the control of the CLR (Common Language Runtime) is subject to several constraints and as such obtains consequent benefits thereof – such code is known as managed code.

On the contrary, unmanaged code does not run under the control of the CLR. But, the point to be noted is that managed and unmanaged code can work together.

Q. 506 What are the value types allowed by C#?

ANS. In addition to the thirteen simple types such as *bool, char,decimal, double, float, int* etc. C# allows enumerations, structures and nullable types, all of which are value types.

Q. 507 What is the decimal data type intended for?

ANS. The *decimal* type is indeed the most interesting C# numeric type intended for use in monetary/financial calculations. It can successfully represent up to 29 decimal places without any rounding errors, a fact that makes it especially useful for computations involving money/finance.

Q. 508 Is there any special significance of the char data type in C#?

ANS. Unlike most other languages such as C++, which use the standard 8-bit ASCII character set, C# uses a 16-bit character type called Unicode, which is large enough to accommodate all of the characters found in all the human languages including Chinese, French, German, and, of course, English.

Q. 509 What do you understand by a widening and a narrowing conversion?

ANS. When one type of data is assigned to another type of variable, an implicit widening conversion takes place automatically in C# if the two types are compatible and the range of the destination type is greater than that of the source type. In all other cases, you need to apply a cast. When a cast includes a narrowing conversion such as from a *float* to an *int*, information may be lost due to truncation, e.g., if the value 1.14 is assigned to an integer, the resulting value will be just 1 and 0.14 is lost.

Note: *You may like to compare this concept with Java. For this, you are advised to refer to chapter 1.*

Q. 510 What is the difference between the use of the prefix increment ++x and the use of the postfix increment x++ in C# and Java?

ANS. There is essentially no difference between the use of the postfix increment x++ and the prefix increment ++x in C# and Java. If you know how to use these operators in one of these languages, you can use them the same way in the other.

Q. 511 What is the difference between short-circuit logical operators || OR and && AND in C# and Java?

ANS. The short circuit logical operators || OR and && AND operate in the same manner in both C# and Java.

Q. 512 Can you name an operator in C# that takes three operands?

ANS. The ternary operator with the most general form:-

exp1 ? exp2 : exp3;

(if exp1 is true, exp2 becomes the value of the whole expression else exp3 becomes the value of the whole expression)

Note the use of the ternary operator in Java as well. It operates the same way.

Q. 513 Can you create a 'for' loop without any conditional expressions? What does it amount to?

ANS. Leaving the conditional expressions in a *'for'* loop makes it an infinite loop that will run forever:-

```
for ( ; ; ) // intenti nal infinite loop
{
  ..............................
  ..............................
}
```

An infinite 'for' loop can be created in Java the same way.

Q. 514 What does the foreach loop do?

ANS. The *foreach* loop cycles through the elements of a collection.

Note that there is a for-each style loop in Java as well but without the foreach keyword.

Q. 515 What do the break and continue statements do? Bring out the main point of difference between them.

ANS. The break statement causes an early termination of the loop, whereas the continue statement causes an early iteration of the loop. *Again, note that the break and continue statements work the same way in Java.*

Q. 516 Explain the use of the keyword new.

ANS. The keyword new is used to create objects, e.g.

Room classroom = new Room();

Here, classroom by itself does not contain the object (Room).

Rather, it contains a reference to it.

On the other hand, consider:-

int i = 100;

Here, i contains the value 100 since i is a variable of type *int*, which, in turn, is a value type.

Again, consider:-

Room classroom1 = new Room ();

Room classroom2 = new Room ();

```
classroom2 = classroom1;
Room classroom3 = new Room ();
classroom2 = classroom3;
```

After the execution of this sequence, classroom2 refers to the same object (Room) as classroom3. The object (Room) referred to by classroom1 is unchanged.

Note: *The keyword new works in essentially the same manner in Java.*

Q. 517 Can new be used with value types?

ANS. Yes, although new is mainly meant for reference types.

For example,

```
int k = new int ();
```

initializes k to zero.

Q. 518 Point out the difference between C++ and C# as regards release of previously allocated memory.

ANS. In C++, the delete operator is used to free memory that was previously allocated. But, C# uses a different, more trouble-free approach, viz. *garbage collection*.

Note: Also, try to note the *similarity* between *Java* and C# in this respect, viz. *garbage collection*.

Q. 519 What is the purpose of the destructor in C#?

ANS. We can define a method in C# that shall be called just prior to the object's final destruction by the garbage collector. This method is known as the destructor, which can be used in some highly specialized situations to ensure that the object is destroyed / terminated cleanly.

Q. 520 What do you understand by 'this'?

ANS. When a method is called, it is, by itself, passed a reference to the invoking object, i.e. the object on which the method is called. This reference is referred to as 'this'.

Note: Try to see *Java's* 'this' reference. Do you note any *differences*?

Q. 521 Can you elaborate on the concept of jagged arrays?

ANS. In general, when we create a two-dimensional array, we are creating what is a rectangular array with the length of each row being the same for the entire array, e.g. a 2 x 3 array implies an array of two rows with three elements in each row. But, C# allows you to create a special two-dimensional array called a jagged array, which is an array of arrays, where the length of each array can differ. In this way, we can have a table where the lengths of the rows differ, e.g.

```
int [ ] [ ] jag = new int [4] [ ];
jag [0] = new int [10]; // length of first array is ten
jag [1] = new int [2]; // length of second array is two
jag [2] = new int [5]; // length of third array is five
jag [3] = new int [8]; // length of fourth array is eight
```

Note: There is a concept of *jagged arrays* in Java as well. Try to see the difference in the declaration of *multi-dimensional arrays* in C# and Java. It would not be possible to take up the complete discussion here. However, if interested, you can refer to the authors' works – *"The Essentials of Java"* & *"The Essentials of C# 4.0"* in this context.

Q. 522 Can you point out the main difference between C/C++ strings and C# strings?

ANS. In C/C++, strings are simply arrays of characters terminated by the '\0' null character whereas in C#, string is a built-in data type. In fact, in C#, strings are objects and thus, reference types.

Q. 523 Can the contents of strings in C# be changed?

ANS. No, strings in C# are immutable (see also **Q.** 586). This might seem to be a drawback but since unused string objects are automatically garbage collected, you can simply create a new string with the desired changes.

Q. 524 What are C#'s access modifiers?

ANS. In C#, member access control is achieved through four access modifiers, namely, public, private, protected and internal. The protected modifier applies only in case of inheritance; the internal modifier applies mostly to the use of an assembly, which for C# loosely implies a deployable program / library. When a member of a class is modified by the public specifier, then that member can be accessed by any code in your program. If a member of a class is specified to be private, it can then only be accessed by other members of its class so that methods in other classes will not be able to access a private member of another class.

Note: Try to see *Java's* access specifiers. What *differences* do you note?

Q. 525 What is the use of the ref and out keywords?

ANS. By means of the ref and out keywords, it becomes possible to pass any of the value types by reference.

Q. 526 Is it possible to have a variable number of arguments in C#?

ANS. Yes, it can be achieved by means of the *params* modifier which represents an arbitrary number of parameters.

Note : Can a variable number of arguments be used in *Java*? Left as an exercise for *you*!

Q. 527 What is the use of the object initializers?

ANS. The primary use of the *object initializers* is with the anonymous types created in a LINQ expression. *Object initializers* provide a means to create an object and initialize its fields and properties.

Q. 528 Can you elaborate on the use of the optional arguments?

ANS. By means of optional arguments, you can specify a default value for a method's parameter. This feature has been introduced in C# 4.0.

Q. 529 Can optional arguments result in ambiguity?

ANS. One problem that can result while using optional arguments is ambiguity. This occurs when a method having optional arguments is overloaded.

Q. 530 What do you understand by named arguments?

ANS. Named arguments is a feature related to passing of arguments to a method. This feature has recently been introduced in C# 4.0. With the help of named arguments, one can specify the name of the parameter to which an argument applies.

Q. 531 Specify the forms of the Main () method available in C#.

ANS. The following four versions of Main () are currently available in C#:-

(i) static void Main ()

(ii) static int Main ()

(iii) static void Main (string args[ ])

(iv) static int Main (string args[ ])

Q. 532 Elucidate the role of the keyword static.

ANS. In general, a class member has to be accessed through an object of its instance. But, it is possible in C# to create a member that can be used by itself, without any reference to a specific instance. To create such a member, you have to precede its declaration with the keyword static. Besides static variable and methods, we can even have static classes, which have two significant uses. First, a static class is used to contain a set of related static methods. Second, a static class is needed when creating extension methods, which relate mostly to LINQ.

Q. 533 Point out any two restrictions on static methods?

ANS. First, a static method cannot have a *'this'* reference. Second, a static method can directly call only other static methods of its class.

Q. 534 When an operator is overloaded, does its original meaning get lost?

ANS. When we overload an operator relative to a class, none of its original meanings is lost. It is just that a new operation / meaning relative to that class, gets added. For instance, overloading the - operator to handle removal of a node from a linked list does not alter its original meaning relative to integers, i.e. subtraction.

Q. 535 What are indexers used for?

ANS. Indexers provide the means by which an object can be indexed like an array. Array indexing is done using the [ ] operator. It is possible to define the [ ] operator for the classes one creates, but it is not done using an operator method. Rather, we use an indexer.

Q. 536 What are properties used for?

ANS. Properties offer a streamlined approach to manage access to the instance data of a class.

Q. 537 Are indexers and properties related to each other?

ANS. Indexers and properties are related to each other as both of them depend upon another feature of C#, viz. the get & set accessors.

Q. 538 Can you overload an indexer?

ANS. Yes, an indexer can be overloaded. The version executed shall be the one that is the closest type-match between its parameter and the argument used as an index.

Q. 539 Does an indexer require an underlying array?

ANS. It is not necessary that an indexer necessarily operate on an underlying array. Rather, it must simply provide a functionality that seems to be 'array-like' to the user of the indexer.

Q. 540 What is the main difference between a private variable and a property?

ANS. Suppose, you want to limit the range of values that can be assigned to a field. It is possible to achieve this aim by means of a private variable along with methods to access its value. However, a property offers a much better, more streamlined way to achieve the same goal.

Q. 541 What do you mean by an auto-implemented property?

ANS. Auto-implemented properties with the most general form:-

prop_data_type prop_name { get; set; }

where, *prop_data_type* refers to the data type of the property and *prop_name* refers to its name, were introduced in C# 3.0.

Auto-implemented properties made it possible to implement very simple properties without having to explicitly specify the variable managed by the property. Instead, the compiler was assigned the task of automatically supplying the underlying variable.

Q. 542 Can properties be overloaded?

ANS. No, you cannot overload a property. But, you can have two different properties with both accessing the same variable.

Q. 543 Can a property be passed as a ref or out parameter to a method?

ANS. No, since a property does not specify a storage location, it cannot be passed as a ref or out parameter to a method.

Q. 544 Can you use a different access modifier with the get and set accessors than the one used for their indexer / property?

ANS. By default, the get and set accessors have the same accessibility as that of their indexer / property. But, you can use a different access modifier as well, e.g. if the indexer / property is public, you can give get or set its own access modifier such as private.

Q. 545 Both the base class and the derived class can have their own constructors. So, what constructor is responsible for building an object of the derived class – the one in the base class, or the one in the derived class, or both?

ANS. The constructor for the base class constructs the base class part of the object and the constructor for the derived class builds the derived class portion of the object.

Note : *This is similar to the concept of superclass and subclass in Java.*

Q. 546 How does a derived class call a constructor defined in its base class?

ANS. A derived class can call a constructor defined in its base class by using an expanded form of the derived class' constructor declaration and the base keyword in the following manner:-

derived_class_constructor (parameter_list) : base (arg_list)

{

....

....

}

where, *arg_list* specifies any arguments required by the constructor in the base class.

Q. 547 In what order are constructors called in a class hierarchy?

ANS. In a class hierarchy, constructors are called in their order of derivation (*just like in Java*).

Q. 548 What do you mean by method overriding?

ANS. The process of redefining a virtual method inside a derived class is referred to as method overriding. When overriding a method, the name, return type, and signature of the overriding method must exactly be the same as that of the virtual method being overridden.

Q. 549 What do you understand by dynamic method dispatch?

ANS. Dynamic method dispatch is the means by which a call to an overridden method is resolved at run-time rather than at compile time. It is important since C# implements run-time polymorphism this way.

Note : *The concepts of method overriding and dynamic method dispatch work in the same way in Java as in C#.*

Q. 550 Can properties / indexers be modified by the keyword virtual and overridden using override?

ANS. The answer to both the queries is in the *affirmative*.

Q. 551 Can you give one good reason for using overridden methods?

ANS. Overridden methods are another way that C# implements the *'One interface, multiple methods'* aspect of *polymorphism*.

Q. 552 Can an abstract method have a body?

ANS. No, not at all!

Q. 553 Can you use virtual and abstract together?

ANS. An abstract method is, by itself, virtual and there is thus, no need to specify the virtual modifier. In fact, it's an error to use virtual and abstract together!

Q. 554 Can you create an object of an abstract class using new?

ANS. An abstract class does not specify a complete implementation and whence, there can be no objects of an abstract class. Therefore, attempting to create an object of an abstract class using new will lead to a consequent compile time error.

Q. 555 What are the two uses of the keyword sealed?

ANS. (*i*) You can use sealed to prevent a class from being inherited by preceding the class declaration with the keyword sealed.

(*ii*) You can use sealed on virtual methods to prevent further overrides.

Note : Is there a similar keyword in *Java*? Yes – the *'final'* keyword.

Q. 556 What do you mean by boxing and unboxing?

ANS. When an object reference refers to a value type, the value type is said to be 'boxed inside the object and this process is referred to as boxing. The reverse process of retrieving a value from a boxed object using an explicit cast from the object reference to its corresponding value type is referred to as unboxing.

Note : *Are there any differences between C# and Java as regards the concepts of boxing and unboxing? Try to find out for yourself! We would just like to mention that there are concepts of auto-boxing and auto-unboxing in Java.*

Q. 557 Is the object class a universal data type? If it is, what are its pitfalls?

ANS. The *object* class is indeed a universal data type in C# and it is possible to use an object reference to refer to any type of data. This makes it possible to get past C#'s otherwise impregnable / strong type checking. But, this must be avoided as far as possible since it can lead to unexpected errors and bugs. Indeed, it's best to save *object's* universal nature for highly special situations. More importantly, true generics are available ever since C# 2.0, and this feature enables you to easily define classes and algorithms that work automatically with different data types in a type-safe manner.

Note : *Does Java too have such a similar superclass universal in nature? Yes, it has! Find it out!!*

Q. 558 Define an interface in C#.

ANS. An interface defines a set of methods that will be implemented by a class. An interface, by itself, does not implement any method. In this way, we see that an interface is a purely logical construct that describes functionality without defining any implementation whatsoever.

Q. 559 What is the main point of difference between structures and classes?

ANS. Structures and classes are similar to each other except that structures are handled as value types whereas classes are treated as reference types.

Q. 560 What is the similarity and difference between interfaces and abstract classes?

ANS. Interfaces are syntactically similar to abstract classes. But, in an interface, no method can have a body. Thus, an interface does not provide any implementation at all. It tells what is to be done but is completely silent about how it is to be done. Once an interface is specified, any number of classes can implement it. Moreover, one class may implement any number of interfaces.

Q. 561 How will you choose between an interface and an abstract class?

ANS. When you can fully describe the concept in terms of 'what it does' without any need to specify 'how it does it', you should use an interface. However, if you need to include at least some implementation details, you should use an abstract class to represent your concept.

Q. 562 When would you prefer to use a structure instead of a class?

ANS. In general, if you need to just store a group of related data, but don't need to operate on that data through a reference and don't need inheritance, structures are a more efficient choice and should be preferred to classes.

Q. 563 Can an enumeration be used to control a switch statement or as a control variable in a 'for' loop?

ANS. Since enumerations represent integer values, they can easily be used to control a switch statement or as the control variable in a 'for' loop.

Note : *There are enumerations in Java as well. However, there remains many a difference between C# and Java in this respect.*

Q. 564 What are an exception and an exception handler?

ANS. An exception is an error which occurs at run-time. Exception handling streamlines error handling by allowing the program to specify a block of code, called an exception handler, which is executed automatically in case of an error. Exception handler eliminates the need to manually check the success / failure of each specific operation or method call. In case an error occurs, it is processed / handled by the exception handler gracefully.

Note : Once again, try to see *Java's* exception handling mechanism. Do you note any *differences*?

Q. 565 Can you elaborate on the consequences of an uncaught exception?

ANS. In general, if your program does not catch an exception, it will be caught by the run-time system, which, in turn, will report an error and terminate the program abnormally / ungracefully.

Q. 566 What is the major benefit of exception handling?

ANS. One of the major benefits of exception handling is that it enables your program to respond to an error and then continue running, that is, handle the error gracefully, and then continue further.

Q. 567 What are the pitfalls of using the 'catch all' handler as a means of dealing with exceptions?

ANS. The inappropriate use of the *'catch all'* handler can result in situations where errors that would otherwise be detected during testing would go unnoticed. It is also difficult to correctly handle all types of exceptions with a single *'catch all'* handler. The *'catch all'* handler should therefore be used rarely in certain specialized and exceptional situations.

Q. 568 Can you have a try block followed by a finally block with no catch clauses?

ANS. Syntactically, when a finally block follows a try block, no catch clauses are technically required. In such a case, the finally block gets executed after exit from the try block, but no exceptions are handled in such a case / event.

Q. 569 Elucidate the use of the checked and unchecked keywords.

ANS. Overflow exceptions in arithmetic computations are controlled by the keywords – checked and unchecked. To ignore the overflow, unchecked is used and to catch the overflow exception, checked is used.

Q. 570 What is a stream in C#?

ANS. C# programs perform Input / Output through streams. A stream is an abstraction that produces / consumes information. A stream is liked to a physical device by the I/O system.

It is useful to note that all streams behave in the same manner irrespective of the physical device they might be linked to.

Note : *Do streams in Java behave the same way? Left as an exercise for you!*

Q. 571 Name the standard console I / O streams.

ANS. *Console.In, Console.Out,* and *Console.Error* are the three standard console I / O streams.

Q. 572 How is binary data read and written?

ANS. Binary values of the C# built-in types is read and written using the *BinaryReader* and *BinaryWriter* streams, respectively. It is pertinent to mention over here that this data is read and written using not its human readable text format but using its internal, binary form.

Q. 573 Define a delegate and an event.

ANS. A delegate is a means to encapsulate a method. It is useful to note that a delegate in C# is similar to a function pointer in C/C++. An event is a notification that an action has occurred. Delegates and events are related since an event is built upon a delegate.

Q. 574 What do you understand by multicasting?

ANS. In simple language, multicasting is the creation of a chain of methods that shall be called by itself when the delegate is invoked; this chain can be created by instantiating the delegate, then using + or += operator to add methods to the chain, and - or -= operator to remove methods from the chain.

Q. 575 In what way are delegates useful?

ANS. First of all, delegates are useful as they support events. Second, delegates provide a means to execute methods at run-time without having to precisely know what those methods are at compile time. This ability of the delegates comes in especially handy if we want to ereate a framework which allows components to be plugged in.

Q. 576 Name the two types of lambda expressions.

ANS. The two types of lambda expressions are the expression lambdas and the statement lambdas.

Q. 577 How does an event work?

ANS. An object that has an interest in an event registers an event handler for that event. When the event occurs, all registered handlers represented by delegates are invoked.

Q. 578 Define a namespace.

ANS. A namespace is, in essence, a declarative region, which provides a way to keep a set of names separate and away from conflict with another.

Q. 579 Can namespaces be nested, one inside another?

ANS. The answer to this query is in the *affirmative.*

Q. 580 List the C# preprocessor directives.

ANS. Following is the required list of C# preprocessor directives:-

(i) #define

(ii) *#elif*

(iii) *#else*

(iv) *#endif*

(v) *#endregion*

(vi) *#error*

(vii) *#if*

(viii) *#line*

(ix) *#pragma*

(x) *#region*

(xi) *#undef*

(xii) *#warning*

Q. 581 What do you mean by generics?

ANS. Generics imply parameterized types. They provide a streamlined and type-safe approach to deal with different data types as compared to the universal object class. They also promote reusability of code. Generics were introduced by C# 2.0 and they have revolutionized the C# language ever since their inception.

Note : *Generics have also been introduced in Java and are somewhat similar to templates in C++. However, differences remain.*

Q. 582 Can properties/indexers/operators be generic?

ANS. Properties/indexers/operators cannot be generic. But, they can be used in a generic class to make use of the generic type parameters provided therein.

Q. 583 Explain in brief the utility of LINQ.

ANS. LINQ (*Language Integrated Query*) gives C# the ability to generate queries for any LINQ compatible data source. Moreover, the syntax used for the query remains the same irrespective of the data source so that the syntax used to query data in a relational database is the same as the one used to query data stored in an array, for instance. There is no need to use SQL or any other mechanism not related to C# so that the query capability is fully and wholly integrated into the C# language.

LINQ can also be used along with SQL, XML files, ADO.NET Datasets as also with C# collections and arrays. Thus, we see that LINQ provides a uniform platform to access data in general.

Q. 584 What do you understand by nullable types?

ANS. A *nullable* type is a special version of a value type that is represented by a structure. In addition to the values defined by the underlying type, it can also store the value null. In this way, we see that a *nullable* type has the same range and characteristics as its underlying type but has the additional capability to represent a value, which indicates that a variable of that type is unassigned. It may also be noted that only value types have *nullable* equivalents.

Q. 585 Differentiate between dynamic type and the object class.

ANS. In one way, the dynamic type is similar to the object class since it can be used to refer to any type of object. The difference is that in case of dynamic, all type checking is deferred until run-time whereas with the object class, type checking still takes place at compile time.

Q. 586 How can you create a string in C# that is mutable?

ANS. A mutable string in C# can be created by means of the *StringBuilder* class, which is in the *System.Text* namespace.

Note : Compare and contrast the way a *mutable* string is created in *Java*.

Q. 587 What do you understand by multithreading?

ANS. C# has built-in support for multithreaded programming. A multithreaded program contains two or more parts that can run concurrently. Each such part is called a thread, and each thread defines a separate path of execution. A text editor formatting its text and printing at the same time is a good example of multithreading. In this way, we see that multithreading is a specialized version of multitasking.

Q. 588 What is meant by TPL?

ANS. TPL (*Task Parallel Library*) is one of the most important features added to the .NET Framework by version 4.0. This library enhances multithreaded programming in two ways. First, it facilitates the creation and use of multiple threads. And, second, it automatically makes use of multiple processors.

Q. 589 What is meant by PLINQ?

ANS. Another important feature added by .NET 4.0 is PLINQ (*Parallel Language Integrated Query*). PLINQ enables you to write queries that automatically make use of multiple processors and parallelism wherever appropriate. It enables the addition of parallelism to a query with minimal effort.

Q. 590 While using the TPL, what are the two basic ways in which you can add parallelism?

ANS. Data Parallelism & Task Parallelism.

Q. 591 Elucidate the utility of collections.

ANS. Collections simplify many programs by providing off-the-shelf solutions to several common but at times difficult to develop data structures. For instance, there are built-in collections that support dynamic arrays, linked lists, stacks, queues, and hash tables.

Q. 592 What is the ArrayList class?

ANS. The *ArrayList* class supports dynamic arrays, which can grow or shrink as per the user requirements.

Q. 593 What is a Hashtable?

ANS. *Hashtable* creates a collection which uses a hash table for storage (the hash table, in turn, stores information using a mechanism known as hashing).

Q. 594 Define a SortedList.

ANS. *SortedList* creates a collection that stores key / value pairs in sorted order, based on the value of the keys.

Q. 595 On what principle does a Stack operate?

ANS. Stack is a *"First-in, Last-out"* list. To visualize a stack, imagine a stack of plates on a table. The first plate put down is the last one to be retrieved.

Q. 596 What is the principle behind the Queue?

ANS. Queue is a *"First-in, First-out"* list, i.e. the first item put in a queue is the first item retrieved from it. Queues are common in real life, e.g. lines at a bank or railway reservation center are queues.

Q. 597 What is a BitArray?

ANS. The *BitArray* class supports a collection of bits. Since it stores bits rather than objects, its capabilities are different than those of other collections.

Q. 598 Elaborate on the role of the enumerator.

ANS. Quite often, one needs to cycle through the elements in a collection, e.g. you may want to display each element. One way to do this is by means of the *foreach* loop. Enumerator provides another way for the same.

Q. 599 What is the utility of the collection initializers?

ANS. C# includes a feature called the *collection initializer*, which helps to initialize certain collections. The syntax is similar to an array initialization.

Q. 600 What types of comments are supported by C#? Does it support XML documentation comments?

ANS. C# supports three types of comments – the first two are // and /* */. The third type is based on XML tags and is called a documentation comment or an XML comment. A single line documentation comment begins with /// while a multiline documentation comment begins with /** and ends with */.

Such documentation comments, in general, precede the declaration of things like classes, namespaces, methods, properties and events; you can embed information about your program into the program itself using these documentation comments and on compiling the program, you can have these comments placed into an XML file as well.

You are advised to compare and contrast the type of comments supported by Java for yourself (refer Chapter 1 in this context).

> ***Note :*** We have briefly referred to certain *similarities* and *differences* between *Java* and C# as regards various topics in the foregoing text, which could be of vital importance from the ***"INTERVIEW"*** point of view. As already pointed out, it would not be possible to take up a complete discussion of these here. However, you can refer to the authors' works – ***"The Essentials of Java"*** & ***"The Essentials of C# 4.0"*** in this context.

■

Appendix

THE JAVAAPI PACKAGE

The JAVAAPI (*Java Application Programming Interface*) is made up of fifty-nine libraries called packages. We enumerate below the important ones (for full details, you are advised to consult the *index.html* of the *API* sub-directory of the *docs* directory of the Official Java Documentation):

java.applet	:	Supplies the intefaces and the class necessary for the creation of Java applets, enablling you to display images and read audio files.
java.awt	:	Supplies the interfaces and classes necessary for the creation of GUI, in addition to graphics and drawings.
java.beans	:	Supplies intefaces and classes in relation to the JavaBean development platform, enabling the creation of software components that are reusable as beans.
java.io	:	Supplies the interfaces and classes that access the system entrance/exit flux.
java.lang	:	Supplies the interfaces and classes that are fundamental to Java Programming. It is the core of the Java language.
java.math	:	Supplies the interfaces and classes that operate on floating point values, or very large integers.
java.net	:	Supplies the interfaces and classes that handle network applications such as the handling of sockets and URLs.
java.rmi	:	Supplies the interfaces and classes that create Java applications in the form of distributed objects, enabling the calling of the methods of distant objects.
java.security	:	Supplies the interfaces and classes that implement the digital signatures and certification of Java components.
java.sql	:	Supplies the interfaces and classes that connect to databases through SQL.
java.text	:	Supplies the interfaces and classes that create character strings from objects and that convert them into other objects.

java.util : Supplies the interfaces and classes that handle random numbers, time, date, or object collections.

javax.accessibility : Supplies the interfaces and classes that extend the functions of GUIs, enabling the implementation of assistance technology such as Braille terminals, or voice-recognition systems.

javax.swing : Supplies the interfaces and classes that extend the java.awt package by supplying enriched components for the management of the GUI. The advantage of javax.swing over java.awt is that you can make an application in which the GUI automatically adapts to the system on which it is running, or takes on an aspect defined by the programmer.

org.omg.CORBA : Defines the architecture of the OMG CORBA bus in order to transit distributed objects in a Java client/server application.

org.omg..CosNaming : Supplies the interfaces and classes that offer a file naming service for Java IDL.

org.omg.CosNamingContext-package

: Supplies the classes and exceptions used by the *org.omg.CosNaming* package.

■

ACRONYMS

AI	Artificial Intelligence
API	Application Programming Interface
AWT	Abstract Window (or, Windowing) Toolkit
CAD	Computer Aided Design
CAE	Computer Aided Education
CAI	Computer Aided Instruction
CAM	Computer Aided Manufacturing
CGI	Common Gateway Interface
DBMS	Data Base Management System
DLL	Dynamic Link Library
DOS	Disk Operating System
E-mail	Electronic Mail
FAQs	Frequently Asked Questions
FIFO	First In, First Out
FTP	File Transfer Protocol
GIF	Graphics Interchange Format
GUI	Graphical User Interface
HTML	Hypertext Markup Language
HTTP	Hypertext Transfer Protocol
I/O	Input/Output
IDE	Integrated Development (or, Developer) Environment
ISP	Internet Service Provider

IT	Information Technology
JDK	Java Development (or, Developers') Kit
JIT	Just-In-Time (Java bytecode Compiler)
JPEG	Joint Photography Engineering Group
JVM	Java Virtual Machine
LIFO	Last In, First Out
MIME	Multipurpose Internet Mail Extension
PC	Personal Computer
POP	Post Office Protocol
SMTP	Simple Mail Transfer Protocol
SQL	Structured Query Language
TCP/IP	Transmission Control Protocol/Internet Protocol
URL	Uniform Resource Locator
WWW	World Wide Web
Y2K	Year 2 Thousand

■

GLOSSARY

3 GL Third-generation language such as C, COBOL, FORTRAN or Pascal that provides developers with considerable flexibility at the expense of ease of use. Most of 3 GLs can handle such detailed tasks as direct memory manipulation and physical disk access, which most 4 GLs cannot handle. 3GLs are, however, much more complex and require much more development time for applications.

4 GL A term applied to languages designed for interacting with the programmer, often used to define languages used with relational databases such as SQL. The intent was to imply that such languages are a step up from 3GLs and are generally preferable for creating database applications and for use with popular development tools.

Abstraction The act of representing the essential features of something without including the unnecessary details.

Algorithm A sequence of precise and unambiguous instructions for solving a problem in a finite number of operations.

Applet A small application unable to run by itself.

Application Programs Software designed for a specific purpose such as payroll, inventory control etc.

Applications Specific uses for a program. With MS-Word, you can, for example, create letters, mailing lists, resumes, and so on.

Artificial Intelligence A branch of computer science that deals with computers which possess reasoning, learning, and thinking capabilities resembling those of human beings.

Base Class Also *Super Class*; new classes can be created/derived from it.

Byte Consisting of 8 bits. A bit is either 0 or 1.

Chip A thin wafer of silicon on which integrated electronic components/circuits are deposited/stored.

Class It unites data and the code/methods acting upon the data; it is the basic language construct in C# for creating user-defined data types.

Coding The process of writing computer instructions in a programming language.

Compiler A system software package that converts a high-level language to the machine language form.

Computer Aided Design Use of computers to automate design operations.

Computer Aided Education A general term that refers to teaching with the help of a computer.

Computer Aided Instruction *See* Computer Aided Education.

Computer Aided Manufacturing Use of computers to automate manufacturing operations.

Constructor It is a method with the same name as its class. It is invoked automatically , by default, when an instance of a class i.e., an object is created. However, the user can define his own constructors as well to instantiate an object of the class.

Cyberspace A synonym for the Internet.

Database A collection of data files integrated and organized into a single comrehensive file system, which is arranged to minimize duplication of data and to provide convenient access to information within that system to satisy a wide range of user needs.

Database A collection of data files integrated and organized into a single comrehensive file system, which is arranged to minimize duplication of data and to provide convenient access to information within that system to satisy a wide range of user needs.

Data Base Management System A general-purpose software package used as a tool for building individual database systems.

Data Hiding It means that the implementation details are hidden from the user by providing a suitable interface.

Data Member	A variable declared in its class definition.
Debugging	The process of finding and correcting program errors/bugs. There are, in general, two types of bugs in a program, viz. syntax and run-time bugs.
Default Parameter	A parameter whose value is already provided for at the time of method declaration and this value is used by default if the corresponding actual parameter is missing at the time of the method call.
Derived Class	A class that inherits properties/attributes from a base class.
Documentation	Documentation of a software system involves collecting, organizing, storing, and otherwise maintaining a complete historical record of programs and other documents used/repared during different phases of the system.
Dynamic Allocation	In Java, objects are *dynamically allocated* from a pool of free memory using the *new* operator.
Dynamic Binding	Also known as *run-time or late binding* as it postpones the binding of the method call till run-time.
Early Binding	Also known as *static or compile-time binding* as in this case, the method call is bound at compile-time.
Electronic mail	A general term used to describe the transmission of messages by the use of computing systems and telecommunication facilities.
Encapsulation	It means binding of the code and the data into a single unit free from external interference. This concept is achieved by means of the *class* mechanism.
End user	Any individual who uses the informatiion generated by a computer based system.
Exception	An unusual but predictable abnormal condition in a program used to notify the error to the user and avoid disruption of the running program.
Exception Handling	It is the means by which the actual notification is done to make the user aware of the *exception* and avoid abnormal program termination.
Fifth Generation Computers	Fifth generation computers shall be introduced shortly. These computers will use a large number of processors working concurrently and independently. Simpler programming languages and knowledge based system implementations are expected in this generation of computers.

File	A collection of related records.
Fourth Generation Computers	Computers built between the period 1975 to date. They use large scale integrated circuits, semiconductor memories and powerful high-level languages and operating systems.
Garbage Collection	In Java, memory is dynamically allocated using *new* operator. However, *new* can fail as there might not be sufficient memory to allocate/create the desired object. For this reason, there is a need to recover free memory from unused objects. In lanuages like C++, recovery of previously allocated memory is handled manually using the d*elete* operator. But, Java uses a much more sophisticated approach, viz. *Garbage Collection.*
Generics	It is a technique for defining software components that have more than one interpretation depending on the parameters' data type. It allows the declaration of data items without specifying their exact data type. These data types are resolved at the time of their actual usage at run-time.
Inheritance	It involves derivation of new classes from existing ones thus, enabling the creation of an hierarchy of classes *simulating* the real world. This phenomenon enables *reuse* of existing code and elimination of tedious repetitive work.
Instance	A variable or an object of a class is referred to as an *instance* of that class.
Hard Copy	Printed/Filmed output from a computer device in human readable form.
Hardware	The physical components of a computer system such as electronic, magnetic and mechanical devices are referred to as hardware.
Header	Text/Graphics that appear at the top of every page.
High-level Language	A programming language whose structure is application oriented and is independent of the structure of the computer.
Input/Output	Pertaining to the techniques, media, and devices used for man-machine interaction.
Information	Information is the result of data manipulation or data processing which can be used to help people make decisions.
Information Technology	Information Technology (IT) encompasses any combination of equipment (hardware) that facilitates the acquisition, creation, modification, retrieval, storage and transmission of information using

electronic media. Thus I includes both computing and communication technology. Various aspects of IT are hardware, software, connectivity, telecommunications, science and human-computer interface.

JIT — *Just-In-Time.* Java bytecode is translated into executable code by the JIT compiler.

Machine Language — A low-level language that is directly understandable by the computer system. Each model of a computer has a unique machine language.

Member — Data and methods defined within a class are called its *members*. Also, *see* Private/Protected/Public Members.

Message Passing — A *message* is a request sent to an object; *message passing* is the process of invoking an operation on an object.

Method Overloading — Methods having the same name but differing in the number of parameters or their data types.

Nibble — Half a byte; 4 bits.

new — The *new* operator allocates memory at run-time (this is referred to as *dynamic allocation* of memory) for an object and returns a reference to it. This reference is then stored in a variable. Thus, in Java, all *class objects* must be *dynamically allocated* and *new* can be used to create an object of any *class type*.

Object — An *instance* of a class is called an *object* or a variable of that class. This is much nearer the real-world entity than the *abstract* concept of a *class*.

OO — *Object-Oriented.*

OOD — *Object-Oriented Design.*

OOP — *Object-Oriented Programming.*

Operator Overloading — The same *operator* can be used for carrying out different operations.

Pass by Reference — In this case, the *address* of an actual parameter is *implicitly* passed to a method.

Pass by Value — A *copy* of the actual parameter is passed to the method in this case.

Password — A code by means of which an user gains access to a computer system. It is used for security purposes/reasons.

Personal Computer	A small and inexpensive computer (usually a microcomputer) used by individuals for personal applications such as entertainment, home management, and hobbies.
Polymorphism	It allows for one name/*interface*, many operations/*methods*.
Private/Protected /Public Members	A class member accessible only to other members of the class is called a *private member*; a class member with the same access characteristics as the *private* member except that it is inheritable is called a *protected member*; finally, a class member accessible both within and outside its class is called a *public member*.
Real-time Systems	Pertains to on-line computer processing systems which receive and process data quickly enough to produce output so as to be able to control, direct, or affect the outcome of an ongoing activity/process.
Reusability	In Java, *reuse* of code is achieved by the concept of *class* hierarchy/ *mechanism*.
Scope	The part of code where a variable is visible is called its *scope*.
Simulation	Simulation implies representing and analyzing properties/behaviour of a physical or hypothetical system by the behaviour of a system model.
Soft Copy	Computer output which is displayed on the screen of a terminal without a permanent/printed copy.
Software	The set of computer programs, procedures, and associated do cumentation related to the effective operation of a computer system is referred to as software.
Stack	A memory in which the information stored last is on top and is retrieved first; also known as *LIFO* storage.
Static Member	A *static member* of a class is shared by all the instances of that class.
Stream	Programs perform *Input/Output* through streams. A *stream* is an abstraction that either produces or consumes information. For example, there are byte, character, and binary *streams*.
Structured Programming	A top-down software development and programming technique that employs *modular* procedural decomposition into *subtasks*. This is the traditional style of *programming* just in contrast to *Object-Oriented Programming*.
Structured Query	Structurted Query Language is better known as its abbreviated

Language	form - *SQL*, a relational data-access language created by IBM. Most database server engines use *SQL* as a standard way of accessing data from client applications.
Subclass	*See* Derived Class.
Super Class	*See* Base Class.
System	*System* is the *class* used by all Java programs.
Throughput	The total amount of useful processing carried out by a computer system within a given time period. It is a measure of the effiiciency of the computer system.
this	When a method is invoked, it is implicitly passed an argument which is a reference to the calling *object* and this reference is referred to as "*this*".
UNIX	A popular operating system for 32 and 16-bit mini and micro computers that was designed by Bell Telephone Laboratories, USA.
Web Camera	A simple web camera consists of a digital camera attached to a computer through USB or parallel port. In the digital camera, light strikes an array of photosensitive diodes instead of a film. Software associated with the web cam (camera) grabs a still image from the camera at a regular interval (say, 30 seconds). the software then turns that image into a normal JPEG file and uploads it to the web server.
World Wide Web	Also called Web, www, and W3, an interlinked collection of hypertext documents (Web pages) residing on Web servers and other document, menus and databases available via URLs (Uniform Resource Locators).

■

ABOUT THE CD-ROM

This part of the book about the included CD-ROM is divided into three sections:

(I) What's on the CD?

(II) Using the CD, and

(III) System Requirements.

(I) WHAT's ON THE CD?

The CD Included in 'Java / J2EE Interview Questions (with Ready Answers)' contains elements specifically selected to enhance the usefulness of the book. The CD contains the following elements/items:

- An extensive "Sample Java Code" including Sample Items, Servlets, Struts, and so on;
- "Interview Preparation" material including Interview Handling, Sample Interview Checklist, Sample Resume and TenTypical_Java_Int_Ques, the last one being a set of Ten Typical JAVA INTERIEW QUESTIONS.
- "Software" including Eclipse Setup, Enterprise Architect 4.51 and that pertaining to COCOMO. Out of these, the first one is used in Functional Testing, the second one as an UML case tool, and the third one in Functional Analysis and Quality Assurance.

(II) USING THE CD

To access the contents from the CD follow these steps:

- *Insert the CD into your computer's CD-ROM or DVD drive;*
- *Double-click My Computer → CD-ROM or DVD drive (as the case may be)*
- *A folder named CD_ROM is displayed on the screen;*
- *Double-click on the folder and the three folders, viz. "Interview Preparation". "Sample Java Code", and "Software", are displayed on the screen.*
- *Double-click on the folder of your choice to view and use the three folder items as described in (I) above.*

(III) SYSTEM REQUIREMENTS

Make sure that your system meets the minimum set of requirements listed as under: (Otherwise, you may encounter some or the other problem using the CD.)

- A 1 6 GHz processor or faster;
- 512 MB or more of RAM;
- 1 GB or more of free hard disk space;
- A monitor with a minimum screen resolution of 1,024 x 768 pixels;
- A CD-ROM or DVD drive attached to your computer;
- Supported operating systems are Windows XP Service Pack 2, Windows Vista (32-bit or 64-bit with SP1), Windows 7 (32-bit or 64-bit);
- You need to install JDK 7 (Java SE 7), Web browsers like Internet Explorer or Firefox, and Acrobat Reader 9 (or a higher version).

NOTES